THE PRIME MINISTERS WE NEVER HAD

'Prime ministerial politics is a rare example of a field in which the losers are often more interesting and more impressive than the eventual winners. Steve Richards deserves applause for noticing this, and exploiting it with great empathy and close argument in this excellent book. He is one of the shrewdest political commentators we have; and unusual in apparently liking politicians.'

Andrew Marr

'Britain's unusually capricious system of selecting its prime ministers means some very gifted leaders have been left on the shelf. There is no one better qualified than Steve Richards to blow away the cobwebs, and to tell us which of them might have made better prime ministers than the rum lot we sometimes got.'

Anthony Seldon

'This is another insightful and entertaining work from Steve Richards, who remains among the brightest and best of British writers and broadcasters.'

Nick Timothy

'A story of slamming doors and sliding doors. Terrific insights on the great prime ministers we didn't have from one of the shrewdest political commentators we're lucky to have.'

Jon Sopel

'A compelling account of the nearly men and women of Number Ten. Steve Richards is a must-read writer on politics, with the rare talent of being both fun and informative.'

John Crace

Steve Richards is a political columnist, journalist, author and presenter. He regularly presents *The Week in Westminster* on BBC Radio 4 and has presented BBC radio series on Tony Blair, Gordon Brown, David Cameron and Theresa May. He also presented the BBC TV programmes *Leadership Reflections: The Modern Prime Ministers* and *Reflections: The Prime Ministers We Never Had*. He has written for several national newspapers, including the *Guardian*, the *Independent* and the *Financial Times*. He also presents a popular political one-man show each year at the Edinburgh Festival and across the UK. His last book was *The Prime Ministers: Reflections on Leadership from Wilson to Johnson*.

THE PRIME MINISTERS WE NEVER HAD

Success and Failure from Butler to Corbyn

STEVE RICHARDS

Atlantic Books
London

Published in hardback in Great Britain in 2021 by Atlantic Books, an imprint of Atlantic Books Ltd.

10 9 8 7 6 5 4 3 2 1

A CIP catalogue record for this book is available from the British Library.

Hardback ISBN: 978 1 83895 241 9
E-book ISBN: 978 1 83895 243 3

Printed in Great Britain by Bell and Bain Ltd, Glasgow

Atlantic Books
An imprint of Atlantic Books Ltd
Ormond House
26–27 Boswell Street
London

WC1N 3JZ

www.atlantic-books.co.uk

—

CONTENTS

To my parents, Keith and Val.

INTRODUCTION

Compare a list of modern prime ministers with the names of the prime ministers we never had. Why did one group succeed where the other failed? Was Harold Wilson a bigger figure than Denis Healey? Was John Major more prime ministerial than Michael Heseltine? Why did Edward Heath reach Number Ten while the more deft and experienced Rab Butler failed to do so in spite of making several attempts?

In drawing up the list of prime ministers we never had in the following pages, I apply two simple qualifications. Those included must have been regarded at some point in their careers as a likely or probable prime minister. As well as being viewed in this flattering light, they must also have had a serious chance of making the leap. The feasible opportunity is as important as the perception of greatness to come.

In my last book on modern prime ministers there could be no dispute as to who was included. Starting with Harold Wilson, each one of them walked into Number Ten and ruled with varying degrees of fragility. No reader could ask why Edward Heath or James Callaghan were part of the sequence. They were prime ministers. The theme of this book, however, is not quite so definitive.

To take an example, some might point out that Neil Kinnock and Jeremy Corbyn lost two elections and Ed Miliband lost one. They all feature in the coming pages. How could they qualify when they lost elections by significant margins? The answer is straightforward. All three were leaders of the Opposition who were regarded as possible winners of future elections. Kinnock was favourite to win the 1992 election, or at least be prime minister in a hung parliament. Miliband was perceived similarly in the build-up to the 2015 general election. Indeed, Miliband spent the evening on election day with advisers compiling his first government, a sad novelistic image in the light of what was to follow a few hours later. Corbyn was not so methodical, but after wiping out the Conservatives' majority and considerably increasing Labour's vote in the 2017 election he was briefly and justifiably viewed as a possible prime minister – even if, at times, he struggled to see himself in such a light.

Nearly all the others included in this book did not lead their parties, despite it seemingly being a fundamental precondition for becoming prime minister. Roy Jenkins was the SDP's first leader but never led the Labour Party, although it was as a Labour Cabinet minister that Jenkins was first seen as a potential prime minister. The other non-leaders included were seen for long phases of their careers, or in some cases more fleetingly, as likely party leaders and prime ministers. In some cases, every word uttered at key phases in their careers was seen through the prism of a leadership bid. For a time, the likes of Michael Heseltine, Michael Portillo and David Miliband could not cross a road without prompting analysis of how the manoeuvre would impact on their ambition to become prime minister.

Part of the mystery I seek to solve is that some of the prime ministers we never had were better qualified than those who got the top job. A few had the qualities to be big change-makers too: strong personalities tested by challenges, and possessing the capacity to convey their mission with an accessible flourish. Roy Jenkins, Michael Heseltine, Denis Healey, Ken Clarke and Rab Butler were authoritative as public figures and quickly acquired deep ministerial range. Healey, Clarke, Jenkins and Butler were chancellors at times when the economy wobbled precariously, while Heseltine's ministerial challenges included replacing the widely loathed poll tax and reviving some run-down inner cities – the latter being not the most fashionable crusade at the height of Thatcherism in the early 1980s.

Heseltine was never chancellor, although the characters in this book show that occupying that role is not necessarily a route to becoming prime minister anyway. In modern times, only John Major and Gordon Brown moved directly from Number Eleven to Number Ten. James Callaghan had also been chancellor, though much earlier in his career. He was Foreign Secretary immediately before moving into Number Ten. Chancellors are often seen as future prime ministers, yet they rarely make it to the very top.

Healey was chancellor for more than five years in the wildly turbulent 1970s, a feat of endurance to say the least. He emerged as a substantial figure and a TV celebrity, a triumph given that he had taken a range of deeply unpopular decisions. As chancellor, Ken Clarke guided the UK economy to a position of reasonable strength by 1997, while being as exuberant a performer as Healey and Heseltine in the media and the conference hall. After the Conservatives' 1997 election defeat, Clarke topped the opinion polls as the most popular candidate in the party's leadership contest. He did so again during the leadership contests he fought in 2001 and 2005. He never won.

As well as being chancellor, Rab Butler was a radically reforming Education Secretary, a modernizing party chairman and a thoughtful Home Secretary. When Conservative prime ministers he served under were ill, Butler stood in. He never acquired the crown.

Roy Jenkins was another chancellor who never became prime minister. He was almost as well qualified as Butler: a reforming Home Secretary, a chancellor who steadied the boat after Labour had been forced to devalue the pound, and a president of the European Commission who returned from Brussels to help launch a new force in British politics, the Social Democratic Party (SDP) – which, for a time, appeared to be sweeping away all before it. Jenkins was also a brilliant biographer, mainly of those who did manage to become prime minister. He had devoted followers in the Labour Party and then in the SDP. When Harold Wilson became paranoid about threats to his leadership he was especially neurotic about Jenkins, a figure who some in his party and much of the media regarded as incomparably more substantial than the Labour leader. But it was Wilson who won four elections; Jenkins never became prime minister. This book explores the reasons why.

When John Major felt increasingly fragile as prime minister, he worried about the threat posed by Heseltine and Clarke. Yet they were largely loyal to him. The one he had most cause to worry about was Michael Portillo, adored by Margaret Thatcher and her followers, a figure with serious ambition and charisma. In the mid-1990s, Portillo was seen as Thatcher's heir and the successor to Major. Yet before long Portillo was not even an MP anymore, and he discovered that his passion for power had faded to the point where the flame hardly flickered at all.

While Gordon Brown was still prime minister, some Labour MPs urged David Miliband, then Foreign Secretary, to launch a challenge. Miliband was Labour's equivalent to Portillo in some respects. He considered making a move against Brown, and there was much talk in parts of the Labour Party and the media of Miliband launching a successful leadership challenge. In the end he did not act. A few years later, in the 2010 leadership contest, David began as favourite to win but was defeated by his younger brother, Ed. Some in the Labour Party and the media still regard David as the lost leader, the one that would have led his party back to power. Nonetheless, if David had become leader there probably would have been a thousand columns and knowing judgements asserting that the party had elected the wrong brother. Perceptions of leaders are fickle and can quickly change.

There is a single chapter on the Miliband brothers, as their tense, discordant dances towards the crown were staged more or less at the same time. They had similarities, unsurprisingly, and yet were far apart ideologically. Both contributed to the fall of the other. Both were decent and thoughtful. Yet they form a dark chapter – two brothers who became ambitious, or perhaps had ambition thrust upon them, and who did not fulfil their desire to reach the top.

There is only one woman on this list and she only just met the criteria, a sad reflection on the male-dominated world of British politics, especially Labour Party politics. Potential female prime ministers in the Conservative Party became prime minister. Margaret Thatcher and Theresa May would have qualified for this book if they had not secured the superior qualification of moving into Number Ten. In the Labour Party there is a case for Margaret Beckett and Harriet Harman. Both might have been formidable prime ministers, but neither went through a phase when they were considered as likely candidates. To her regret, Harman never stood for the leadership, and she acquiesced when Gordon Brown did not make her deputy prime minister after she had won the deputy leadership contest in 2007, a considerable triumph in a strong field of candidates. If she had insisted on being made deputy prime minister or had stood and won the 2010 leadership contest, she may have become a prime minister or another that we never had. She did not do so.

Margaret Beckett held a range of Cabinet posts including Foreign Secretary, and was also acting leader when John Smith died in 1994. She was a formidable voice when Labour was in power and when it struggled in opposition after the 2010 election – always authoritative, and more experienced than most of her colleagues who flourished in the New Labour era. Beckett had been a minister in the 1970s, and was on the left as the party erupted into civil war after the 1979 election defeat. Such was her range and depth that she had the capacity to contextualize and weigh up significance as apparent crises erupted most hours of each day. A calm perspective is a rarity in the frenzy of modern politics.

Her only realistic chance of becoming a potential prime minister was if she had won the 1994 leadership contest. However, Tony Blair was the victor by a big margin; he'd been seen as the winner from the moment he announced his candidacy. Famously, the only question in the summer of 1994 was whether it should be Blair or Brown. Rightly or wrongly, even at the height of their careers, neither Harman nor Beckett were spoken of as potential prime ministers. Harman never saw herself in that role. Beckett dared to hope that her role might be permanent when she became temporary leader. When Blair entered the race, her hope vanished.

Barbara Castle is included in this book. She did not envisage becoming prime minister either, although she was flattered to be described sometimes as the politician who might be 'the first woman prime minister'. Like Harman, she did not stand in a single contest to be leader. Castle makes the list on the basis that for a short time she was the most prominent woman in British politics, and was seen by her admirers in the Labour Party and the media as a potential prime minister.

Quite a lot of the perceptions are retrospective in her case. During Labour's 2020 leadership contest the candidates were asked regularly for their favourite past Labour leaders. The response of Lisa Nandy when taking part in a Channel Four debate was for a non-leader: 'Barbara Castle was the best PM Labour never had.' In a leadership contest, every utterance is picked apart; this was a subtle response, avoiding the dangerous symbolism of backing an actual leader from the past. Nandy's choice also showed that Castle's legacy had endured. The former Labour Cabinet minister Patricia Hewitt spoke similarly a few years earlier: 'Barbara Castle should have been Labour's – and Britain's – first female prime minister. What a role model she would have been: passionate, fiery and absolutely committed to social justice.'[1] Indeed, while reflecting on her own career, Margaret Beckett also made the case for Castle being the Labour prime minister we never had.[2]

Castle had many of the qualities required for leadership: burning convictions, charm, energy, and the ability to communicate the reasons for her beliefs to an audience that might not automatically share them. She also had a skill for forming genuine friendships with some of the biggest figures, always helpful when riding towards the top. Harold Wilson admired and liked Castle. She greatly respected him, observing often that if Wilson had stayed on as prime minister instead of resigning in 1976, Labour would have won in 1979.

Castle did not become the UK's first woman prime minister. Margaret Thatcher got there in 1979. In the mid-1970s, Castle noted in her diary that her fellow Cabinet minister, Shirley Williams, had become Wilson's favourite: 'Harold is singling out Shirley for special and repeated praise… The newspaper stories about her becoming prime minister are increasing.'[3] But, like Castle, Williams never thought she would acquire the crown: 'I was excited that people were saying it, but I never took that PM stuff very seriously. I knew it wasn't going to happen. I don't think I'd have been a terribly good prime minister. Or I would have been either very good or hopeless.'[4]

Williams is an interesting case. At her peak, polls suggested she was hugely popular with the wider electorate; she was committed and politically courageous, with a melodious voice. The sound of a leader's voice matters. Williams's was far more engaging than Margaret Thatcher's. Castle's diaries are punctuated with jealous references to how Williams was admired by both Wilson and the media. But in spite of her popularity, Williams was defeated at key moments, losing her seat in 1979, failing to hold Crosby for the SDP in 1983 having won a famous by-election there following her defection from Labour, and not winning a Cambridge seat in 1987. She never stood in a contest to be leader of either Labour or the SDP, although she became leader of the Liberal Democrats in the House of Lords, a relatively minor post. Williams never got into a position where she could be feasibly seen as the next prime minister; indeed, as she moved closer to such a place, voters rejected her. Williams failed to secure a safe seat for life, one of the fundamental qualifications for leadership. As a result, she suffered the weird experience of being hugely popular nationally – and with the likes of Harold Wilson – while living in justified fear of losing her seat.

There are three men who emphatically do qualify for the dubious honour of inclusion but do not feature in the book. Two Labour leaders, Hugh Gaitskell and John Smith, would almost certainly have become prime minister. Iain Macleod, Edward Heath's chancellor after the 1970 election, might well have done. All three died prematurely. They are not included because, sadly, there is no mystery as to why they failed to reach the very top.

There is another category of politicians who do not qualify for inclusion in my list: those who might have been great prime ministers, even if they stood no realistic chance of reaching the very top. The case can be made for more or less anyone depending on your point of view. The former Conservative leader William Hague often gets quite a few votes when this game is played out on the radio or in articles. He does not make this book because there was not a single moment while he was Conservative leader after the 1997 election when he or anyone else thought he would win the subsequent election. When he was duly beaten in 2001 he resigned as leader, spending more time playing the piano, writing good books and earning decent money on the speech-making circuit. By the time he returned to the fray as shadow Foreign Secretary and then Foreign Secretary under David Cameron, all ambition had been sated. This does not mean he would not have made a good prime minister. It means he was never widely seen as a potential prime minister when he was politically active or had a realistic chance of reaching Number Ten.

On the other side, the same boundaries apply to the former Cabinet minister Alan Johnson, who was charming, decent, a natural communicator and experienced as a minister. He too might have thrived in the top job. But, as he has reflected, he did not win the party's deputy leadership contest in 2007 and never fought a contest to be leader. Johnson struggled when Ed Miliband made him shadow chancellor.

In cases like Hague and Johnson, there are no mysteries to solve. They did not become prime minister because they had no chance – whatever their strengths of character. This is not a book based on my views or anyone else's about who might have been a great prime minister. Such a book could be longer than *War and Peace*.

The failures of those included in this book require deeper explanation and exploration. All those who meet the criteria of 'prime ministers we never had' appeared to be in a position where the crown was within their reach. None of them seized the glittering prize, yet this book is not by any means a study of failure. The doomed figures were high achievers in varying ways. Some, like Jeremy Corbyn, were bewildered by how high they climbed. Most were disappointed they did not climb higher, but they had already achieved much in government or as leaders of the Opposition. The prime ministers we never had are very different from each other but are bound by one tantalizing common question: why did they fail to make the final leap? That is the question this book seeks to answer. Each chapter is not a full account of a political life. That would also make Tolstoy's novels seem slim. Instead, the characters and their specific strengths and flaws are assessed, to discover why they got so seemingly close and yet in the end were so far from seizing the crown.

——

The demands on those who do reach the very top are immense. The coronavirus that began to rage across the UK in March 2020 presented even greater challenges in terms of leadership than the financial crash of 2008 did. There will be more pandemics, testing not only the health of a country but its economy too. The UK's tottering social care provision was exposed tragically during the Covid-19 pandemic, but remedying the squalid fragilities of a lightly regulated sector will be expensive and complex. The NHS too is underfunded compared with health systems in equivalent countries. Meanwhile, climate change will only be addressed by leaders of vision ready to take tough decisions that might well be unpopular, at least in the short term. And now that the UK has left the EU, its place in the world is less clearly defined. The UK itself is vulnerable, as Scotland and Northern Ireland stir in different ways. Robust and resolute leadership is evidently required. But quite often the robustly resolute do not become prime minister, while those ill-suited to meet the titanic demands of leadership make it to Number Ten. Why is this?

The answers matter partly because if a prime minister has an overall majority, they wield considerable power. After his personal triumph in the December 2019 election, Boris Johnson was in a strong enough position to decide almost single-handedly his government's response to the pandemic in the spring of 2020, as well as the form that Brexit would take – two historic sequences that would have been different under an alternative prime minister. There are endless similar examples of the near-presidential conduct of prime ministers, from Margaret Thatcher's monetarist economic experiment to Tony Blair's decision to back President Bush's war in Iraq. These were partly personal crusades, and they would have taken a different form if others had made it to Number Ten.

I avoid too much counter-factual speculation. This is not a book about 'Prime Minister Neil Kinnock' or 'Prime Minister Ken Clarke'. Obviously, the UK's path would not have been precisely the same if any of the figures in this book had become prime minister. Whether the UK would be in a better place is inevitably another subjective judgement. We all have our own views, based on where we stand politically. However, I do make the case that if Heseltine had won the Conservative leadership contest in 1990, the course of history in the UK would have been dramatically different.

Similarly, if Kinnock, Ed Miliband or Corbyn had won general elections, the UK would be in a different place, as their victories would have meant a change of governing party. But how much space would any of them have had as prime minister? If Corbyn had won, he might not have secured an overall majority, and would have faced the constraining hell of the global pandemic as well as having to spend energy and time on addressing the still-unresolved Brexit question. Ed Miliband assumed he would be a prime minister in a hung parliament in 2015. Such a context would have limited his radical instincts, as would the dynamics in the Labour Party at a time when those who did not share his leftish views held senior positions. Nonetheless, if Miliband had won in 2015, there would have been no Brexit referendum. Miliband had bravely opposed the proposition in the election, and got little credit for his stance even from pro-EU newspapers. In the 2015 election, the pro-European *Financial Times* urged its readers to vote Conservative. In a near-incomprehensible editorial, the even more pro-European *Independent* argued for a return of the Conservative/ Liberal Democrat coalition.

Kinnock, in 1992, also worked on the understanding that if he became prime minister it would be in a hung parliament. In such a context, he would have had to spend much energy on assembling support to win votes in the Commons, and would have had a tense relationship with his chosen chancellor, John Smith. As prime minister, John Major faced the nightmare of the Exchange Rate Mechanism (ERM) crisis in September 1992. Kinnock might have done too, although he has always maintained he and Smith would have adopted a different approach on gaining power. Gazing through the speculative fog, what is clearer is that Labour was more or less united in its approach to Europe. Major's difficulties in legislating the Maastricht Treaty might have been avoided under Kinnock.

In truth, we will never know what would have happened if any of those in this book had become prime minister. Speculation is as fruitless as guessing what happens to characters in a novel without a clear ending. Subtle writers sometimes decide not to give a definitive resolution; our time as readers is better spent trying to make sense of what the author has decided to convey. Similarly, in the equally subtle and febrile world of politics, it is more fruitful to focus on what did happen to the prime ministers we never had, and to discover the reasons why they did not get to Number Ten.

With the exception of Rab Butler, I have known to varying degrees the prime ministers we never had that are featured in this book. As with the prime ministers in my previous book, I found them all more complex and interesting than the way they were often perceived or portrayed. I interviewed Roy Jenkins several times towards the end of his life, about politics and his biographies of Gladstone and Churchill. He was always generous with his wine at any time of day. On one occasion, the journalist John Lloyd and I went to interview him at his office in the Lords at 11 in the morning. Good wine was served. But Jenkins was also generous on a much more important level. He was widely mocked as a grand and lofty figure, but he had a refreshing and counter-intuitively modest curiosity, often asking about others in politics and the media. After interviews, he was always keen to talk about what was happening and how I as a columnist chose topics and individuals as themes.

Jenkins once observed to me, accurately, how difficult it was for columnists in the era of New Labour and weak opposition, when the 'only two dominant figures are Blair and Brown… in previous decades there were a greater range of big figures to write about on both sides.' I was struck that, at the end of a mountainous career, Jenkins was still fascinated by the art of column writing.

Denis Healey was equally engaged and more mischievous when I interviewed him a few times, mainly about his period as chancellor in the 1970s. The interviews were decades after he was at the Treasury. He was passionate about the era in which he had played a part, and less curious, I sensed, than Jenkins about what was happening when Labour returned to power in 1997.

Barbara Castle was so mischievous she made me laugh out loud on the few occasions I interviewed her or met her. In the chapter on her, I quote extensively from one of my interviews, during which she revealed whether or not she had an affair with her friend Michael Foot. She was nearly blind at the time I knew her, and yet she could see sharply all that was happening in the early phase of the New Labour era. My exchanges with these three prime ministers we never had were all towards the end of their lives, all personal political ambition spent. They were free to reflect.

I got to know Neil Kinnock much better after he ceased to be Labour leader, and I continue to meet up with him regularly. The *Observer* columnist William Keegan and I have spent many long, convivial lunchtimes drinking too much wine and discussing politics with him. He can be as fun and insightful now as I remember him being when he was a rising star in the Labour Party. I recall observing him from a distance then: the youthful orator who could fill every hall in the land; the guest on TV chat shows; a star of the left who turned on Tony Benn at a pivotal moment. Then he became leader and endured nine years of hope and hell. I note that when he reflects on his time as leader, the pain is still there – as well as the ability to laugh as he highlights the farcical absurdities of leading Labour as the party went through a phase when it was almost impossible to lead.

All the prime ministers that never were challenge the caricatures that defined their public image. Perhaps Michael Heseltine does so most of all. At least that is what I found on the few occasions I interviewed him or spent a bit of time with him. He might have been a performer and intensely ambitious, but he also possessed a deep seriousness and sense of responsibility. When I asked him in a BBC radio studio about his party and Europe after he had left the Commons, he almost shook with anger and sorrow. I observed a similar surprising intensity in a different context. In the autumn of 1992 he was president of the Board of Trade in John Major's government, and struggling with his decision to close several deep coal mines. Tory MPs were in revolt. Unusually, Tory-supporting newspapers backed the miners and not the Conservative government. My then BBC colleague John Pienaar and I had lunch with Heseltine at the height of the crisis. Heseltine deployed every implement on the table – knives, forks, salt and pepper pots, unused plates and glasses – to show what he was trying to do with the mines and to explain the support he was giving to those who would lose their jobs. I noticed that his hands were shaking as he moved the implements around. He had found the crisis traumatic and it had taken a toll on him, not because of the impact on his leadership ambitions but because of the burden of the responsibility. In terms of mastering policy implications he was not frivolous as Boris Johnson could be, or casually shallow as David Cameron often was. There was a weightiness to Heseltine.

Yet it was the Etonian duo, Cameron and Johnson, who made it to Number Ten.

I interviewed Michael Portillo for a Radio 4 series on those who had lost their seats or elections at key moments in their careers. Famously, Portillo lost his seat in Labour's 1997 landslide. He not only had to accept defeat but adapt also to the fact that voters were thrilled by his humiliation. 'Were you up for Portillo?' became the slogan of the night. He spoke openly about the saga and the degree to which it triggered a new outlook on politics and life. But he also admitted that, years later, he still looked at whoever was prime minister with a degree of envy.

To some extent, Portillo also had curiosity. When I was a guest on BBC One's *This Week*, the political show in which Portillo formed an engaging double act with the Labour MP Diane Abbott, he was the most interested in the answers to questions and the least predictable in discussions. Curiously, there was the same enigmatic quality when he was at his peak as a potential prime minister as there was later, when he became more of a TV celebrity. He had changed as a public figure and yet the basis of his charisma had not. From seeking to be prime minister to becoming a TV presenter he was charming and engaged, yet also reserved, distant and self-contained.

I knew the Miliband brothers best of all, liked them both and found the leadership contest in which they were both candidates something of a nightmare, as did many other political journalists. During the New Labour era, I met up with them often – separately of course. I also saw a fair amount of Ed when he was leader and in the aftermath of his election defeat in 2015. The careers of the two Milibands took an unlikely course. Only Jeremy Corbyn can beat them in his even more bizarre political journey. They began as

assiduously thoughtful special advisers, working behind the scenes
in opposition and then in government – David committed to Tony
Blair and Ed to Gordon Brown. Although they were written about
often, they were not public figures for many years. They seemed
fairly content with their background roles while others battled it
out in public. Yet they became prominent politicians speedily once
they had secured safe parliamentary seats. After which their careers
developed with a weird intensity, partly fuelled by the fraternal
rivalry but also by the way personal ambition took hold of them as if
from nowhere. I did not get the impression they started out aching
to lead their party or were even wholly sure at the beginning they
wanted to become MPs. Yet both ended up ferociously determined
to lead, more or less at around the same time.

The least likely course of any figure in this book was the one
taken by Jeremy Corbyn. He makes the Milibands' journey seem
normal. Corbyn had no desire to be a leader even when he stood for
the leadership contest in 2015. His rise and fall is one of the most
remarkable stories in modern British politics. I used to interview him
regularly, long before he became leader, when I presented GMTV
live early on Sunday mornings. The production team discovered
that Corbyn was willing to come to the studio, often at short notice,
as he lived nearby. Over coffee afterwards he was always polite and
modest. After he resigned as leader, some commentators suggested
that Corbyn was a vain narcissist.[5] I have never met a politician who
was less vain. No doubt after he became leader the idolatry that
greeted him at public events partly went to his head. It would go
to the head of any human being. Before then, he was content to be
a local MP and vote against his party leadership in the Commons
on a regular basis. When he was leader I occasionally bumped into
him jogging near Finsbury Park in north London. By then he had

good cause to be wary of nearly all journalists, but he was always pleasant and unassuming in conversations.

During the period Corbyn was leader he never went in for personal attacks on anyone, even to the point that he struggled to launch an onslaught against Theresa May or Boris Johnson at Prime Minister's Questions. Similarly, he was too decent to sack virtually anyone on his frontbench or in his office. These were failings in the context of leadership. A leader must be ruthless. And these were by no means his only flaws as a leader. Unsurprisingly, as an MP who had given no thought to leadership, he struggled to lead. I suspect that, far from being a narcissist, he was relieved on many levels not to have been prime minister. Even so, he got closer than many expected. In the aftermath of the 2017 election I had conversations with several Labour and Conservative MPs who told me, in the midst of the chaos of Theresa May's premiership, that Corbyn could well be prime minister before very long. He never was.

Like those in my previous book, *The Prime Ministers: Reflections on Leadership from Wilson to Johnson*, the chapters that follow are based on a series of unscripted BBC talks, each one recorded in a single thirty-minute take. Some of the talks are still available on BBC iPlayer or YouTube. The themes, lessons and epic dramas are explored at much greater length in this book.

The prime ministers who never were form as much of a soundtrack to our lives as do the prime ministers. At their peak they were each talked about and analysed as much as the occupants of Number Ten were. Hope is a driving force in politics, explaining why so many keep going in spite of the overwhelming pressure. The characters in this book dared to hope that they would be prime minister. Their hopes were dashed, but each of them had good cause to dream.

1

RAB BUTLER

Rab Butler is the original prime minister we never had. Butler is one of those rare former Cabinet ministers whose name and deeds are still often cited. When they are, an observation usually follows, along the lines of, 'Ah yes, Rab Butler, the best prime minister we never had'. Indeed, the persistent claim forms the subtitle of a recent biography of Butler, although the author wisely adds a question mark.[1]

The judicious question mark has its place not so much because of the adjective 'best'. That is a subjective judgement. Rather, the justified doubt is over whether Butler was ever in a strong enough position to become prime minister, in spite of his remarkable career. On so many levels Butler was supremely well qualified. No one else in this book can compete with him in terms of experience and range. He held multiple roles for decades: a reforming minister, a modernizing party chairman and a stand-in prime minister. Butler had a high profile on the political stage from the 1930s until the Conservatives were defeated in the 1964 election. In each post he had a profound impact. Butler was not a 'here today, gone tomorrow' politician. He was a change-maker.

There is a striking contrast between Butler's ministerial career at points when he might have become prime minister and the careers of some of those who did climb to the very top. Tony Blair and David Cameron had no ministerial experience when they became prime ministers. Margaret Thatcher was only briefly Education Secretary. John Major had held two of the most senior jobs, Foreign Secretary and chancellor, but only fleetingly.

Compare those examples of limited or no ministerial experience with Butler's mind-boggling range. As a junior minister in the early 1930s he played a significant role in implementing plans that helped India become autonomous from the British Empire, a highly charged mission that included the handling of opponents within the Conservative Party – not easy for a senior minister, let alone a junior one. During the war he was responsible for education, passing the Education Act of 1944, one of the few examples of legislation that was still cited for its significance half a century later.

After the Conservatives were slaughtered in the 1945 election, Butler was a reformer in opposition, seeking ways of synthesizing Tory values with the fresh challenges and assumptions of the post-war era, one in which Labour ruled with a big majority. Blending a party's traditional values with changing orthodoxies is an art form. Although not exuberant as a public performer, Butler was an artist in terms of encouraging his largely reluctant party to move with the times. As a result, the Conservatives soon resumed their traditional role of winning elections.

When he was made chancellor in October 1951, Butler faced the demands of strengthening a fragile post-war economy. There were oscillations in terms of progress and his own popularity, as there are for all chancellors who serve for more than a moment or two. But on the whole, the economy was stronger by the end of his spell at the Treasury than at the beginning. Butler moved on to become an innovative Home Secretary under Harold Macmillan in the late 1950s, as well as performing several other tasks. He was briefly Foreign Secretary in the run-up to the 1964 election. He even stood in when the actual prime minister was ill, on two highly sensitive occasions.

Most Cabinet ministers do not last for very long. They soon find they are not up to the job, fall out with their leader, or get bored too easily. Some are moved from department to department without staying long enough to leave any significant mark. Butler's political CV is daunting and this is only a brief introductory summary. He had more experience than several incoming modern prime ministers put together.

Here is a depressing lesson of leadership: for aspiring leaders, there is greater safety in having no past of significance than one of such depth that controversies and consequences are recalled when the crown moves into sight. Butler's patient, practical reforming zeal propelled him to the top of his party, but it was also a significant obstacle in the way of him becoming prime minister.

———

The proposals to give greater self-government to India were complex and highly contentious. Winston Churchill was one of many Conservative MPs who looked on warily at what the youthful Rab Butler was doing – an intimidating prospect. Party members were equally concerned as Butler in his role as junior minister put the case for what became the Government of India Act in 1935.

Butler was a genuine modernizer, unlike many more recent figures in the Conservative Party who have claimed this vaguely defined epithet for themselves. In the case of India he faced one last defiant cry from old-fashioned imperialists and took them on politely. Butler had a good relationship with local party members in his Saffron Walden constituency, but even they felt compelled to 'express great apprehension lest the granting of self-government to India... may be injurious to the British Empire'.[2] His first move as a minister was substantial but it alienated a significant section of his party. Genuine reformers are bound to antagonize those within their party who cling to the status quo.

In seeking change, Butler was not dogmatic. His determined pragmatism was on display from the beginning as he patiently sought ways of bringing doubters with him. He insisted regularly in the Commons that the proposals in relation to India were the product of compromise and determined expediency; they represented what Tony Blair would later call the 'third way'. The British government retained a right to intervene if it judged governors in India were ruling irresponsibly. Self-government depended partly, and vaguely, on the consent of the Westminster government.

Inevitably, this third-way approach did not satisfy more ardent imperialists. Churchill and his supporters established the India Defence League, a pressure group committed to keeping India as part of the British Empire. In response, Butler was involved in setting up the Union of Britain and India, whose name articulated the ambiguity of the limited leap towards self-government. And so in his first ministerial role, Butler was at the heart of a divide within the Conservative Party, implementing seismic changes in a cautious manner. If there was a template for Butler's career, this was it.

One of Butler's great enduring strengths was fully formed from the beginning: his eagerness to work with non-Conservatives, including policy specialists and those from other political parties. He had consulted widely over self-government for India. In doing so he pushed at the boundaries of what a section of his party would accept, and yet he sought to manage internal dissent as subtly as possible, which was another of his talents. Churchill praised Butler even as he vilified more senior ministers, quite an achievement for the youthful politician. Butler had been careful to treat Churchill with solicitous respect in the Commons and in private meetings. He was alert to the political mood at any given time and knew Churchill was a potential leader. More immediately, Butler recognized that the great ego would erupt less ferociously if treated with charming deference.

There were other strengths. From the beginning of his career Butler was a doer who derived satisfaction from implementing policies as much as from the theatre of politics. Some colleagues thought him closer in certain respects to a civil servant, mastering detail and looking towards putting policies into effect. This was a misjudgement, mistaking his capacity for work and his self-effacement as the traits of a technocrat. Butler was ideologically rooted on the centre right, a politically deft one-nation Conservative capable of finding the means to bring about ends, forging new alliances and creating a consensus around thorny issues. He did not have the temperament of a civil servant. He was a constructive and creative Conservative politician.

When Butler was made president of the Board of Education in 1941 the same patterns recurred. There was already a broad but fragile political consensus about the need for sweeping changes to education provision. As is often the case with an apparent consensus, when specific measures were proposed there was little agreement within parties, let alone between them.

The need for reform of schools had been widely recognized since the end of the First World War. In 1918, still exerting a restless radical verve, Liberal prime minister David Lloyd George had passed an Act aimed at raising the school leaving age and giving more responsibility to local authorities to run schools in place of overstretched churches and other religious institutions. The changes were never implemented, largely due to resistance from parts of the Conservative Party. Butler's triumph as Conservative Education Secretary was to realize the essence of Lloyd George's vision.

By the outbreak of the Second World War, Butler was getting used to making moves that challenged orthodoxies in his party. For some Conservatives, education was still seen as a religious responsibility even though their perception was at odds with reality. Churches did not have the resources or the inclination to meet the demand for school places. As with his plans for India, Butler had to deal with the wariness of Churchill, who was now a wartime prime minister rather than a formidable backbencher. Churchill wanted Butler to focus on schools delivering as best they could in wartime conditions. Butler insisted that the education system needed to adapt more fundamentally to modern conditions. He was much less demonstrative than Churchill but far more ambitious, at least in terms of domestic reform.

Again, Butler looked beyond the boundaries of the Conservative Party, calculating rightly that in the national wartime government he would have the support of Labour ministers – including the deputy prime minister and Labour leader, Clement Attlee. In making the case for more secular education and a school leaving age of fifteen, rising to sixteen, Butler cited the left-wing political philosopher R. H. Tawney as much as he did more conservative advocates of change.

As with his approach to India he was not recklessly inexpedient. He sought again a third way, although in doing so from the right

Butler was more at ease with embracing some on the left than Blair tended to be when he navigated this deceptively tricky terrain as Labour prime minister. Blair was not known for citing Tawney very often, while Butler was freer to do so as he wooed Labour figures.

Butler was a navigator of what was possible, and more of an incrementalist than his internal opponents dared to realize or acknowledge. Following complex negotiations with religious leaders, a majority of the Anglican church schools were effectively absorbed into the state system. As part of the compromise, a third of them received higher state subsidies while retaining autonomy over admissions, curricula and teacher appointments. Churches had lost some of their grip but by no means all. Well into the twenty-first century, some church schools would still be targeted by middle-class parents who discovered an attachment to Christianity in order to secure a place for their children. Butler's historic education policies had distinct limits and yet marked a radical break with the past.

The most enduring reform of the 1944 Act established secondary education at the age of eleven, while abolishing fees for state secondary schools. The Act also renamed the Board of Education as the Ministry of Education, giving it greater powers and a bigger budget. Subtly, the legislation was both a move towards greater centralization and an assertion of localism, with councils acquiring more responsibility for local schools. The Act hinted at a much bigger vision of how to manage a public service through robust central and local government. The hint was not followed through, however. Following decades of confused corporatism in the 1960s and 1970s, the UK government opted for weaker central government and moribund local government after 1979, a combination that led to a more atomized state. By then, Butler's one-nation conservatism was out of fashion.

Even so, the 1944 Act became totemic. On its sixtieth anniversary, the chief inspector of schools, David Bell, noted in a lecture:

> It is no wonder that the 1944 act is often referred to as the Butler act, as a measure of the respect for Rab Butler's contribution to the development of state education. The fact that we continue to work towards his educational goals reflects the high quality of his forward thinking and the debt we owe him for stimulating and guiding great steps forward in educational provision in this country. It is time now for the generations who have benefited from Butler's visionary thinking to repay that debt, and seek to improve further the life chances of the generations to come.[3]

Not many Cabinet ministers have their name associated with reforms that are the subject of a lecture decades later. Most are not associated with reforms while they are ministers. Yet Butler was a cautious visionary. His changes meant that, although pupils had at last the benefits of a later school leaving age, they faced the prospect of selection at eleven, an arbitrary age for a child's long-term fate to be determined. Some church schools continued to flourish and became part of a new elite.

In spite of the reactionary strands of the legislation, the Act marked a big leap on both practical and ideological grounds, guaranteeing British children an education until they were at least fifteen. In some respects, Butler was framing arguments about a more benevolent state that came to underpin the 1945 Labour government. This does not mean Butler was by any means a figure of the left, but he was willing to contemplate a bigger role for government, not least in the context of the 1940s and the Second World War. He was ahead of his party on this – the only place for a genuinely reforming minister to be, but not one that necessarily endears a potential leader to local members. Butler was as personally ambitious as any of his Conservative Party contemporaries, but he was a tireless reformer who did not always calculate how this left him in terms of becoming leader.

After Labour's victory in 1945, Butler became a thoughtful opponent. Quite a lot of the Conservative frontbench was surprised to be out of power after the war. Butler kept going, applying the same intelligent energy as he had done in government. Here too there are parallels with the approach of Tony Blair and Gordon Brown in the build-up to the 1997 election. They were obsessed with the question of why Labour kept losing elections, and they sought, with varying degrees of success, to synthesize the values of their party with the attitudes of the voters who'd abandoned them – or who'd never supported them to begin with. Both became prime minister. Butler performed at least as effective an act of synthesis for the Conservatives, but he did not become prime minister.

After Attlee's victory in 1945, Churchill's instinct was to attack Labour with a renewed ferocity without looking too closely at his own party. He was a restlessly impatient loser. Butler was less complacently bombastic, recognizing there was little to be gained from mounting an onslaught that by implication challenged the judgement of the voters. Attlee had won a landslide. Butler knew the Tory message had to be much more sophisticated than 'the voters got it wrong'.

As head of the party's research department, Butler published a series of charters that blended Tory support for enterprise and individualism with a recognition of government responsibilities and the importance of direction from the centre. He cited his Education Act as one model. Voters had backed a Labour government to make radical change in relation to the role of the state, and Butler did not believe the Conservatives could ignore what had happened. This did not make him a left-wing figure, much as Labour's 1997 manifesto, although cautious, was not a programme of the right. The Tories' manifesto in 1950 was a third-way programme that stressed the security of the individual while also being more supportive of trade unions. The Butler-inspired policies proposed to denationalize where practical and to retain state ownership if that delivered efficiencies. Butler had in mind Robert Peel's 1834 Tamworth Manifesto, which had sought to adapt the Tory Party to fast-changing times.

The Conservatives gained ninety seats in the 1950 election, reducing the Labour majority to five, a major advance. Compare this partial comeback with what happened after their even bigger defeat in 1997, when the party was defeated again in 2001. It lacked a Butler-type figure. After 1945, Butler did more than any other Tory to convey a sense that his party was adapting to new times without changing its values, a tricky balancing act and one that did not always meet with Churchill's approval.

By 1951 the Conservatives were back in power and Churchill was prime minister once again. Although Butler had played a substantial role in reviving his party, the Tory right was not grateful. Some MPs were wary of Butler's liberal instincts and his willingness to move beyond what they regarded as traditional conservatism. It was the recurring pattern: Butler made a difference, and in doing so he alienated some on his own side. With some misgivings, Churchill made Butler chancellor. He shared the doubts felt by sections of the Conservative Party. Was Butler too liberal? Was he too willing to move on the terrain occupied by Labour? The answer to both questions was 'no'.

Butler's reputation at the Treasury soared, fell and rose again, arguably the best that chancellors can hope for. A few chancellors endure a largely hostile reaction during their entire tenure at the Treasury. None enjoy universal praise. Most go up and down in popularity, which is why being chancellor is not a safe route to becoming prime minister. Neither Roy Jenkins nor Denis Healey made it to the top. James Callaghan did, but only after retreating to other posts for many years. John Major was lucky in being chancellor for such a short time, delivering only one budget. It is testimony to Gordon Brown's wilfulness and agility that he went from being Labour's longest-serving chancellor to the occupant of Number Ten, but as his reputation rose and sank several times at the Treasury he agonized over whether he would ever get the top job.

Butler was chancellor at a challenging time. He inherited a significant balance of payments deficit, a key test of economic fragility then and for several decades to come. He responded to the UK's post-war economic vulnerability by instigating another of his New Labour–like third ways. This time he was an early version of Gordon Brown rather than Tony Blair. In his first budget, in 1952, he promised 'realism and hope', close in its attempt to reassure and inspire to Brown's 'prudence for a purpose'. Towards the end of his reign at the Treasury, *The Economist* wrote about 'Butskellism', detecting a coming together of Butler's policies and those of Labour's Hugh Gaitskell. Gaitskell had been chancellor when Labour was defeated in the 1951 election. Butler replaced him in the new Conservative government, and Gaitskell became Labour's leader. There was something to the Butskellism assessment: Butler accepted elements of a mixed economy, as did Gaitskell. Both were advocates of what is now known vaguely as 'fair taxation'. In one of his budgets, Butler introduced tax cuts that were paid for by an excessive profits tax. Gaitskell might have done the same.

But the elements of Gaitskell's approach that Butler shared tended to be policies more readily associated with a Conservative government. As shadow chancellor, Butler had supported Gaitskell's plan to increase defence spending, to be paid for with a new prescription charge – the emblematic bargain that provoked the Cabinet resignations of Aneurin Bevan and Harold Wilson. For a Conservative, there are benefits to hailing a policy that divides Labour. David Cameron did the same when he praised Tony Blair's public service reforms after he became Conservative leader in 2005.

Butler was not on the left and Gaitskell was not a Conservative. Yet the term 'Butskellism' became a motif in the 1950s because it mischievously captured the methods of two figures adopting new approaches that attracted suspicion. At first, Butler was a prudent chancellor, deciding like Roy Jenkins would in the late 1960s that he had no other choice. But by the time of his second budget, in 1953, the economy was coming back to life. As it revived, Butler was widely seen as the great success of the Churchill peacetime government. The same happened to Gordon Brown and several other chancellors when they presided over apparently robust expanding economies.

———

It was while Butler was chancellor that he first got close to the pinnacle of power. In the summer of 1953, Churchill had an unreported stroke that kept him out of action. This was the first episode of an extraordinary three-part drama in which Butler had a chance of being prime minister. Churchill's Foreign Secretary, Anthony Eden, was undergoing a series of major operations and was also politically inactive for a time. The UK government was almost as incapacitated as it became when the coronavirus struck Boris Johnson and other senior figures in the spring of 2020.

The illness of prime ministers played a big part in Butler's career. In 1953, the healthy Butler chaired several Cabinet meetings before Churchill returned to the fray. Like most prime ministers, Churchill could not give up. Still, for Butler the act of chairing Cabinet meetings in his absence was a potent one. He was carrying out prime ministerial duties.

Yet it was Eden who was finally selected as Churchill's successor in April 1955. With Eden apparently healthy again, Butler did not stand much of a chance. For years there had been a sense of inevitability that when Churchill finally went it would be Eden's turn. The assumption at the top of the Conservative Party was that Eden had waited long enough and must be given his opportunity to lead. Eden's succession was similar to that of Gordon Brown in 2007; after a long wait, Brown was unstoppable. Though there was one significant difference. There was no alternative as substantial as Butler when Brown was crowned unopposed, after the bizarre leadership contest in which he was the only candidate. But, however weighty, Butler did little more than look on as Eden finally got his wish and moved into Number Ten.

Part two of this saga followed more speedily than anyone could have anticipated. This was Butler's more substantial opportunity to acquire the crown. His failure to do so would cause him more anguish than anything else in his career.

The next vacancy in Number Ten was triggered by the dramatic fall of Eden as a result of the Suez Crisis that erupted in the summer of 1956. The ingredients of the crisis are darkly familiar – early examples of what would become distinct features of post-war

British foreign policy. They took the form of what was known later as 'British exceptionalism'. At first, Eden and his fickle supporters in the Conservative Party and the media displayed a strident sense of a uniquely mighty Britain. Yet the bombastic facade disguised a neurotic insecurity about the UK's place in the world. The combination was seemingly a contradiction in terms, but the two elements were intimately linked. There are many echoes arising from the Suez drama: a need to appear strong in ways that unintentionally reveal weakness; a Labour leader sensing a need to seem supportive of military action; a media hailing the 'courage' of a military adventure only to turn and condemn 'weak' leadership. The ingredients were still in place, albeit in different forms, when Tony Blair made his moves towards the Iraq War, and when Margaret Thatcher instigated the Falklands War. However, in both those cases the prime ministers went on to win further elections. Suez destroyed Eden.

All hell broke loose when Egypt's president, General Nasser, nationalized the Suez Canal in July 1956. The canal had been jointly owned by Britain and France and, in response to Nasser's action, British exceptionalism and insecurity flared up. At first, the newspapers were jingoistic, demanding that something must be done, just as they did decades later when the Argentinian junta seized the Falkland Islands. The Labour leader, Hugh Gaitskell, felt compelled to join the outrage, comparing Nasser's conduct to that of Mussolini and Hitler.

In keeping with his decision to resign over Neville Chamberlain's appeasement of Germany in the 1930s, Eden was ready to act. The Second World War still loomed large, as it did when Thatcher and Blair instigated their military adventures: in one televised broadcast, Eden echoed Gaitskell and explicitly compared Nasser to the dictators of the 1930s.

As UK prime ministers are prone to when calculating military interventions, Eden made an assessment of how the UK stood in relation to the US. He assumed that, at the very least, President Eisenhower would not oppose military action. This was a fatal error. Eisenhower wanted all peaceful routes to be explored. Quickly, Eden discovered how dependent the UK had become on the economic and military might of the Americans. With the US threatening to withdraw financial support from sterling, the Cabinet was no longer united in its nationalistic bullishness. At one point, Harold Macmillan, who had replaced Butler as chancellor, threatened to resign unless a ceasefire was called.

The newspapers turned. As they did, Gaitskell also became an opponent of the military intervention. Having been praised for his Churchillian leadership, Eden became isolated, both at home and on the international stage. He had no choice but to end the military operation in November 1956, before much progress had been made.

The past had determined the assumptions of all the key players, distorting their judgement, as it would with future leaders in subsequent military interventions. In particular, Butler's approach was framed by the 1930s. Back then he had been a strong supporter of appeasement, placing him in a wholly different position to Churchill, Eden and Macmillan, who had all famously opposed Neville Chamberlain's foreign policy. Partly because of his personal history, Butler felt the need to at least partially back Eden and be seen to do so. He had been a dove in the 1930s. Now he must be a little more hawkish. In the early weeks of the crisis, Butler tried to restrain Eden, but to little or no effect. This time his third-way approach alienated both sides. In arguing for a more restrained approach he infuriated the gung-ho supporters of military action, while his failure to restrain the prime minister earned him the opprobrium of the plan's opponents.

Arguably, Butler's attitude was more consistent than that of his rival. Macmillan started out all for the use of force. He did not advise Eden to move cautiously. Then he made the leap to the other side. Publicly, Butler defended Eden and Suez, while privately he was more critical. Of course, the nuanced approach rarely works when the UK is involved in military action: some Cabinet ministers and Tory backbenchers regarded Butler as a figure they could not wholly trust, the supporter of appeasement now almost supporting military action but not quite doing so.

Macmillan was more skilled at being devious. The art of deviousness is an important qualification for leadership and difficult to pull off. It must pass largely undetected. A politician cannot succeed in their manipulative moves if everyone suspects them of being a schemer. In his response to Suez, Macmillan was more of an artist than Butler. Macmillan also had the space to equivocate, both as chancellor and because he'd opposed appeasement and therefore had no need to prove his muscularity.

Macmillan's support for Eden's policy at first was sincere. Yet when the fragility of the enterprise was becoming clear, he discreetly questioned the strategy of the chiefs of staff and argued as chancellor that no risks should be taken until the US gave its full support. He made the case on the grounds of the economic situation. Butler was now Leader of the House, no longer in the Treasury, and had no such ministerial cover for a shift towards overt scepticism, or lacked the suppleness to find a protective shield.

By November 1956, Eden was too ill to continue as leader and took a break in Jamaica. Butler deputized again, as he had done for Churchill. As Eden's stand-in and deputy he had no choice but to be even more overtly loyal. Both Butler and Macmillan addressed the 1922 Committee of backbench MPs that month. Butler made clear his concerns about Suez but was in effect acting prime minister, and he struggled to be both loyal and disloyal simultaneously – again part of the artistry required of potential leaders. Macmillan was less constrained and used his limited space ruthlessly, highlighting the economic risks of a failed military venture. Sometimes events and circumstances conspire to place Cabinet ministers in a position where only one route is available to them. This was the case with Butler as Eden moved towards his doom. The obstacles on the route prevented Butler from becoming prime minister.

Eden never returned to lead. In January 1957, his doctors advised him to stand down on health grounds. This left Butler and Macmillan as the only two figures seen as possible successors. Unusually for him, Butler was more confident than he had cause to be. Normally, he was a perceptive reader of the political rhythms and possessed a fairly well-developed sense of where he was placed at any given time on the stage. This time he misread badly. In his overconfidence, Butler even went as far as preparing a statement that would form his televised prime ministerial address to the nation. He was acting prime minister, after all, and after the traumas of Suez dared to assume the smoothest transition to him being the actual prime minister.

He never stood a chance. Macmillan was a more textured politician who had managed his rise to the top with a greater sense of self-interest. He was the better Commons speaker, witty and combative, who'd made his mark as a successful Housing Minister, then a post of Cabinet rank, and as a stabilizing chancellor. Macmillan and Eden had been on the same side in the defining appeasement debate. In the years that followed, Macmillan had managed to retain better relations with Eden than Butler had. Eden never fully trusted Butler.

The party's chief whip, Edward Heath, had a duty to inform Butler that he had not 'emerged' as Eden's successor. This was the era in which the outgoing leader and the Cabinet in effect chose the successor. Only three Cabinet ministers supported Butler, with most of the rest backing Macmillan. Acquiring the ruthlessness to bear bad news was an early test of leadership for Heath. He told Butler he was not the chosen one with characteristic bluntness, but not even the subtlest of politicians could have sugared that particular pill. Butler never fully recovered from the shock. The degree to which he was taken aback revealed a naive side to his character: he was perceptive about others but not always wise about how others saw him.

Uniquely, Butler had a third chance to become prime minister. Most prime ministers we never had managed to get tantalizingly close to the summit once, or perhaps twice. Some never got much beyond base camp. Butler kept going in an era when the lure of quitting politics and making millions or becoming a TV star played little part in the calculations of ministers burdened by dashed hopes.

To soften the blow of his failure to succeed in 1957, Macmillan gave Butler the Home Office, which he took on while continuing as Leader of the House of Commons. Always hungry for work, he subsequently added a third string to his bow, that of party chairman, following the successful 1959 general election. While Macmillan saw himself as a global leader, Butler was once again a driver of domestic reform. He was a long-serving and relatively liberal Home Secretary while fulfilling other demanding roles. Butler was as prominent and active as ever, without establishing much of a rapport with Macmillan. Given the blows to his leadership ambitions, he possessed freakish levels of political stamina.

When Macmillan fell ill in the autumn of 1963, it was Butler yet again who stood in, even making the leader's speech at the annual party conference, an event that became an unofficial leadership contest. By October, Macmillan had stood down on the advice of his doctors. Macmillan spent quite a few years half regretting that he followed the instructions of his medical advisers. He was not seriously ill and lived for many years after he resigned. Part of him recognized, however, that illness gave him the excuse he needed to get out with dignity as darkness descended on his leadership, with the Profumo affair, the 'night of the long knives' Cabinet reshuffle, and economic storms brewing. The Profumo saga involved spies, secrets, ministerial lies in the House of Commons and affairs with glamorous women – not an easy mix for Macmillan to play down in the media and beyond. Meanwhile, his reshuffle had been too obviously part of the panic-stricken mood. Amid the bloody mayhem, the Opposition leader, Harold Wilson, popped up to declare, 'The prime minister has sacked half his cabinet... the wrong half.' Wilson had learned the art of wit from observing Macmillan closely. Most successful leaders deploy wit like a weapon, though the likes of Margaret Thatcher show there are exceptions to this particular rule.

Even from his hospital bed Macmillan had significant influence over who would succeed him. At the very least, he wanted others apart from Butler to have a chance. Macmillan had told Butler privately more than once he would be the successor. But he had indicated the same to Lord Hailsham. Neither prevailed. Wielding Prospero-like powers from above the political fray, Macmillan did not go out of his way to help Butler, or indeed Hailsham, become the next prime minister.

Macmillan later told Hailsham that he had decided Butler 'didn't have it in him'.[4] Macmillan could be perceptive about colleagues and opponents, but this particular judgement was arguably wrong. Alec Douglas-Home became the chosen one, resigning from the Lords to become prime minister. Douglas-Home was a less substantial figure than Butler and an easier target for Harold Wilson. The Labour leader pitched himself successfully as a modernizer, in contrast to the outdated aristocrat Douglas-Home. Wilson might have struggled more against a modernizing figure like Butler.

Macmillan had been wary of Butler since the 1930s, despite them both being positioned on the 'one nation' wing of the party. Macmillan had his own name for his third way, the 'middle way', and wrote a book with this title. Butler called his memoirs *The Art of the Possible*. Both men were pragmatists. Both were fascinated by the art of politics – reaching a consensus to bring about reform, the framing of arguments to win a case, and how to perform in the theatre of politics. In spite of this common ground, the two of them fell out badly early in their careers and their relations never fully recovered.

As part of Macmillan's wider curiosity about politics and economic policy, he was fascinated by Oswald Mosley during the phase when Mosley was a left-wing minister in the tottering Labour government. In May 1930, Mosley resigned from Ramsay MacDonald's government over its refusal to adopt a stimulus package largely aimed at reducing unemployment. Most Tories were delighted at Mosley's departure and they backed MacDonald's attempt to cut public spending. The exception was Macmillan. He wrote to *The Times* defending Mosley's resignation as a principled act that challenged the 'game of politics'. In an illuminating and partially courageous analysis, Macmillan noted that parties often contested elections on promises or pledges they would not meet, adding, 'if these rules are to be permanently enforced, perhaps a good many of us will feel that it is hardly worth bothering to play at all. Sir Oswald Mosley thinks the rules should be altered. I hope some of my friends will have the courage to applaud and support his protest.'[5]

The next morning a riposte was published signed by four Conservatives, one of whom was Butler: 'When a player starts complaining "that it is hardly worth while bothering to play" the game at all it is usually the player, and not the game, who is at fault. It is then usually advisable for the player to seek a new field for his recreation and a pastime more suited to his talents.'[6] The elegant style, playing with the metaphor in Macmillan's letter, suggested Butler was the instigator. At least, that was Macmillan's view.

The exchange shone much light on the youthful duo. Macmillan was out of Parliament when he wrote the letter, but he had every intention of returning. His observations seemed braver than they were. He was hailing a Labour resignation rather than a Conservative act of disloyalty. He was not necessarily agreeing with Mosley's economic interventionism, although he was fairly sympathetic at the time. Macmillan was celebrating conviction and integrity, and displaying a romanticized view of politics in which heroic individuals rather than team players should flourish. Inevitably, when he became prime minister he took a more orthodox approach to collective responsibility.

Butler's response was a defence of the 'game' as played by both sides and a put-down of Macmillan for apparently not wanting to play by the rules. Yet the reply is also not quite what it seems. Butler was more ambitious than Macmillan when he was a Cabinet minister, working skilfully with non-Conservatives to implement reforms and sometimes pushing at party boundaries while also adhering to the rules of collective responsibility. While unswervingly loyal to the Conservative Party, he was never as tribal as his *Times* letter might have implied. After his career was over, his choice of biographer was revealing in this respect. Butler asked the Labour-supporting former editor of the *New Statesman* Anthony Howard to write the authorized account of his life. Howard was taken aback, but the request was true to the pattern of Butler's character.

The spat between Butler and Macmillan was complicated, but the consequences were straightforward. Macmillan never forgave Butler for his lofty response in *The Times*. He had assumed he was making a legitimate point about principles and electoral mandates, and he was shocked to have been demolished by Conservative colleagues. At the very least, Macmillan was disinclined to do Butler favours in relation to becoming prime minister. This was borne out by subsequent events – first when Macmillan beat him to become prime minister in 1957, and then when he acted ambiguously during the dramatic autumn of 1963. Douglas-Home served as prime minister until the 1964 election. Wilson won by a narrow margin before securing a landslide victory in 1966. Butler's long political career was over.

———

Macmillan's ambivalence towards Butler points to another lesson of leadership: aspiring leaders stumble if they antagonize too many influential figures. Butler failed to establish a rapport with Eden or Macmillan. Both used him as their deputy without helping him to succeed. Butler was pursuing his leadership ambitions when Conservative leaders were not elected but emerged, though he would not have been more successful if leaders had been elected by MPs or party members. In a long career he had been too effective as a policymaker and party modernizer. Even his admiring local party had been wary of his role in delivering a degree of self-government in India. Others disapproved of his education reforms. Some were wary of his liberal instincts as Home Secretary. By 1957 – and even more by 1963 – Butler hadn't the space for a broad pitch.

He also made one fundamental policy misjudgement, another factor as to why he did not become prime minister. His support for Chamberlain's appeasement policies in the late 1930s is an example of a stance taken by an aspiring leader from which there is no escape in the years that follow. The issue was so highly charged and of such consequence that the positions of the key players at the time were never forgotten. Eden's resignation from Chamberlain's government over appeasement helped him to become prime minister years later. Butler's support for Chamberlain was on colleagues' minds when they turned away from him. Perceptions of a potential leader's past can play a big part in determining their fate.

Those raging debates over appeasement took place early in Butler's political career, raising questions within the Conservative Party about his judgement as a possible leader. Towards the end of his career he failed to pass an altogether different test of leadership that had nothing to do with his stance on contentious policies. Leadership is partly a performance, and the Conservative party conference of 1963 provided Butler with a potentially glorious opportunity to perform – one he squandered. With Macmillan out of the picture, Butler was in effect delivering the leader's speech, a gift for a prime ministerial candidate as the party considered who to choose next. While not a scintillating orator, Douglas-Home had thrilled the conference with his speech earlier in the week.

Butler opted for cautious dullness in his 'leader's speech'. He was never a great speaker, even if he could be witty and elegant in debate. He chose not to be funny or particularly stylish in his lacklustre address.

This failure to rise to the occasion was echoed in 2005 at the Conservatives' annual gathering, when, in a more formal setting, candidates gave speeches as part of their bid to become leader. Then it was the favourite, David Davis, who blew it, and David Cameron who was deemed to have delivered a triumphant address. Davis's speech was not that bad and Cameron's was not especially good, but perceptions form fast at party conferences. In 1963, ministers, MPs and activists left the conference in Blackpool disappointed by Butler's contribution. In the aftermath, there was no great internal clamour for Butler to succeed Macmillan.

His support for appeasement in the 1930s, his early falling out with Macmillan, and his failure to match the noisy excitement of a feverish party conference in 1963 were specific factors that go some way to explain why a brilliant reforming minister was blocked from becoming prime minister. There were also character flaws that were in play throughout his career. Butler was determined and resilient, but he was not ruthless. Acquiring the leadership is partly a matter of timing, but also of tireless determination. When Eden and Macmillan were vulnerable as prime ministers, Butler was seen at times as a natural successor. But he never went for the kill. In the midst of the fast-moving drama in 1963, Butler could not face turning on his rivals, especially Douglas-Home whom he respected and regarded as a friend. Later, he observed, 'I had against me such a terrific gent… if I had had the most ghastly walrus I might have done something.'[7] Butler might have even waited quite some time to face down a ghastly walrus. He was brutal when he had been unwise to have been, tearing a young Macmillan apart, and then was far too restrained when engaged in a battle with old friends at the top of the Conservative Party.

Butler was also unlucky to face Macmillan – a charming, thoughtful, devious and witty rival on the same wing of the Conservative Party – at the height of his powers. And Eden appeared to be at least as formidable when he succeeded Churchill. Even the informal contest in 1963 was fought out by some of the more impressive figures in the party's recent history. Butler's most immediate rivals were Douglas-Home and Hailsham, but Iain Macleod, Reginald Maudling and Edward Heath were hovering – all with distinct qualities and experience, and each making calculations about their own future. Here is perhaps the simplest explanation of all as to why Butler did not become prime minister: he was up against some of the most weighty figures in post-war Conservative Party politics.

———

There was no fourth chance for Butler. Three missed opportunities to become prime minister were more than enough. With Labour in power for six years after the 1964 election, he left active politics and became Master of Trinity College, Cambridge, as well as a Tory peer. Compared with most Cabinet ministers, Butler's political career had been a triumph. His impact in each department as a Cabinet minister or junior minister had been both immediate and enduring. His modernization of the Conservative Party was deep, when such projects can be shallow. But becoming a prime minister places an aspiring leader on a far bigger stage, with more power to shape events. On the basis of his ministerial career, Butler would probably have made full use of the stage – more subtle than Eden in his handling of Suez, more focused on domestic reform than Macmillan, and a tougher opponent against Wilson in the 1964 election than Douglas-Home. Such is the complex relationship between aspiring leaders and their parties that Butler never stood a chance of finding out how well he might have done. He appeared to be closer to the very top than he ever was.

Despite the internal tensions that he generated, Butler remained reasonably comfortable with his party throughout his career, however much he was on its liberal side and despite senior figures conspiring to stop him from becoming prime minister. In some respects, Butler's nearest equivalent within the Labour Party was Roy Jenkins, also a formidable Cabinet minister who implemented historic reforms. Like Butler, Jenkins was on the liberal wing of his party.

There was another similarity too: Jenkins was seen as a possible prime minister at more than one time. But Jenkins's career was far more turbulent than Butler's, and after six years as a dominant Cabinet minister he became deeply uncomfortable with his party in a way that Butler never did. For Jenkins and the Labour Party, the consequences were seismic.

2

ROY JENKINS

Roy Jenkins is unique among the prime ministers we never had. He was seen as a potential prime minister in two different parties, first when he was a Labour Cabinet minister in the 1960s and then as leader of the SDP in the early 1980s, during the new party's heady honeymoon. By his own conduct Jenkins proved to be the least tribal of the prime ministers we never had, and yet he had his own tribe of devoted followers. The 'Jenkinsites' were social democrats and liberals, sometimes a combination of the two. They yearned for him first to be a Labour prime minister and then to be a prime minister who broke the mould with the SDP. Jenkins also had prominent admirers in the media. Arguably, they all hoped to see him in Number Ten with a greater intensity than Jenkins did himself, although their hero was not without considerable personal ambition.

For Jenkins, the honour and burden of being hailed as a likely prime minister began when Harold Wilson became vulnerable after winning a triumphant landslide in 1966. The government was forced to devalue the pound in 1967, a humiliation from which Wilson never fully recovered. Following the devaluation, the newspapers turned on the prime minister. In some respects, the government lost its sense of purpose and direction. Suddenly, Wilson seemed less dynamic and self-confident.

While Wilson struggled to retain his enigmatic zest, Jenkins flourished as his new chancellor, having already been a reforming Home Secretary of epoch-changing significance. Even if Jenkins had not felt a flicker of ambition, the dynamic of an apparently weak prime minister and a Cabinet minister in masterly control of his brief was bound to trigger feverish speculation in the media and within parts of the Labour Party. In the aftermath of the devaluation, newspapers reported Wilson's vulnerability and the private hope of some Labour MPs that Jenkins might replace him. The speculation fed on itself, as it always does.

When a prime minister is in trouble, space opens up for the more successful Cabinet ministers. Harold Wilson was in a surprisingly fragile place from the late 1960s. By 1968, the chances of Labour winning the next election looked slim, in spite of the government being buttressed by a landslide majority and facing a publicly awkward leader of the Opposition. The Conservative leader Edward Heath had already been beaten in the 1966 election, and looked far from comfortable as he navigated his restless party towards the next election. Even so, Labour's poll ratings fell from 41 per cent in September 1967 to 30 per cent in February 1968.[1] The by-election results were as disastrous as the poll ratings. In May 1968, Cecil King, the chair of the *Daily Mirror* and Wilson's only reliable supporter among the tabloids, turned on him and wrote: 'Britain is threatened with the greatest financial crisis in history. It is not to be removed by lies about our reserves but only by a fresh start under a fresh leader.'[2]

King's assessment reflected the political mood in the late 1960s. Patrick Gordon Walker, admittedly sacked in a Cabinet reshuffle, concluded around the same time that 'Wilson was finished'.[3] In his diary, minister Richard Crossman predicted that Jenkins would be the likely successor if Wilson fell, while the prime minister's closest ally in Number Ten, Marcia Williams, admitted, 'Things really are black.'[4] King also assumed or hoped that Jenkins would take over. He and Crossman were by no means alone.

In a speech at a May Day rally in London in 1969, Wilson felt the need to address speculation, ongoing for more than eighteen months, that his leadership was under threat. He did so with characteristic wit: 'May I say, for the benefit of those who have been carried away by the gossip of the last few days, that I know what's going on. [pause] I'm going on, and the Labour government's going on.'[5] Wilson had been battered by dissent within sections of his own party as well as attacks from newspapers that had previously hailed him as a great modernizer. Early in his leadership, the *Mirror* and several other normally non-Labour newspapers paid homage, much as they would to Tony Blair many years later. Wilson had been a media star.

But the tide turned after Wilson was forced to devalue the pound. Enforced devaluation condemns prime ministers to being viewed with disdain for years to come. Those who have to do it are never wholly content again. John Major faced even greater difficulties when he was forced to leave the Exchange Rate Mechanism in 1992.

Wilson moved the chancellor at the time of devaluation, James Callaghan, to the Home Office. Wisely, Callaghan had asked to be moved, realizing he would not have the authority to guide the government through the economic and political storms that were bound to follow the devaluation. Jenkins succeeded Callaghan at the Treasury, after which he was seen as a potential prime minister.

It is a tribute to Callaghan's wily stamina that he became prime minister, at a point when Jenkins was soon to leave the Commons and never return as a Labour MP.

Few in the late 1960s would have predicted such a twist. Then, Jenkins was widely perceived as the chancellor who had calmed the economic storms. Ken Clarke enjoyed similar approbation when he replaced Norman Lamont as chancellor soon after the ERM crisis.[6] Clarke was seen as a possible alternative to John Major, as Jenkins was to Wilson. But there was a big difference. On the whole, Clarke respected Major, whereas Jenkins had little admiration for Wilson at that time.

As Wilson stumbled seemingly without political purpose, Jenkins took the tough decisions on public spending, tax and interest rates.[7] He had been a liberal Home Secretary and proved to be a disciplined chancellor who followed a prudent path – reasons why he became a favourite of a media that tended to be socially liberal and fiscally conservative. The same applied to a section of the parliamentary Labour Party. This was the period when fans of Jenkins became 'Jenkinsites'. In the late 1960s, there were no 'Healeyites' and no 'Bennites', although that was to change. Before long, Tony Benn had his intense admirers too. But Healey never benefited from the same ardour.

Alert to the threats posed by his colleagues, Wilson regarded Jenkins with particular neurosis. Crossman noted in his diaries that Wilson was 'suffused with a jealousy that shocked me' about Jenkins.[8] Crossman was not easily shocked when reflecting on rivalries, ambition and leadership. He must have seen Wilson when he was in an especially troubled mood. On one level, it was a tribute to Jenkins that in a Cabinet with some considerable heavyweights he was the one Wilson was worried about. On another, Wilson's wariness was a big problem for Jenkins. There was no space for a constructive relationship based on mutual trust. This did not impede Jenkins as a policymaker. But those loyal to Wilson in the Cabinet and beyond began to share his suspicion. Like Eden and Macmillan in relation to Rab Butler, Wilson did not set out to do Jenkins many favours.

Wilson had cause to be wary. Jenkins's range of interests and experiences was one of the widest in the Labour Cabinets of the 1960s and 1970s, and he was in a competitive field. This was an era when a deep curiosity about politics, the arts and the media was common in Labour Cabinet ministers. Arguably, Jenkins's lust for life exceeded that of his rivals. From his days as a student at Oxford onwards, he got intense pleasure from writing, reading, women, wine and politics. No wonder Churchill was one of his heroes. Both Jenkins and Boris Johnson wrote biographies of Churchill; Jenkins had many more Churchillian characteristics than Boris Johnson, and wrote a much better book.

Somehow or other Jenkins crammed a huge amount into each day, his energy undimmed by a prodigious consumption of wine. He had a great enthusiasm for the company of others, a useful skill when moving upwards in politics, and formed many passionate friendships. Jenkins's authorized biographer, John Campbell, goes as far as to suggest that, at Oxford, Jenkins had an affair with Anthony Crosland, another giant of post-war Labour politics.[9] This may not have been the case. Andrew Adonis, Jenkins's original choice to be his biographer, is emphatic the affair did not happen. Adonis is certain that while Crosland was keen, Jenkins was not.[10] One way or another, with the affairs he did have and his many friends from a range of circles, Jenkins knew how to enjoy life.

In terms of his political personality, Jenkins had a declamatory style as a speaker that made him seem grand at times. Famously, he could not pronounce the letter 'r' and was often mocked as 'Woy Jenkins'. Yet he was a compelling communicator – an underestimated part of his repertoire, and an important requirement of leadership. The best prime ministers are political teachers, making sense of what they are doing or trying to do, and this was a talent Jenkins possessed. He could also be a witty speechmaker and, like Rab Butler, he deployed understated wit, an effective way of winning over an audience.

There are many examples. Here is one that evokes his style. Noting in a Commons debate the farce of a few senior intelligence officers regarding Wilson as a communist spy, Jenkins declared, 'The idea that Harold Wilson, with his light ideological baggage, could be an agent for the Soviet Union is frankly absurd.'[11] The phrase 'light ideological baggage' is typical of Jenkins: funny, mischievous and accurate.

He was also robust enough to respond to other formidable orators. On another occasion in the Commons when Jenkins was chancellor, Enoch Powell challenged him over his approach to the economy. An intervention from Powell was guaranteed to electrify the Commons. There was a pause as Jenkins stood at the despatch box, a hesitation that worried his supporters. Had Powell got the better of him? Then Jenkins looked up at Powell and delivered his imperious, improvised response: 'The Right Honourable gentleman's logic as always is impeccable, but since he invariably starts from false premises he's bound to reach false conclusions.'[12] Jenkins could hold his own with the best political speakers of the twentieth century.

He wore expensive suits, drank vintage claret, and spent weekends playing tennis and cultivating relationships. Yet he was nowhere near as stuffy or precious as he could appear to be. He had an intense interest in other people and a desire to engage that was fairly egalitarian. Local voters, political journalists, prime ministers and other prominent politicians might attract his attention. In his early years as an MP he wrote well-reviewed biographies on H. H. Asquith, Arthur Balfour, Sir Charles Dilke and Stanley Baldwin, all big Liberal and Tory figures from the late nineteenth and early twentieth centuries.

His interest in Liberal prime ministers, in particular Asquith, gave some definition to his own public image. He was widely seen, and to some extent saw himself, as a Labour liberal, at ease with the Liberal Party at a time when his senior colleagues tended to patronize Liberals or view them with indifference. In the 1980s, Jenkins's liberal instincts were to play a part in his final rise and fall. In the 1960s, they helped to make him the most successful minister in Wilson's Cabinet.

Jenkins's reforms as Home Secretary defined the permissiveness of the late sixties as much as any feted rock group from that decade. Indeed, Jenkins's mastery of legislative change shows why politics matters. It is through power that lives can be changed, perhaps more so than through protest or music. The Beatles' *Sgt. Pepper's Lonely Hearts Club Band* might have transformed pop culture for ever. Demonstrations in the late 1960s on a range of issues might have become totemic. But as an elected Home Secretary, Jenkins changed what people could and could not do.

While John Lennon called for peace and love, Jenkins initiated police and prison reforms aimed at making it harder for the courts to jail people indiscriminately. Jenkins gave strong personal support to David Steel's Private Members' Bill that led to the Abortion Act in 1967, making abortions legal and available up to twenty-eight weeks of a pregnancy. Private Members' Bills are normally doomed, but when Steel's proposal looked likely to be dropped due to insufficient time, Jenkins helped ensure that it received enough parliamentary space to pass. He voted for it in every division. Jenkins and Steel shared a mutual respect that would take on considerable significance as Jenkins later sought an alternative, but even thornier, route to Number Ten than the one he contemplated as an ambitious Labour Cabinet minister.

Jenkins's first tenure at the Home Office, during the mid-1960s, was characterized by a commitment to social liberalism. The resolute consistency is highly unusual. Most Home Secretaries stagger from one crisis to another without leaving a distinct legacy. Jenkins had a determined sense of purpose that transcended unpredictable eruptions of events. One instance of this can be seen in his support for Leo Abse's bill for the decriminalization of homosexuality, a proposal Jenkins described as an 'important and civilising measure'.[13] Jenkins craftily arranged proceedings so that he could speak in favour of the bill from the frontbench as Home Secretary, without claiming to represent the entire government. In addition to this, he abolished the use of flogging in prisons, supported measures aimed at ending censorship in the theatre, and announced that he would introduce legislation banning racial discrimination in employment. This took legal form in the Race Relations Act, passed once Jenkins had moved to the Treasury.

Most Cabinet ministers seek to please the ruling prime minister. They have no greater ambition, at least while a prime minister is commanding and popular. Harold Wilson, a social conservative, did not share the same passion as Jenkins for a more permissive or 'civilized' society, as Jenkins sometimes described his legislative crusade. Wilson's indifference did not deter Jenkins, however.

While it is to Wilson's credit that he gave Jenkins the space to implement his reforms, Jenkins showed his leadership potential by pursuing his own distinct agenda, knowing full well that the prime minister was not a great enthusiast. Ministers become fully formed as public figures when they follow their own convictions rather than seeking to please their prime minister. If Jenkins's priority had been to keep Wilson happy, he would not have delivered so many social reforms.

If Wilson and Jenkins had got on better, they would have been a potent double act, with Wilson representing the social conservatism of many Labour voters in the north of England, as well as elderly Conservative supporters, and Jenkins speaking for metropolitan progressives. But the two were not close. Only later, when Jenkins wrote his memoirs, did he come to value Wilson as a unifying leader who had given him some of the most senior posts in his governments. Jenkins even wondered whether Hugh Gaitskell, to whom he was much closer, would have been as generous in his patronage.[14]

Jenkins's changing view of Wilson was typical of his Cabinet colleagues. They fumed about him while they worked in the same Cabinet, and then recognized how well he had done to keep such unruly ministers together.[15] Aspiring leaders rarely see the constraints under which prime ministers lead at the time. Their ambition would likely be stifled by too much empathy for the candidate they contemplate replacing. The exceptions are Ken Clarke in relation to John Major, and Denis Healey who was a big admirer of James Callaghan both at the time and in retrospect.

After the enforced devaluation in 1967, Jenkins came to the government's rescue as chancellor. Although his approach had none of the reforming romanticism he'd exhibited at the Home

Office, he decided on the path he wanted to take and kept to his chosen route, much as he had in his previous post. Unsurprisingly, his ultimate goal as chancellor was a return to strong economic growth after the crisis. The path he chose involved considerable fiscal discipline and patience. Above all, he depended on restoring stability to the fragile currency, a move that would strengthen the economy as a whole. This was his project. Unlike Gordon Brown, Labour's longest-serving chancellor, he did not have the space or the time to aim for much more, or to establish the purpose behind the prudence.

For Jenkins, stabilizing the economy was a daunting objective given the confidence-sapping devaluation crisis. Looking back in 2020, Dick Taverne – a close friend of Jenkins, and a Labour MP who left the party long before the formation of the SDP – conjured up Jenkins's bleak inheritance when he became chancellor. Taverne recalled how *The Times* wondered whether the UK economy might suffer a dark and long recession, one that would bring about the premature collapse of the government. *The Times* had its own agenda, but it reflected the excitable mood at the time.[16]

In Jenkins's view, sustained economic growth could only be achieved by moving towards a surplus in the balance of payments. He pursued deflationary policies, including cuts to public spending and increases in taxation in order to ensure that resources went into exports rather than domestic consumption. He had no choice but to seek to win back confidence in the markets and the media, thereby earning space to pursue more social democratic goals – precisely Brown's strategy after Labour's victory in the 1997 election. In the New Labour era, Jenkins formed a close relationship with Tony Blair, but as a chancellor he was similar to Brown. In managing the economy, both Jenkins and Brown were cautious social democrats.

While it is true that Jenkins was closer than most of his colleagues to the spirit of the Liberal Party, he remained a social democrat. He was not an economic liberal like the later Liberal Democrat leader Nick Clegg. But Jenkins did have an affinity with the party of Lloyd George and later David Steel and Charles Kennedy, who were both opponents of the coalition that Clegg formed with the Conservatives in 2010. Early in the twenty-first century, Jenkins was to observe: 'The problem with voters in Britain is that they want US levels of taxation and European standards of public services.'[17] This was a social democrat implicitly putting the case for higher taxes to pay for better public services. He wrote the words after Labour's 2001 election victory but before Blair and Brown had dared to make the case for higher taxes in order to pay for improvements to the NHS. The same social democratic instincts informed his approach to being chancellor in the late 1960s, but his space to manoeuvre was extremely limited and time was short. The next election was already moving into view.

After Jenkins became chancellor in 1967, the markets remained stormy, only calming when Britain's current account hit a surplus in May 1969. Despite signs of a stable economy, his 1970 pre-election budget was cautious and there were no overt giveaways. Ken Clarke applied the same approach in his budget before the 1997 election.

Jenkins was praised for his prudence, until Labour lost the election and some in his party blamed him for not being more generous. This was a red herring. As Jenkins wrote in his memoir: 'Contrary to popular myth it caught the political mood better than a more generous budget would have done and therefore I did not and do not feel that Treasury caution was in any way responsible for the Labour defeat in the 1970 election.'[18]

Admittedly he is a biased narrator, but there is no evidence to suggest his budget was the reason for the defeat. Other, more potent factors led to Labour's unexpected loss, including voters' doubts about Wilson's leadership and the speculation that colleagues, including Jenkins, were plotting to remove him. There was also a wider disillusionment with a tired government that had ruled haphazardly for six years.

Whatever the controversy around his final budget, Jenkins emerged from the Labour government as one of its big figures, widely seen as an effective Home Secretary and chancellor, arguably the two toughest briefs for a Cabinet minister. For a short time after the 1970 election, Jenkins continued to be viewed as a potential prime minister.

Wilson was deeply shocked by the defeat. Losing elections is unavoidably painful for prime ministers; they tend to see it as personal rejection. To lose unexpectedly is even more of a setback. In today's more impatient and speedy political era, a leader who loses an election is unlikely to survive in the post for very long. In the slightly less frenzied media climate of 1970, Wilson hit on his own third way: he neither resigned nor was forced out, but for a time he more or less disappeared from public view. Yet he went on to win two more elections and a referendum on the UK's membership of the Common Market. And despite all the speculation around Jenkins, nothing happened. The reforming Home Secretary, successful chancellor, commanding speaker and prolific writer would only be a member of Wilson's Cabinet once more. He returned to the Home Office after the February 1974 election, before leaving for Brussels to become president of the European Commission, never to be a minister again.

———

Yet Jenkins had a second extraordinary chance to make it to Number Ten, or so it seemed for a time. In 1981, he was instrumental in the formation of the SDP, a new political party led by four former heavyweight Labour Cabinet ministers. Parties are often divided, but usually stagger on. When he was leader, Wilson described the Labour Party euphemistically as a 'broad church'. For the likes of Jenkins, the church became too broad. Jenkins was the prime mover in a rare formal schism.

Political reporters are often too quick to say that British politics is dramatic, exciting and unpredictable, but the early 1980s really was a period of historic change. Margaret Thatcher was prime minister, and her economic revolution was underway. Inflation rose and unemployment soared as she embarked on a monetarist experiment. Inner city riots ensued. The Cabinet was divided over the approach of Thatcher and her assiduous chancellor, Geoffrey Howe. Yet the Conservative Party remained more or less intact.

On the other side, Labour elected Michael Foot as its leader in 1980. As Thatcher moved the Conservatives towards the right, Labour turned to its most left-wing leader for decades. Thatcher versus Foot represented an altogether different battle to Wilson versus Heath.[19] Even before Foot became leader, Jenkins sensed there might be a gap in the so-called centre of British politics, one that a new political party could fill.

Jenkins had left the Cabinet to become president of the European Commission in 1977. Normally, such a marked departure from the cut and thrust of domestic politics would signal the end of prime ministerial ambition. Such ambition was not uppermost in Jenkins's mind but he was a political addict, and he could not wholly look away from British politics even while enjoying himself at the European Commission in Brussels.

His unique journey back to the highly charged political situation in the UK began when he delivered the Richard Dimbleby Lecture in November 1979, a few months after Margaret Thatcher had won the election and as Labour was embarking on a post-mortem that quickly became a civil war. In his lecture, Jenkins floated the idea of a new political party without provocatively calling for its formation. He spoke of the 'strengthening of the radical centre', saying:

> I believe that such a development could bring into political commitment the energies of many people of talent and goodwill who, although perhaps active in many other voluntary ways, are at present alienated from the business of government, whether national or local, by the sterility and formalism of much of the political game. I am sure this would improve our politics. I think the results might also help to improve our national performance.[20]

Jenkins's speech was vague in many respects. Those who speak of the 'radical centre' tend to be unclear about what they mean in policy terms, and also where their ideological instincts lie. But Jenkins was deliberately stirring the pot. His pitch was far too abstract but his timing showed his artistry. He had held many conversations in the early 1970s with disaffected Labour MPs and former MPs about setting up a new party. At the time he'd sensed rightly they were being premature. As the decade drew to a close, he finally saw an opportunity.

Having semi-departed from the Labour Party when he became president of the European Commission, Jenkins had the space and inclination to challenge orthodoxies and assumptions about the inevitable dominance of the two main parties in the UK. Yet this could never be a solo project. For a new party to have any hope of succeeding he needed the charisma of Shirley Williams, the weight and flair of David Owen, and the organizational talents and strategic insights of William Rodgers. The former Labour Cabinet ministers became the 'Gang of Four' when the Social Democratic Party was launched in 1981. From the beginning there were tensions and differences of approach, but Rodgers later noted the centrality of Jenkins's attempts to at least give the new party some sense of ideological purpose: 'Without Roy, the argument behind Dimbleby – "a strengthening of the radical centre" – would have been welcomed but without excitement; and without Dimbleby, a new party would have lacked a prospectus.'[21]

With the Dimbleby Lecture, Jenkins had provided the embryonic SDP with a route map of sorts. After the formal launch, he proceeded to give the project more momentum. In some respects, he was the most courageous of the Gang of Four, daring to contest the Warrington by-election in the autumn of 1981, a seemingly safe Labour seat. This was a big risk for him. If he had been heavily defeated, the project and his role in it would have ground to a halt.

Close to the opposite happened. A more vivacious and natural campaigner than his rather grand presence might have suggested, Jenkins came near to winning, securing 42.4 per cent of the vote. In his speech at the count, Jenkins neatly conveyed his sense of personal triumph: 'This is my first defeat in 30 years in politics... and it is by far the greatest victory in which I have participated.' He was right. Like Jeremy Corbyn in the 2017 general election, he had both lost and been triumphant.

Meanwhile, the SDP was well ahead in national polls, sometimes by a dizzying margin. One or two polls gave the SDP–Liberal Alliance more than 50 per cent of the vote. (The alliance between the two parties was formed in June 1981, only a few months after the launch of the SDP.) Jenkins was seen as the likely leader and, given the scale of the SDP's popularity in particular, a possible prime minister. The SDP flourished at the height of Margaret Thatcher's first wave of unpopularity, as Michael Foot struggled to make his mark as leader of a still-troubled Labour Party. Foot was facing the dual problem of a formal schism and the bitter deputy leadership contest between Denis Healey and Tony Benn.

Jenkins did not have to wait much longer for an actual by-election victory. He was elected as the SDP's first leader soon after winning Glasgow Hillhead in 1982. A realistic reader of the rhythms of politics, Jenkins dared to conclude that he had a chance once more of reaching Number Ten. He went as far as outlining a plan to William Rodgers that would make Rodgers his first chancellor if the SDP–Liberal Alliance formed a government. After fraught discussions with the Liberal leadership, in the build-up to the 1983 general election Jenkins was given the title 'prime minister designate' – a clumsy attempt to convey that the new political party had a statesman at its helm even if he was an old-fashioned campaigner. However awkward the contortion, Jenkins is the only prime minister we never had to secure a title that included the words 'prime minister'.

———

In reality, the 'prime minister designate' was much further away from Number Ten as SDP leader than when he'd been a Labour Cabinet minister. Most aspiring prime ministers do not aspire credibly for as long as Jenkins did. The durable credibility of his seeming closeness to the very top is testament to his leadership qualities. Yet Jenkins was not as close to Number Ten as at times he appeared to be, even if he might have flourished in the role. Here are the reasons why.

Returning to the late 1960s, Jenkins may have been riding high, but Wilson's leadership was not so dismal to have justified an attempt at toppling him. At that time Jenkins was a chancellor seeking economic stability. It would have been an act at odds with his stabilizing mission to trigger a period of volcanic political instability by seeking to depose a prime minister. Jenkins, the reliably solid chancellor, would have become a different political personality: a risk-taking, reckless, self-aggrandizing assassin. Probably, he would not have even successfully carried out the assassination. Almost certainly, Wilson would have survived the attempt to remove him.

After Labour's landslide victory in 1966, Wilson would not have taken his bow voluntarily. He would have resisted, arguing with some justification that he was a vote-winner who could hold the party together. When Michael Heseltine challenged Margaret Thatcher's leadership as she persisted with the deeply unpopular poll tax, the Conservatives were well behind in the polls and they had recently lost a by-election in the supposedly safe seat of Eastbourne. Thatcher had also provoked the resignation of two senior Cabinet ministers, Nigel Lawson and Geoffrey Howe, since her election victory in 1987. Howe's departure was the immediate trigger that brought about her fall, but in some ways Lawson's resignation as chancellor a year earlier was as destabilizing for her leadership. She had been prime minister for more than eleven years when Heseltine finally made his move.

There were no calamities on this scale for Jenkins to cite as justification for attempting to remove Wilson, who had been prime minister for a relatively short period compared with Thatcher in

1990. Jenkins would have caused mayhem and probably lost. The sense at the time – that he had a chance and blew it – was wrong.

After Wilson lost the 1970 election there was slightly more of an opening for Jenkins. Wilson was no longer the election-winning leader, but an increasingly lacklustre political force who had been defeated by Edward Heath, a poor party leader who was soon to struggle as prime minister. Yet Jenkins was doomed to paralysis once more, for a reason that applies to several of the prime ministers we never had. From 1970 onwards, Europe played havoc with British politics – or, to be more precise, British politics could not cope with the issue of Europe. Parties split. Tory prime ministers fell. Potential prime ministers never became prime ministers. And the issue of Europe killed off Jenkins's chances of leading the Labour Party.

After the 1970 election defeat, Jenkins focused largely on whether the UK should be part of the Common Market, as it was then called – an unavoidable focus as Heath instigated the negotiations that led to the UK joining in 1973. Jenkins was a passionate pro-European, but at this point the majority of Labour MPs and activists were opposed to joining. As leader of the Opposition, Wilson ducked and weaved to prevent his party falling apart. Unity was his overwhelming objective.

In the autumn of 1971, in a key vote on the issue in the Commons, Wilson voted against membership along with most Labour MPs. This did not mean Wilson was a passionate opponent of Britain joining the Common Market. Rather, he considered his opposition to be a necessarily pragmatic act of leadership. In contrast, Jenkins led sixty-nine Labour MPs to vote with Heath in favour of membership.

Looking back in his memoir, Jenkins's admirer Roy Hattersley concluded that this was the moment when the schism in the

Labour Party started to take shape, even though the split did not formally occur until 1981.[22] Over the next few months, Jenkins agonized about his position as deputy leader. Some of the more charismatic stars on the left were acquiring greater definition with their opposition to Common Market membership. Tony Benn had become a highly articulate opponent. Michael Foot had always been against. Peter Shore had an almost Churchillian style of oratory as he put the case for Britain staying out. Increasingly, they were the heroes of the party activists, especially Foot and Benn. There were intense internal tensions over whether or not Labour should call for a referendum before the UK joined; and, more strategically, over whether Labour should use the issue to bring down Heath's government.

After five months of twists and turns, Jenkins resigned as deputy leader. He could not credibly stay on when Labour seemed to be moving so far from his position on Europe. This was a key moment in terms of Jenkins's personal ambitions. A figure who resigns as deputy is unlikely to be leader in the future, a point that wasn't lost on him: 'During the winter and early spring months of 1971–72 the prospect that I would one day be Prime Minister, which for three or four years until then had seemed more likely than not, was quietly but ineluctably slipping away from me.'[23] Jenkins was the first British politician to resign from a senior post over the UK's membership of what became the European Union. Plenty from both the main UK parties would resign or be forced out of much bigger posts in the years to come.

For Jenkins, the first Commons vote over the UK's membership, in 1971, marked a turning point. Labour was moving leftwards and against membership. He and his allies were in a different place. One of them, Dick Taverne, left the party to fight and win a by-election in Lincoln in 1973, as the Democratic Labour candidate. One of his causes was Europe. Taverne had discussed the possibility of a new party with Jenkins during the by-election and Jenkins had quite rightly told him the timing was wrong. Even so, by then the issue for Jenkins was a matter of when, not if. And a figure having these kinds of discussions about a new party was never going to be leader of the one he was contemplating leaving.

Meanwhile, some of Jenkins's other allies called on him in their battles with their local parties. Jenkins spoke at a meeting in Newham in defence of its local MP, Reg Prentice. Local members wanted to deselect Prentice. Perhaps their instincts were right; Prentice went on to make a much bigger leap than Taverne: he joined the Conservatives. Jenkins's commitment to those at odds with their local parties suggested a figure drifting away from his party rather than surging to its top. A political party won't elect a candidate who is obviously facing away from the direction of travel.

This was the state of affairs by the time of Labour's 1976 leadership election, in which Jenkins stood but made little impact. James Callaghan was the victor, the demoralized figure that Jenkins had replaced as chancellor in 1967. Michael Foot came second.

But Europe and Labour's ideological tide were not the only reasons Jenkins did not become Labour leader or prime minister. Character played a part almost as much as the external circumstances. Like Rab Butler, Jenkins was not ruthless or daring enough to seize the crown and to make the most of the limited opportunities, nor was he willing or inclined to woo a Labour Party moving further away from his politics. He was not tribal in the way that Denis Healey and Roy Hattersley were – two other Cabinet ministers resisting some of the moves leftward.

Like Hamlet delaying the revenge of his father's murder, Jenkins could always find reasons for not making a move against Wilson. Jenkins's memoirs are punctuated with tantalizing moments and retrospective regret. He describes the excitable mood in 1968 as possibly his best chance. With his deep understanding of history, Jenkins recognized echoes from the previous decade:

Looking back... I think that those troubled summer days of 1968 were for me... the equivalent of the same season of 1953 for Rab Butler. Having faltered for want of single-minded ruthlessness... he then settled down to a career punctuated by increasingly wide misses of the premiership. People who effectively grabbed the prime ministership – Lloyd George, Macmillan, Mrs Thatcher – do not let such moments slip.[24]

This is a persistent theme of Jenkins's career. After the parliamentary vote on Common Market membership in 1971, another of his fans, the Labour MP Robert Maclennan, suggested Jenkins should contest the leadership. Maclennan was quiet, decent, yet passionate. He briefly became leader of the SDP in 1987 as the party descended into terminal chaos. Like Jenkins, he was a social democrat who was alarmed when the Liberal Democrats moved towards smaller-state economic liberalism under Nick Clegg. Maclennan thought Jenkins would have lost but also have established himself as the heavyweight successor to Wilson. 'In retrospect I think he was right,' Jenkins noted of Maclennan's advice in 1971.[25]

Jenkins's retrospective regret was misplaced. A challenger who loses rarely gets another chance – a reason for Boris Johnson's withdrawal from the Conservative leadership contest in 2016. Johnson sensed, with good cause, that his ambition was better served by pulling out rather than losing.

Jenkins noted the gap between Wilson's jealous paranoia and his own lack of brutal wilfulness: 'Wilson became needlessly worried about a challenge from me to his leadership. It was needless because I probably would not have had the deadliness to stand and would not in any event have won.'[26]

The term 'deadliness' is revealing. Jenkins knew he was being called upon to commit a metaphorical killing of a leader who still commanded significant support within the Labour Party. He was not up to the task. In contrast, Margaret Thatcher was deadly enough to kill off the career of Edward Heath; Tony Blair had the ruthless streak to stand for leadership despite knowing this would leave Gordon Brown devastated and angry; and Boris Johnson was willing to destroy both Theresa May and David Cameron. Jenkins was not so single-minded in his ambition.

On this matter, Jenkins concluded candidly: 'I always sense that I would enjoy being prime minister more when it was over than while it was taking place. This thought set limits to the thrust of my ambition. No doubt also it raises the question of how truly at ease I was with power. It is not a thought which I suspect much troubled the minds of the great determined leaders of history.'[27]

Jenkins is not an entirely accurate reader of his own political mind. No doubt there was an issue with the intensity of his ambition. Like Denis Healey, he had a greater range of interests and passions than most of those who become prime minister. Also, there were times when he showed a lack of wilfulness. Yet Jenkins did possess a ruthless streak, more so than he recognized when he wrote his memoirs. As a Cabinet minister, he largely ignored Wilson and pursued his various objectives with unyielding determination. In the 1960s, he was by some margin the most single-minded Cabinet minister in terms of policy implementation. Later, he made several big calls, first by stating the case for a new political party and then by standing in risky by-elections. While still a Labour member he defended his colleagues in their dark battles with local parties, which wasn't easy given the anger directed at some Labour MPs.

Perhaps a Thatcher or a Lloyd George would have made the most of the narrow opportunities to lead that arose in Jenkins's career, but even that is questionable. Thatcher challenged Heath after he lost two elections in a single year. Although Wilson lost in 1970, he still had two significant election wins to his credit. Thatcher's act of ruthlessness was less daunting than taking on Wilson in the late 1960s would have been.

After 1970, the Labour Party moved away from Jenkins and there was nothing he could do about it. He could have been as brutally ambitious as Lloyd George and Thatcher combined, and he still would not have become leader of his party. He was at odds with the majority of MPs and activists on the matter of Europe and, over time, several other issues too. The internal differences made Jenkins seem more right-wing than he was, a misperception widely shared by increasingly influential party members. The gap between activists and Jenkins was partly one of temperament. As another ally, David Marquand, noted later: 'He was a quintessential insider in a party funded by and for outsiders; a man of power, not of protest.'[28]

For all the speculation around Wilson from 1968 until his resignation in 1976, no one challenged him – a vivid example of how most prime ministers remain in place despite media speculation about their imminent demise. Even Theresa May kept going for longer than many pundits expected after she lost her party's small overall majority in the early election she called in 2017.[29]

Jenkins was convinced Labour would lose the election in February 1974. He planned to fight the ongoing battles within the party while maintaining tentative conversations with some allies about a new party. But against expectations Wilson won, or at least won a few more seats than the Conservatives, and was able to form a minority government. To his bewilderment, Jenkins was made Home Secretary for the second time.

This period was darker for Jenkins than the glittering 1960s. He faced the nightmare of IRA terrorism, including the Birmingham pub bombings which killed twenty-one people and injured many others. The bombings took place in November 1974, a month after Wilson had won another election and secured a small overall majority. By then, Jenkins's disillusionment with Wilson and the Labour Party was deepening. After failing to make much of an impact in the 1976 leadership contest, he willingly left British politics and went to Brussels. But Jenkins's appetite for British politics was undimmed. His diaries spanning his four years as president of the European Commission convey a sense of pleasure at his new role. His break from British politics also gave him the chance to navigate a distinct route back.[30]

———

Even so, the phase in which Jenkins helped to form and then lead the SDP was also one in which all paths to Number Ten were blocked from the beginning. Although the SDP soared in the polls for a short time in 1981, the party never had a hope of winning an election. Jenkins and other senior members blamed the Falklands War for bringing momentum to a halt. This was a red herring.

The SDP was doomed from the start, its fate sealed when the likes of Denis Healey and Roy Hattersley, with views close to those of the defectors, stayed in the Labour Party. Their resistance to the lure of the fleeting glamour of a new political force meant that Labour was going to remain a broad church even if some of its stars had left. The SDP was a party of the centre left, which meant there were two parties battling for the anti-Tory vote. The schism guaranteed electoral victories for Thatcher, a point that wasn't lost on her. She became much bolder after the Labour split, before the Falklands War. Her most significant Cabinet reshuffle took place in September 1981, when she sacked or demoted the so-called wets who opposed her economic policies and brought in contentious allies such as Norman Tebbit. The Falklands War erupted the following spring.

In order to prevail in a general election, the SDP had to destroy Labour. Instead, Labour and the SDP fought to be the main opposition party, with Labour strong enough to be the bigger party in the Commons however well the SDP performed in terms of votes. Labour was in trouble but still strong in parts of the north of England, as well as Wales and Scotland. In the second decade of the twenty-first century, Labour was to become weak in all those parts of the UK, but in the 1980s the SDP had no hope of taking many seats in these areas. In the same way that prime ministers last in their post much longer than the speculation about their imminent fall often suggests, so the two bigger parties tend to endure.

There were also internal tensions at the top of the SDP that made the project more fragile than it appeared. Jenkins was keener on a close relationship with the Liberals than David Owen, who emerged as a formidable rival to Jenkins. Owen had more respect for the Labour Party than he did for the Liberals, who on the whole he viewed as a bunch of amateurs. The differences were not only emotional. Owen regarded himself as a robust social democrat and saw Jenkins as closer to being a liberal. This is the problem with the notion of a 'radical centre'; the term is so vague it can span entirely different values and policies. The reality was more complex. Jenkins was a social democrat who got on well with the Liberal leader, David Steel, who was himself rooted on the left of centre. In 2019, Change UK, another political party born out of a split, suffered even more dramatically from a lack of ideological clarity. It collapsed within a year. The SDP was impressively long-lasting by comparison.

Under Jenkins's short leadership, the SDP and Liberal parties worked fairly well together; but after the honeymoon, setbacks in by-elections and disappointing opinion polls fuelled tensions between the two sides. Bill Rodgers and David Steel worked tirelessly to divide the seats between the parties for the forthcoming 1983 general election. David Owen looked on warily, convinced that the SDP should be campaigning as a separate force.

The biggest setback for the SDP came shortly before the election. New parties need a sense of momentum best achieved via sensational by-election victories. In March, a crucial by-election was held in Darlington, where Labour was defending a relatively small majority. The seat was seen as fertile terrain for the SDP, and senior party figures were rarely out of the constituency during the campaign. But the same commitment was also true of Labour's stars. It was a mighty battle, like a mini general election.

The contest in Darlington was emblematic of the SDP's impossible dilemma. Labour was still a force, albeit an erratic one. In Darlington, Michael Foot rediscovered his oratorical verve. Denis Healey packed out halls. So did Neil Kinnock. Roy Hattersley was on witty form. Labour's candidate was a respected, competent local figure, while the SDP selected a candidate who was out of his depth and embarrassed by the mischievous questioning of *Newsnight*'s legendary by-election reporter, Vincent Hanna. Labour won the seat. The SDP came third, well behind the Tory and Labour candidates.

For Jenkins, the period from the Darlington by-election to the June general election was the most humiliating of his career. He was seen by some in the SDP and beyond as a liability and a poor communicator. Halfway through the 1983 campaign, Steel summoned Jenkins to a meeting at his house in Ettrickbridge, a tranquil village in the Scottish Borders. This was an incongruous setting for a bloody battle. The meeting became known as the 'Ettrickbridge summit', a grand title almost justified by the scale of Steel's ruthlessness. During the gathering, Steel proposed that Jenkins keep a lower profile, meaning Steel in effect would become leader of the campaign for the SDP–Liberal Alliance. Steel had held no Cabinet post and yet the junior figure in the duo was effectively telling his senior that he was hindering the alliance's chances. In comparison, Jenkins had been chancellor and Home Secretary twice, then president of the European Commission.

Jenkins refused to accept such a demotion, but after this his confidence was undermined and he staggered to the finishing line with less verve than he had displayed in the early days of the SDP. There was little sign of the exuberance he had shown during the Warrington and Glasgow by-elections. When the SDP came third in the general election, not far behind Labour in terms of votes but miles behind as far as seats were concerned, Jenkins had little choice but to resign. Owen had been breathing down his neck from the beginning and was not going to wait any longer. Once again Jenkins's path to Number Ten had been blocked, even if he dared fleetingly to assume the SDP would 'break the mould of British politics' and, in doing so, propel him towards the very top.

Yet after the fall of the SDP, Jenkins's influence was greater for a time than the late careers of the other prime ministers we never had. When Tony Blair became Labour leader in 1994, he turned to Jenkins as a mentor. Blair bypassed the former prime minister James Callaghan, who was still active. Callaghan was hurt by Blair's indifference and his dismissive description of Labour's past being 'old Labour'. In an interview, Callaghan described himself mischievously as 'original Labour'.[31] For Blair, Jenkins was a more obvious choice as a guide; the figure who had deployed the conveniently vague phrase 'radical centre', which Blair made use of with the same imprecision. Jenkins also taught Blair that the split among progressives was fatal in the twentieth century, allowing the Conservatives to win most elections.

The two of them were both close and far apart. Jenkins was on one level less tribal than Blair. He left the Labour Party, set up the SDP and later became a Liberal Democrat. Yet Jenkins was more centre-left than Blair. The early SDP programmes were to the left of New Labour. David Owen regarded Labour's 2017 election manifesto under Corbyn as similar to the SDP–Liberal Alliance's pitch in the 1983 campaign when Jenkins was leader. Owen made this observation approvingly, even if he and Jenkins had fallen out on several fronts at the time.[32] Jenkins was much keener on constitutional reform than Blair and more overtly pro-European. But early on in Blair's leadership, Jenkins was a mentor in a limited way.

Part of Blair was keen on a formal relationship with the Liberal Democrats, but he was never a fan of electoral reform. In order to maintain relations, Blair pledged a referendum on the issue in the 1997 election. After winning a landslide, he asked Jenkins to lead a commission on a new voting system. Jenkins wrote a characteristically elegant report, making this dry topic come to life.

He toured the country giving talks on his proposals, but Blair was never personally committed to the cause and much of his party was opposed. Blair did not hold the referendum, one of several decisions that fuelled Jenkins's disillusionment with him. In his last speech in the Lords, Jenkins declared his opposition to Blair's support for the war in Iraq. His relationship with Blair illustrated his capacity for influence and also his ultimate impotence – a dazzling figure no longer in a position of power. Even so, Jenkins is unique in having three strikingly distinct phases to his political career: a reforming Cabinet minister, the first leader of the SDP, and an early influence on a landslide-winning Labour prime minister, even if his influence wasn't as great as he'd hoped.

The rest of his post-SDP life was as varied as his political career had been. He became chancellor of Oxford University, a post of ceremony and internal politics to which he was wholly suited; he continued to play some sports, and drank good wine. His curiosity was undimmed, as was his capacity for friendship. He met the author Robert Harris regularly to discuss politics and have an enjoyable gossip. Harris was younger by several decades, but although Jenkins could lapse into a sense of his own grandeur, he was not stuffy or self-absorbed.

Most impressive, however, was Jenkins's commitment to his literary work. He continued to write books, including his weighty biographies of William Gladstone and Churchill, which were remarkable achievements for a writer in his seventies and early eighties. These books were accomplished histories, but Jenkins was also able to place some of the dilemmas and parliamentary highs and lows of his subjects in the context of his own experience. Perhaps surprisingly given his political allegiances, he admired Churchill the more of these two figures.[33]

One way or another, Jenkins remained a key player, right from his student days at Oxford until near the end of his life. But he would have been much more of a player if he had become prime minister. It is tempting to argue that Jenkins achieved more than some prime ministers, but the temptation must be resisted. He had a fuller life compared with many of those that made it to Number Ten, but the prime ministers had a much greater capacity to make a difference. Indeed, Jenkins only had the space to make an impact as a minister because Wilson allowed it.

The UK would have been unrecognizably different if Jenkins had made it to the very top. Instead, he wielded power as a Cabinet minister for a relatively short period of time and had to settle for a limited form of influence after that. But such was his range of interests, he was largely untroubled by the limits that external circumstances and, to a lesser extent, his own character placed on his political ambition.

———

Serving in the same Cabinets as Jenkins from 1964 was the most prominent woman in British politics during that decade. Barbara Castle was ambitious and in some respects better placed than Jenkins in Labour's eternal ideological debates. She was to the left of him and a favourite of Harold Wilson in a way he never was. Wilson gave her Cabinet posts in which she made a distinct mark. Like Wilson, she was aware of the increasing power of television in the portrayal of politicians and shared his fascination with the media. Unsurprisingly, some wondered whether Castle would be the UK's first woman prime minister. How close did she get?

3

BARBARA CASTLE

In the 1960s, Barbara Castle was by far the most famous female politician in the UK. No other woman in politics came close. Indeed, few male politicians enjoyed such prominence. She held three Cabinet posts in the Wilson governments that ruled from 1964 to 1970, and her profile rose as she moved from one department to the next.

Such a neat pattern isn't inevitable. Ministers can easily remain relatively obscure as they are reshuffled regularly. But obscurity was never a risk for Castle – she was not content to perform a managerial role on behalf of her leader. Her relentless, impatient focus was based on deeply held and nuanced convictions. With each complex ministerial remit, her reforming zeal was matched by a fairly well-developed and distinct ideological position. She was a performer too. Some of Wilson's Cabinet ministers were dull and self-effacing. Castle was in the group that adored the political stage.

By any objective assessment, Castle was associated with the implementation or attempted implementation of more substantial policies than the most prominent Conservative female politician in the 1960s and early 1970s. Before she became Conservative leader, Margaret Thatcher had been Education Secretary in the troubled government formed by Edward Heath in 1970, her only Cabinet post. While Thatcher was as striking a figure as Castle, she kept her head down as Heath and his senior colleagues fought draining political battles with the unions and negotiated a route towards the UK's historic membership of the Common Market.

As a loyal minister, Thatcher supported membership of the Common Market and gave the appearance of backing Heath on every other front too. Her real views on Heath's wobbly leadership only became clear after she succeeded him. Similarly, Thatcher's public personality only took full form as a leader. There was an almost self-effacing quality to her presence in Heath's Cabinet and then in opposition up to the October 1974 election when the Conservatives were defeated. Before then, she had publicly declared her view that a woman would not lead the Conservatives in her lifetime. She happily accepted whatever role Heath asked her to perform, though soon the hint of self-effacement would cease to be part of Thatcher's repertoire. Columnists were fascinated by the likes of Iain Macleod, Enoch Powell, William Whitelaw, Sir Keith Joseph and others. Thatcher rarely got a look in, and nor did she seek attention. Her work rate was remarkable and she was fairly content with her middle-ranking role on the frontbench.

Castle's and Thatcher's careers are illuminating counterpoints. This chapter seeks to discover why Thatcher rather than Castle became the UK's first woman prime minister. The comparison helps to make sense of Castle's spectacular and yet haphazard political journey – one that ended earlier than she would have liked, at least in terms of her ministerial career.

As a rising minister, Castle was incomparably different from Thatcher in terms of her public personality. She could be mischievous and extrovert. She had been a journalist briefly and had an understanding of how the media worked. Unlike Thatcher before she became leader, Castle was also at the centre of several raging internal battles. Although she had been on the losing side of some of these conflicts, intense battles can help shape potential leaders. By the late 1960s, she was fully defined, partly to her cost.

A brief summary of Castle's career shows how close she was to the centre of many thorny issues that defined the Labour government and party in the 1960s and early 1970s. She was the first Minister for Overseas Development and had Cabinet status, having argued for the new department in opposition. After the 1964 election, Wilson offered her the chance to set it up. This was not a bad start for an ambitious politician, but it was her next post that made her one of the most famous ministers in the Cabinet. As Transport Secretary, Castle delivered some lasting policy changes. After that she was Employment Secretary, introducing the Equal Pay Act and, with much less success, proposing trade union reforms in her White Paper *In Place of Strife*. Her plans were not implemented by the Labour government at the time, and yet they have been cited regularly since as a model that might have prevented not only the industrial confrontations of the 1970s but also the more severe responses to these from the Conservative governments elected after 1979. After the February 1974 election, Castle was made Social Services Secretary and she was off again with a reforming zeal. She crammed her various ministerial pursuits into the six years before 1970 and then from February 1974 until Wilson's resignation as prime minister in March 1976.

By comparison, Thatcher's record before she became prime minister was more modest. As Education Secretary, she became best known for scrapping free milk for most pupils. Critics of her policy dubbed her 'Thatcher Thatcher, milk snatcher', an unhelpful slogan for an ambitious politician. Thatcher's other main contribution in her only Cabinet post was to introduce more comprehensive schools than Labour Education Secretary Shirley Williams, even though she was no fan of comprehensive education.

Yet it was Thatcher who became the UK's first woman prime minister, a leader who won three general elections, including two landslides. She changed her party and her country beyond recognition. For decades after her dramatic fall in November 1990, the Conservatives were either intoxicated or troubled by 'Thatcherism'. One-nation conservativism, personified by Rab Butler and Harold Macmillan, became a distant memory. The UK, or at least England, remained Thatcherite in its attitudes towards the state and economic policymaking long after she had left Number Ten.

In contrast, Castle left the Commons just as Thatcher moved into Number Ten. Some of Castle's policies were long-lasting but her distinctive soft-left approach to politics, subtler than the 'labourism' of James Callaghan or the vaguely defined 'centrism' of Roy Jenkins, was never fully tested. There was no 'Castleism', whereas shelves creak with books about Thatcherism. Castle's failure to reach the top, and Thatcher's success in doing so, explain how some politicians become leaders and most do not.

———

Both Castle and Thatcher were political addicts by the time they got to university. Castle did not enjoy studying on the whole – she assumed she had failed her PPE degree at Oxford and turned her attention to other interests. She became treasurer of the Oxford University Labour Club, the highest position a woman could hold in the club at the time. Thatcher was also heavily involved in politics at Oxford, although she was a more committed student than Castle.

By 1937, Castle had embarked on her political career. She was a councillor in the north London borough of St Pancras and a journalist on the left-wing *Tribune* magazine before she moved to the *Daily Mirror*. She was far more interested in the media than Thatcher, and more aware of how journalists worked and the rhythm of news. This was a useful skill in a Labour Party that faced a largely hostile media. Most senior Labour politicians from the 1930s onwards did not know how to deal with the way they were reported and were indifferent to finding out, although in the Wilson era that complacency started to change, much as it did again when Tony Blair became leader in 1994.

Perhaps coincidentally, Castle's closest allies in the Labour Party shared her interest in journalism. Wilson became obsessed with the media, though he had never been a journalist. In his early years as Labour leader, he enjoyed the largely flattering assessments in the newspapers and on the BBC. Later he fumed when the media turned. His fascination was constant. Michael Foot was a more distinguished journalist than Castle, an editor of *Tribune* and the *Evening Standard* and a regular TV pundit. Castle and Foot adored each other, though she insisted that their relationship had only been platonic. Foot occasionally hinted that they might have had an affair. At the age of ninety she was adamant that Foot was wrong: 'I love Michael, not in a sexual sense, you understand. I put it that way at Jill Craigie's [Foot's wife] memorial last month because I thought there was no point in pussy-footing around in these areas. Mind you, he likes the flesh-pots, does Michael. I don't know what it is between us, though. He is a very generous man, too generous at times.'[1]

It is impossible to imagine Thatcher reminiscing about a colleague and friend in quite the same way. Here was a late example of Castle's endearing capacity for mischief. She knew how to raise a smile. She also had a determinedly serious side, apparent in her seizing the chance to move on from her role as a councillor when the opportunity came. Castle was elected MP for Blackburn in 1945, the youngest woman in the new House of Commons. She was thirty-four and was soon made Parliamentary Private Secretary (PPS) to Stafford Cripps, who was then president of the Board of Trade. More significantly in terms of her subsequent career, she kept this role when Harold Wilson succeeded Cripps.

Castle was lucky to work for Wilson and she made the most of her good fortune. In the late 1940s, there were few signs of Wilson's leadership potential, but he was to be a rising star during the 1950s and, in 1963, became leader of the party. Wilson and Castle had a close relationship as he moved to the top. Although there were periods when they fell out, Wilson was a genuine admirer of hers and Castle was a sincere fan of his, not only when he was soaring politically but when he went out of fashion too. Wilson's working relationship with Castle illustrates his restless and impatient leadership style: he moved her from one Cabinet post to another, often losing interest in what she was trying to achieve. Still, he remained loyal to her and she was always in the Cabinet while he was prime minister.

Her closeness to Wilson put Castle in a favourable position politically. The same can't be said of Thatcher when she was a frontbencher. Thatcher rose under Heath, who at best found her irritating. Heath tolerated her as Education Secretary and no more than that. In contrast, Wilson went out of his way to promote Castle and sing her praises. She returned the favour. Castle was capable of showing disapproval if she felt the need to do so – she was no subservient sycophant – but most of the time she conveyed affection. Theirs was an unlikely relationship but a strong one, as she reflected during the same interview in which she explained her friendship with Foot:

Oh Harold… Let me make it clear, I was never Harold's mistress. These rumours prevent Harold getting the credit he deserves. Harold believed in women. He believed in their importance in society. He was always looking for ways of promoting women. In a way that still hasn't been properly recognised, Harold was a true progressive. When he brought me into government, he told me he wanted me to go to Transport. I told him I wasn't keen. But he was persuasive, telling me I'd be the first woman to occupy that post. He was the first prime minister to actively promote women in governments.[2]

Castle was on the opposition benches for thirteen years after Labour was defeated in 1951, having had a whiff of power as PPS to Cripps and Wilson. Both she and Thatcher used their phases in opposition to develop ideas and become more fully formed as politicians. Castle became a supporter of Aneurin Bevan in the internal battles against the followers of Hugh Gaitskell. During the same phase, Wilson was identified with the Bevanites after he resigned from the Cabinet with Bevan over the introduction of prescription charges. Wilson was far more pragmatic than the more ardent Bevanites, but the approximate political association in the internal battles further strengthened the rapport between Wilson and Castle. They shared a political cause – or at least appeared to do so.

Thatcher became a Conservative MP in 1959, fourteen years after Castle. She also rose speedily. In 1961, the Tory prime minister,

Harold Macmillan, made her a junior minister at the Ministry of Pensions and National Insurance – the youngest woman to be appointed to the post and one of the few MPs from the 1959 intake to be appointed to the frontbench. Like Castle, Thatcher would face long years in opposition. The Conservatives lost in 1964 and were out of power for six years. During this period Thatcher became a crusader for lower taxes, occasionally exhibiting an exaggerated stridency that would become a permanent character trait later on. This would be to her advantage when she was at her populist peak, but it was close to a fatal flaw towards the end of her career.

In the aftermath of a landslide defeat, Thatcher cheered up activists at the 1966 Conservative Party conference by criticizing what she regarded as the high-tax policies of the Labour government. She described them as being steps 'not only towards Socialism, but towards Communism', arguing that lower taxes were an incentive to hard work. Towards the end of her reign as prime minister she called the Labour leader, Neil Kinnock, a 'crypto communist'. She had an indiscriminate sense of what constituted an attachment to communism, but in her early years of opposition Thatcher acquired an identity as an economic liberal and social conservative. In 1970, she told her local newspaper that she would like to see a 'reversal of the permissive society',[3] a view shared by many elderly activists in her party. The combination of economic liberalism and social conservatism placed her close to the ideological instincts of the party membership, but she was not being calculating in order to woo activists and nor did she frame her beliefs to pose a threat to Heath. She expressed her deeply held convictions or instincts.

As Thatcher was acquiring an identity as a rising star on the Tory right, Castle was proving to be a determinedly daring and innovative Cabinet minister. In leading her new Ministry of Overseas Development as a separate entity from the Foreign Office, she faced a logistical mountain, later saying: 'In taking up the aid responsibilities of so many different departments I inevitably took over numbers of their staff. Their sensitivities had to be dealt with gently and some new slots filled.'[4]

Castle was a great believer in departmental plans. For her they were a focus for a coming together of ideological convictions and practical policy development. They created a sense of mission. In a White Paper published in the summer of 1965, Castle set out the essence of her new department: 'The central purpose of the new ministry is to formulate and carry out British policies to help the economic development of the poorer countries...'[5]

But she faced a structural problem, as is often the case with Whitehall reforms. She and her new department were not fully in control of the theoretical policy areas. The Colonial Office retained responsibility for budgetary aid. The Treasury continued to determine relations with the International Bank for Reconstruction and Development. The Foreign Office had a big say in military aid. Soon Wilson became wary of his own initiative, and the new department quickly ceased to have Cabinet rank.

Castle's new department was not alone. Wilson had set up a Department of Economic Affairs to challenge the might of the Treasury and the economic orthodoxies it espoused. That department did not last very long either. Wilson found being prime minister much harder than he had initially envisaged – a common experience – and he quickly lost enthusiasm for reconfiguring the way the UK was governed, as other more daunting and immediate challenges sapped his energy. Changing Whitehall has always been fraught with difficulty. Many years later, in 2016, Theresa May set up a new Brexit department, the Department for Exiting the European Union. It never functioned properly. Brexit ministers were unclear about their roles, as decisions relating to Brexit seemed to be made elsewhere. The same was true in early 2020 when Boris Johnson's chief adviser, Dominic Cummings, hailed plans for a Whitehall revolution. They got virtually nowhere.

Wilson had become disillusioned with Whitehall reforms but not with Castle. She became Transport Secretary in 1966, a middle-ranking Cabinet post but one buzzing with policies at the time she took over. Although she was disappointed not to have secured a more substantial promotion, there were some attractions for her. She was excited by the challenge of creating an integrated transport system out of the fractured chaos that existed. Wilson did not regard the move to Transport as an insult, noting that the role was high-profile and important since so many newspaper readers were motorists.

At this stage in their respective careers, Castle had an instinct for publicity and a hunger for attention that surpassed Thatcher's by a wide margin. The gap between them remained until Thatcher suddenly became a leadership contender, at which point she also displayed a fascination with and love of photo opportunities and wider media attention. But as Castle's biographer notes, 'No new stretch of motorway was opened, no bypass unveiled, without Barbara in the foreground looking chic…'[6]

Castle was also brave enough to take on the car lobby, introducing the national speed limit and breathalyser tests. As a result she saved more lives than most Cabinet ministers, and acquired an even higher profile. Such policies were easy to understand and easy to oppose or support. The opposition was noisy but she was a passionate advocate:

As I had anticipated, the breathalyser when it was finally launched in 1967 caused a stir throughout the land. My postbag was full of abusive letters, usually anonymous. One of them, scribbled on a torn piece of paper, ran: 'You've ballsed our darts matches up so get out you wicked B'. Another grubby epistle showed a dagger dripping with blood over the words 'We'll get you yet, you old cow'.[7]

Apart from highlighting how anger against politicians was expressed long before Twitter came along, these outbursts also show how Castle was willing to take on causes that would generate hostility until they became part of an accepted consensus. No government would scrap speed limits or breathalyser tests. Indeed, the pattern was to impose greater restrictions in the decades that followed.

Castle was one of the longer-lasting Transport Secretaries, even though she only served three years before becoming Employment Secretary, a role which came with the elevated title of First Secretary of State. Transport Secretaries tend to move on quickly, but she stayed long enough to make her mark. The next Transport Secretary to make a significant impact was Andrew Adonis, who served under Gordon Brown. Adonis became Transport Secretary in 2008 and only agreed to serve in that post if he could launch high-speed rail. He did so.

As First Secretary of State, Castle's profile continued to rise. She became a prominent supporter of the women at the Dagenham Ford plant campaigning for the same wage as their male counterparts. In the 2010 film based on the dispute, *Made in Dagenham*, Miranda Richardson played Castle, making her one of the few Cabinet ministers to have been portrayed by a film star. Most ministers are forgotten about almost immediately. More significantly, Castle pioneered the Equal Pay Act, passed shortly before the 1970 election. This piece of legislation provided some protection for women workers in the stormy decade that followed. Although women were still subject to unfair treatment and lower pay well into the next century, Castle's Act at least gave them some legislative muscle. She set a course that others followed.

There was a significant pattern to this phase of Castle's career – an interesting ideological framework that defied simplistic caricature. Compared with quite a few of her Cabinet colleagues she was excited by the benevolent potential of the state, of what government could do to make lives better. But as an added component, she was not a dewy-eyed romantic statist. As Transport Secretary she looked to modernize the management of British Rail and was by no means automatically sympathetic to pay claims from various unions. This was a significant difference between Castle and most of the Labour Cabinet at the time. As her biographer put it, 'she did not come from the wing of the Labour movement which regarded the party's first task as promoting the interests of the trade union movement'.[8]

Castle saw the government's relations with trade unions as part of a much wider contract. She supported incomes polices even when other ministers resisted, but as part of a modern state in which the government delivered its side of the deal with, for example, the development of an integrated transport policy or a fairer approach to low pay and pensions. Whenever there was a Queen's speech outlining forthcoming legislation, Castle pushed hard for her department to have at least one substantial bill. Her Transport Bill – never fully implemented – included proposals for road pricing and parking charges, with all the money raised going towards better transport, a move that might have benefited the less affluent as much as a pay rise. In her support for hypothecated road charges she anticipated the principles behind the Congestion Charge introduced successfully in London more than thirty years later.

Some of Castle's chauvinistic colleagues saw her assertiveness as an ego trip. Ego played a part in her personality, but there was much more to her than a hunger to make a personal mark on the statute book. She saw legal frameworks as a model to deliver decent public services, social justice and more harmonious industrial relations. Castle was well to the left of New Labour, and was a vocal critic when Tony Blair became leader, but in her wariness of 'labourism', as personified in the 1960s by James Callaghan, and her vision of an active state with real responsibilities, she had one of the more coherent sets of radical visions that deserved more attention at the time – and since.

In contrast, Thatcher did not make history as Education Secretary, though she had less time to do so. Castle was hyperactive in three Cabinet posts over six continuous years until 1970. The Heath government lasted only three and a half years. Thatcher was Education Secretary for the duration. She was as energetic as Castle and even more of a workaholic, although less reflective about the work she was doing. Thatcher had no time to write a diary and did not consider doing so. Castle's diaries are an important document, and they are highly readable, if not always entirely reliable. They cast light on the battles and themes of the Wilson years. Even if Thatcher had been inclined to reflect, she was much less at the centre of torrid events as a Cabinet minister.

Whereas Castle was engaging with Wilson's agenda at close to the highest levels, Thatcher stayed burrowed away at Education. In some ways she was a technocrat in this phase of her career, submerging her ideological instincts to get on with the task at hand. Overall, her record as a minister was nowhere near as extensive as Castle's.

Yet in February 1975, Thatcher became Conservative leader while Castle was in the last year or so of her final Cabinet post. James Callaghan sacked Castle as Social Services Secretary when he became prime minister in 1976. He told her it was time for her to make way for younger people. True to form, she contemplated telling him that he should therefore leave office too.

As Thatcher began the long march towards election victory as Conservative leader, Castle's ministerial career was over.

———

There was a general consensus that Castle's chances of becoming Labour leader and prime minister were destroyed by her passionate support for a new approach to industrial relations. In her biography of Castle, Anne Perkins opens the relevant chapter with a striking sentence: 'The decision to legislate on industrial relations destroyed Barbara's career.'[9] Reviewing Perkins's book, then Foreign Secretary Jack Straw reached a similar conclusion: 'Barbara fell, and never properly recovered, as a result of the humiliating failure of her greatest project – reforming the trade unions.'[10] Straw had been Castle's special adviser and succeeded her as the MP for Blackburn. He knew a thing or two about stormy internal disputes. He was writing his review while Foreign Secretary in 2003, at the height of the Iraq War.

Castle's approach to trade unions, fair and constructive but not sentimental, was ahead of its time. Her attempts in the late 1960s to establish a new framework for industrial relations were doomed from the start. She never had enough support – not at the beginning of her tempestuous journey and certainly not by the end.

Revealingly, she did have the enthusiastic backing of Wilson. That should have been enough. Three years earlier, Wilson had led his party to a landslide victory. Landslide winners can usually do more or less what they want, and expect the meek Cabinet to follow. But Wilson's authority with his colleagues had been undermined by the devaluation crisis in 1967, along with what they saw as his lacklustre and devious approach to leadership. In the context of an already restless Cabinet, Wilson's support for Castle was never going to be enough.

Castle's failure to see that all paths towards reform were blocked reflected what could be her brittle and sometimes misplaced self-confidence. *In Place of Strife* was not an aberration but part of a less flattering ministerial pattern, in which Castle would often be too ambitious in her objectives and her means of achieving them. Unlike Rab Butler and Roy Jenkins, she was not a patient incrementalist. She liked the drama of the big political move, whether it was setting up a new Cabinet department or publishing a contentious Transport Bill.

Castle had cause to act in relation to the unions. In 1968, the year before her proposals were formally published, 4.6 million days had been lost through disputes.[11] Her confidence to act was based partly on a distorting sense from her recent past. In politics, the recent past is a dangerous guide to the immediate future. Many leaders and aspiring leaders turn to the past for guidance, and subsequently move towards their doom.

Castle calculated that she could achieve consensus around her plans partly on the basis of her relative success in dealing with unions when she was Transport Secretary. In this respect, her trauma with the unions was a preview of what was to happen to Edward Heath in the early 1970s. Heath had been successful as Minister of Labour under Harold Macmillan, forming decent relations with the unions. As a result, he acquired a fatal sense that he could work with them in the transformed circumstances of the 1970s. Castle's experience in the 1960s should have been a warning. James Callaghan should have taken note too. He assumed when he became prime minister in 1976 that he would be able to work with his friends in the unions. They gave him an even more hellish time than that experienced by Heath and Castle.

Unlike a lot of her colleagues, Castle had consistently supported price and income controls, regarding them as a means to boost productivity and redistribution – part of her wider vision for an active state. The same balanced view informed her approach to union reform. Her proposals included secret ballots for some planned strikes that threatened the 'national interest'; a right for government to intervene in 'unconstitutional' strikes; and, more widely, a Commission for Industrial Relations that would have had the power to impose settlements in disputes. At the same time, she extended some trade union rights.

Union leaders did not see any balance in her plans whatsoever and were opposed and outraged that one of the Cabinet's left-wingers was challenging them. Partly taking their cue from the unions, most of the Cabinet opposed the proposals without reflecting on them for more than a moment or two. Callaghan's authority had inevitably been considerably diminished by the devaluation crisis that took place when he was chancellor. Few chancellors recover from a devaluation. Callaghan did, at least in terms of his standing within the Labour Party. He did so partly as a result of his unswerving opposition to *In Place of Strife*, a stance that was both sincere and calculated. Without the support of the Cabinet, much of the parliamentary party and the trade unions, Wilson had no choice but to drop *In Place of Strife*. Neither he nor Castle had the authority to impose their will.

The internal coalition opposed to their plans was vast. Callaghan and his wing were not alone. On the other side of Labour's 'broad church', Michael Foot noted the 'clamours for a Labour government to drink the poison that would kill it'.[12] At this point, Foot's politics were miles away from Callaghan's. However, they were wholly united in their opposition to *In Place of Strife*.

Wilson left Castle behind too, at least on this issue. When Labour returned to power in 1974, Wilson made Foot his Employment Secretary. Foot was close to the big union leaders and sought to remain that way. Even though industrial relations became much worse than in the late 1960s, no minister dared mention *In Place of Strife*. Wilson regarded Foot as one of the big successes of his 1974 government, regularly singling him out for praise. Foot did not reciprocate. He and his wife, Jill Craigie, remained stern critics of Wilson for the rest of their lives.[13]

Castle had acted impulsively without seeking wider support, a decision that resembles Theresa May's decision to announce her plan for leaving the European Union without having fully tested the support of her Cabinet and the parliamentary party. May pressed on only to find impossible resistance. Castle persisted for a little bit, but was never going to prevail.

A politician with more guile than Castle might have recovered and retained a chance of getting into Number Ten. Callaghan showed how recovery is possible, in so far as he was a failed chancellor who became prime minister. By 1976, when Labour held its first leadership contest since Castle became a prominent national figure, her views about the need for a new framework for industrial relations were already starting to look far-sighted. Heath's government had fallen in 1974 because of dire industrial relations, and an already exhausted Wilson was drained further by industrial disputes after he returned to Number Ten that year. Callaghan was to go through similar difficulties. If Castle had established a band of Castleites in the parliamentary Labour Party, she might have been able to stand in what became an all-male leadership contest in 1976, claiming vindication for her visionary stand in the late 1960s. But she did not have a significant number of devoted followers, partly because the male-dominated parliamentary Labour Party would barely have considered the idea of electing a woman. And there was another factor. Castle had a capacity to annoy as well as charm. The 1976 contest would have been her only chance to be prime minister and she would have been slaughtered.

In his review of Castle's biography, Jack Straw opens with a revealing observation: 'As her mother was dying, Barbara remarked "that she was endearing, much loved and totally exasperating". Like mother, like daughter.'[14] Straw chooses to highlight at the beginning of his reflections her tendency to cause exasperation. To some extent, Castle was Straw's mentor. He admired her and was influenced by her. He was also exasperated by her.

Imagine the attitude of her colleagues who were not so instinctively supportive. She was a battler, and too often gave the impression that she was battling as an act of vanity. She was a performer but not an actress. Unlike some of her male counterparts, she could not hide her ambition. Instead of building up allies she alienated too many colleagues. According to Straw, she was one of the most 'self-absorbed' people he had ever met. Self-absorption is common in politics and most other fields, but successful politicians are able to hide their fascination with themselves as they seek allies. Evidently, Castle could not do so.

Her sense of timing was also poor. A successful leader can read the rhythms of politics as a conductor reads music. They know when there is trouble ahead and what is possible given the nature of the rhythms. Castle launched big plans without being clear on how she was going to secure the level of support required to execute them. She liked the theatre of the big announcements, when she needed to be more focused on how to deliver. *In Place of Strife* was by no means the only example. She left behind weighty White Papers on other policy areas. Quite a lot of the proposals were not implemented.

She was also a victim of Labour's chauvinistic culture. Many of the Cabinet were self-absorbed, from Wilson downwards, and yet only Castle was regularly described as such. If she had been a man with the same range of skills and experience, self-absorption might have been forgiven. But such was the extent of the criticism she received that it did not seriously cross the mind of Castle, however big her ego, that she might be leader. Indeed, she wondered whether Shirley Williams, a Cabinet minister in Wilson's later government, might be a future leader. Castle chose to be loyal to Wilson for the most part, rather than plan or plot to succeed him. There wouldn't be a female candidate in a Labour leadership context until Margaret Beckett stood in 1994. Beckett had been acting leader after John Smith's sudden death. She was easily defeated by Tony Blair. In Castle's case, after Wilson resigned she was on the backbenches and her Cabinet career was over. The next Labour leadership contest was in 1980, between two male candidates: Michael Foot and Denis Healey. By then, Castle was not even in the Commons.

———

Thatcher infuriated some colleagues far more intensely than Castle ever did. The Conservatives were at least as chauvinistic as Labour. Before Thatcher won they had staged only one other leadership contest, an all-male campaign in 1963 when Heath was the winner. Until 1963, Conservative leaders 'emerged', with only male candidates being considered.

There are, though, key differences between Thatcher and Castle. Thatcher's most intense period of inadvertently provocative self-absorption, when she came to assume that her continuing leadership coincided with national interest, came only after she had been prime minister for several years. In the years before she became leader, Thatcher irritated colleagues – but not to the same extent as Castle managed to do. This was partly because she was far less engaged in big battles as a Cabinet minister compared with Castle. Her relative reticence as a minister was greatly to her advantage when she stood for the leadership. Although she was prominent and distinct as an Education Secretary, she had few clashes with colleagues. Like Rab Butler, on a smaller scale Castle had been too engaged as a Cabinet minister and had created enemies on the various political battlefields as a result.

Rarely a day passed in the 1960s when Castle was not arguing with a senior colleague or pursuing her agenda, whatever the cost to her relations with other ministers and MPs. Thatcher annoyed Heath. She would not have been his chosen successor. But leaders of the modern era, especially leaders that lose general elections, are in no position to choose their successor. In the end, it was to her advantage that Heath did not like her. Their awkward relationship meant that she personified a leap away from the recent past when she stood against him in 1975. Castle's closeness to Wilson helped her rise in the Cabinet, but was not of any use in terms of becoming a leader.

Quite a lot of Thatcher's frontbench colleagues were wary of her when she rose to be a Cabinet minister, and did not see her as leadership material. This was not an issue, as Thatcher did not see herself as a future leader. Ironically, this attitude made it easier for her. When the time was right, Thatcher made her moves speedily, suddenly, and without the years of anguish that can gnaw away at those who ache to be leader and prime minister. When the party's MPs sought a fresh start after the tempests of the Heath era, she could claim to represent the best opportunity. The more experienced candidate, William Whitelaw, had been much closer to Heath and Heath's policies. He became a candidate in the second round of the 1975 Tory leadership contest. Thatcher beat him with ease, rewarded for the courage of challenging Heath in the first place.

On the whole, and partly through luck, Thatcher became identified with popular policies rather than deeply contentious ones, except when as Education Secretary she scrapped free school milk for most pupils. In the key period of her speedy ascent, Heath appointed her as shadow Secretary of State for the Environment. He assumed this middle-ranking assignment would keep her out of the limelight. But instead, over the next few months, Thatcher handed out gifts in the form of policies. She announced her party would abolish the unpopular local property tax that was based on a house's notional rental value. She also pledged to help those struggling to pay back their mortgages. In the dark October 1974 election, she glittered. The Tories lost again but her profile was growing, as Castle's had in the late 1960s. But Castle became famous as a controversial Transport Secretary and for *In Place of Strife*. Thatcher was pleasing voters with superficially attractive policies.[15] At this point, she was not a hugely contentious figure.

Having lost the October election, a significant number of Conservative MPs wanted a new Conservative leader. Their yearning came at precisely the right moment for Thatcher. After that election, Heath put her in the Treasury team where she performed well in the Commons. As she flourished, Thatcher's friend and ally, Keith Joseph, proved his unsuitability for leadership with a series of insensitive speeches and awkward public performances. Aware of his shortcomings, Joseph decided he would not challenge Heath. Thatcher was available to fill the gap, distant from Heath in that he never allowed her to be close to him, evidently on the right and yet without being too precise in her ideology, and she took her chance with ruthless self-confidence.

Castle had no such opportunity and there is little evidence to suggest that she would have responded with the same focus even if she had. She would never have challenged Wilson. As Straw notes, she was insecure and had phases of self-doubt. She was a formidable campaigner and did not suffer fools, but she was never in a position to do what Thatcher did – to leap from being a middle-ranking member of the shadow Cabinet to leader of the Opposition in the space of a few months.

When Thatcher was elected leader of the Opposition in February 1975, Castle was Secretary of State for Health and Social Services. She continued to implement historic policies. In difficult economic circumstances, she legislated so that child benefit was paid directly to mothers. She introduced a range of other measures that involved extracting cash from a Treasury trying to limit spending. Yet she remained on the wrong side of major issues. In the 1975 referendum on the UK's membership of the Common Market, Castle campaigned energetically for withdrawal. In contrast, Thatcher was one of the higher-profile figures campaigning for the UK to remain. Those calling for withdrawal were heavily defeated. Castle soon changed her mind, to the extent that after she left the Commons in 1979 she became an MEP. Thatcher almost changed her mind on Europe too, becoming hostile to the EU as prime minister although she never argued that the UK should leave.

Castle continued to be politically active as she reached ninety. She was a perceptive critic of New Labour, arguing that the statement implicit in the name 'New Labour' – that she and her generation had been part of a failed project and there was now a new vision – was wrong:

> They do not seem to have realised that all governments, whatever their complexion, end in apparent failure. Macmillan was triumphant in 1959 and was biting the dust shortly afterwards. Heath won in 1970 and spent three and half years doing U-turns, looking for the perfect answer. Thatcher was a remarkable woman, but her premiership ended in ignominy. But the current leadership seems preoccupied by the failing of Labour in power and in opposition.[16]

She was right. Thatcher's leadership ended in the most humiliating fashion possible, with much of her Cabinet telling her she had to resign in the dramatic autumn of 1990. In not becoming a leader, Castle had one advantage over Thatcher: after she ceased to be an MP she could make waves without her words being viewed through the prism of her fall. Thatcher's later interventions were viewed almost solely within the context of her brutal removal from power.

In their final years, both Castle and Thatcher were cheered heartily at their respective party conferences. But there was a big difference. Thatcher never spoke at one after she ceased to be prime minister, whereas Castle was applauded when she called for New Labour to be more generous to pensioners. Her voice was as powerful as ever, her frail frame and reddish hair as striking on the conference platform as when she was more physically robust. Although revered, she still lost that particular argument, and the leadership prevailed in its determination to limit its generosity to pensioners. Castle was a great change-maker but too often she was on the losing side of internal arguments. Leaders need to be on the winning side most of the time, or keep well clear of the deadly arguments until they have secured the crown. That is why Thatcher became a leader and Castle did not.

———

Denis Healey was Castle's Cabinet colleague from 1964 and again after the February 1974 election. He was seen as a far more likely prime minister than Castle, even though he too wasn't one to avoid taking a stand on contentious issues that divided his party. In making his case with pugnacious vigour, he acquired an aura of leadership. Yet the reasons he acquired an aura were also the causes of his downfall. The substance of his case and the scale of his pugnacity might have been leader-like, but they also meant Healey would never be a leader.

4

DENIS HEALEY

From the mid-1970s, it was Denis Healey's turn to be seen as a likely Labour leader and prime minister. There were sound reasons for the perception. Healey had more prime ministerial qualities than some prime ministers. Yet the assumption that Healey would lead Labour was based on an illusion, one that is fairly common in British politics.

Politicians and political journalists often pluck a figure out of context and conclude, 'Ah yes, they are an obvious leader.' But the context determines the fate of aspiring leaders as much as their characters do. As with Shakespeare's tragic heroes, character alone does not shape destiny. The immediate backgrounds in which they make their moves, as well as their pasts and the acts of others, play a part in deciding what happens. So it was for Healey in the 1970s until the early 1980s. He was doomed never to be a Labour leader or prime minister, and the obstacles blocking his path should have been more obvious at the time. In addition, his evident tragic flaws were as significant as his epic strengths. In British politics, we choose to see what we want to see. Much of the media and quite a few of his colleagues chose to see Healey as a Labour leader and prime minister when they should have looked more closely at what was happening around him, and them.

It was during Labour's party conference in September 1980 that the assumptions of the media and a significant section of the shadow Cabinet became fully formed in relation to Healey and leadership. They had little doubt about what was to happen next in the party's latest turbulent drama. Following Labour's defeat in the 1979 election, a civil war had erupted almost immediately. Why had Labour lost? Had the leadership betrayed the members and gone to the country with a manifesto that was too cautious and timid? Or had it been too left-wing? Were Labour's economic policies in government the cause of the defeat, or could they form the basis of some kind of renewal in opposition? Should trade unions and party members have more power over the leadership and the policies they espoused? James Callaghan had opted to stay on as leader, but by the early autumn of 1980, more than a year after the general election, he was ready to take an exhausted bow.

Halfway through Labour's gathering that year, the BBC broke the story that until then had only been the subject of much speculation, when one of its political correspondents confirmed that Callaghan was to stand down shortly after the conference was over. Callaghan had wanted to delay the announcement, seeking the space to plan a more controlled exit. Instead, the news of his departure leaked, sparking questions in the middle of the conference about who would replace him. Another leadership contest loomed.

Editors of the ITN early-evening bulletin appeared to have the answer. They ended the news, which had led with Callaghan's imminent resignation, with a teasing shot from the conference hall. The camera began by focusing on Callaghan, sitting close to the centre of the raised platform, and then panned to Denis Healey sitting below in the front row. (Healey was not a member of the party's ruling National Executive, and therefore had no right to be on the platform.) The implication was clear: Callaghan was going and Healey was the obvious successor.

The ITN news bulletin was by no means alone in predicting this neat sequence. The view was shared by most shadow Cabinet members and political commentators. One columnist in *The Times* reported a conversation with another potential contender for the leadership: 'He added when pressed that Mr Denis Healey would be the next leader. Apparently there was no question about that…'[1]

For many years Healey had been spoken of as a future prime minister. He looked the part, had an intellectual capacity well beyond many of those who had been prime minister, and enjoyed high personal ratings in opinion polls for much of his career. He was clever and fun, a potent combination in politics. And Healey was experienced too. By the autumn of 1980 he had been a long-serving and widely respected Secretary of State for Defence and a formidably robust chancellor during the wild economic storms that whirled around the Labour government from 1974 until 1979. Now in opposition, his personal ratings remained high. Callaghan wanted Healey to succeed him and had sought to time his departure accordingly, although not for the first time the outgoing leader's sense of timing was ill-judged. Arguably, Callaghan had already mistimed the calling of the general election, deciding against the autumn of 1978 and delaying until May 1979. And the timing of his resignation was not as helpful to Healey as it first seemed. Nonetheless, the media focus on Healey in autumn 1980 was justified in many respects. Apparently, he was the obvious figure to lead Labour back to power, a big beast to take on what appeared to be the fragile premiership of Margaret Thatcher.[2]

Healey's tenure as Defence Secretary from 1964 to 1970 had established him as a formidable force. The brief is not an easy one for ambitious Labour politicians. The party tends to be less trusted by some voters and parts of the establishment in relation to defence issues compared with the Conservatives. Even those Labour Defence Secretaries who win the respect of the military establishment rarely climb further in politics. The Fred Mulleys, Geoff Hoons, John Huttons and Des Brownes – some of Healey's successors as Defence Secretary – came and went. But Healey had hardly got going in terms of his career after his sustained contribution in that role during the 1960s.

That is partly because he ranged far more widely than others who held the Defence brief in Labour governments. Over nearly six years, Healey impressed the military, the sceptical media and the world beyond the UK with his authoritative grasp of international affairs, which had been a passion of his since he was a student at Oxford in the 1930s. Conveniently for Healey, Harold Wilson's choices as Foreign Secretaries in his 1960s governments were lacklustre or, in the case of the erratically brilliant George Brown, only at their best when sober. Without mighty Foreign Secretaries commanding the attention, Healey shone more brightly on the international stage. Later he described his six years at the Ministry of Defence as 'the most rewarding of my political career. I liked the work… I liked the people I worked with… I was able in my NATO role to work constructively with friends old and new, on what had been my underlying objective in politics ever since my student days – the prevention of world war.'[3]

In the 1950s and early 1960s, Healey had written articles and essays mainly on foreign affairs, his deepest interest in politics but not by any means his only one. His writing contrasted with the prolific output of Roy Jenkins. Healey was gripped by international issues; Jenkins wrote about former prime ministers, more drawn to character in politics.

Healey became shadow chancellor when Labour lost the 1970 election, and showed a similar grasp of economic policy as he had the Defence brief. After the February 1974 election, Healey was chancellor in a hung parliament at a time when inflation was raging and there was industrial turmoil. The outgoing Conservative government had introduced a three-day week in response to the latest miners' strike, in order to ration energy. By the time of the election, the miners were seeking pay rises of around 35 per cent. Inflation was in double figures, at close to 14 per cent, and the inflation rate was to get much higher as the incoming Labour government agreed to pay claims from a variety of unions.

This was the hardest of times to be a chancellor, not least with no Commons majority – and then only a tiny one after the October 1974 election – and a divided Cabinet with several ministerial titans wary of the course Healey was seeking to take. For more than five years, Healey faced sterling crises, public spending emergencies, soaring inflation, and unions refusing to cooperate with pay policies that were anyway seen by him as a last resort. He described pay policies as 'the equivalent of jumping off the second floor of a house, needed only if the rest of the house was on fire'.[4]

This characteristically vivid image reflects a wider ambiguity about incomes policies, the recurring motif of the 1970s. Harold Wilson was elected in 1974 opposed to an incomes policy, in which the government sets the pay limits – often in both the public and private sectors. With typical guile, he adopted one by claiming it was voluntary, but made it enforceable if the guidelines were not heeded. Callaghan had been even more ferociously opposed when mocking Edward Heath's incomes policy, and yet he too adopted one as prime minister. Healey grasped the desperate context in which each one was introduced. The house was on fire.

The Cabinet was divided. Labour was divided. Healey was responding to one crisis after another. He presented more unscheduled budgets than any chancellor in modern times, with some of his addresses euphemistically described as 'mini budgets' when they were packages hastily assembled to prevent the economy from falling off a cliff. In modern times, only the Conservative chancellor Rishi Sunak came close to presenting so many financial statements. Sunak was responding to the pandemic that struck the UK in March 2020, the gravest crisis since 1945. Healey's challenge was almost as daunting.

Yet amid all the economic constraints, Healey found the money for a series of historic reforms – changes that were largely overlooked when a significant section of the party membership came to regard the conduct of the 1970s Labour government as a 'betrayal'. The term 'betrayal' is one of the most emotive in British politics, and it is nearly always an oversimplification. As this vulnerable government staggered from one crisis to another, Healey announced a 25 per cent increase in the state pension, while council house rents were frozen and local authority house building continued on a substantial scale. When the UK economy expanded in the 1980s and 1990s there was a shortage of affordable rented accommodation, largely because of the sale of council houses and the failure to build replacements. There was no such shortage amid the turmoil of the 1970s. Healey also found the cash for the introduction of universal child benefit and statutory maternity leave.

The government Healey was part of is often thought of only in terms of bleak crises, the 'winter of discontent' in early 1979 being the ultimate symbol of the chaos over which it presided. But in near-impossible circumstances it was also a government of historic social reform, and Healey played his part.

The anarchic economic nightmare, though, was a constant theme. At least Healey survived the course, still in place as chancellor in 1979 when Labour lost power. As a feat of endurance alone, this was a substantial achievement, but Healey could also claim to have navigated the jagged economic terrain with a degree of success. By 1979, inflation was falling, from admittedly soaring heights, and the government had got through the hellish phase during which the International Monetary Fund was dictating more or less how much it could spend. The journey had been draining. Even Healey, who always gave the impression of being up for the fight, fell ill at the end of it all.[5] He blamed the never-ending meetings with the unions and the disruptive chaos that followed in terms of strikes and pay demands.

Ministers are often moved from department to department every few months, and yet Healey was Defence Secretary for nearly six years and chancellor for more than five, in a torrid decade. No Labour prime minister moved Healey in a reshuffle. His determined longevity in thorny Cabinet posts was a significant reason why Healey was seen as a potential prime minister.

By 1980, Healey had many other claims to be Labour leader, including a range and depth of interests from a relatively early age. His autobiography, appropriately titled *The Time of My Life*, is one of the best written by a senior British politician in the second half of the twentieth century. Published in 1989, it evokes his rich and varied life.

At eighteen, Healey spent part of his summer cycling in Germany. He spoke German and would soon speak several other languages.

By the time he went to Oxford he had read the great novelists, and his literary hero was Virginia Woolf. His music teacher at school took a shine to him, introducing him to the legendary composers. He read the poets, wrote poetry himself, and enjoyed reciting poems that he had learned off by heart. In addition, he was a good enough photographer to publish a book of photos later in his career. The cliché was that Healey had a hinterland, in his range of passions beyond politics. The observation was repeated so often it understated the aspiring leader's phenomenal cultural curiosity.

As a bonus for Healey and his leadership ambitions, he also had a lightness of touch to accompany his intellectual weightiness and political combativeness. During a Christmas edition of Bruce Forsyth's *Generation Game*, a group of public figures dressed up as Santa Claus and the contestants had to guess who each one was. Healey was one of the celebrity participants, generating big cheers from the audience when he removed the disguise and revealed his identity. Such a positive reaction was by no means guaranteed. Another chancellor, George Osborne, was booed when he presented medals at the London Paralympics in 2012. Appearing out of context is a risk for chancellors, but Healey got a boost from tongue-in-cheek appearances. Mike Yarwood, a brilliant impersonator with his own peak-time show in the 1970s and early 1980s, also helped to humanize Healey with his impressions. Impersonating Healey, Yarwood would dismiss others as 'Silly Billies'. Healey had never uttered the words until Yarwood did, but they soon became his catchphrase.

Healey was a forerunner of those politicians in more recent times who shaped their public image by appearing on the BBC's *Have I Got News for You*. Boris Johnson is perhaps the most memorable of these. But Healey never became prime minister even though, unlike Johnson, when he made his light-hearted TV contributions he had passed an important test of leadership: he had faced and responded to economic crises of historic significance.

———

That was the weighty case in favour of Healey becoming Labour leader when Callaghan stood down – and as we have seen, by the time of Labour's conference in 1980 many assumed he would acquire the crown. But the simplistic singling out of one candidate with leadership qualities overlooked the wider mood of that annual gathering.

Different factions were fighting each other with an intensity that was unique even for the Labour Party. At one noisy fringe meeting on the Monday night of the Blackpool conference, the former Cabinet minister Shirley Williams warned that fascism was not confined to the right; with a dramatic flourish, she declared there was also a 'fascism of the left'. She had in mind her former Cabinet colleague Tony Benn and his devoted supporters, proposing or implementing sweeping internal reforms of the Labour Party and hailing a radical programme of new policies. Williams was still in the Labour Party at this point, but not for very much longer. Her comments were widely reported on news bulletins and formed part of a *Panorama* programme broadcast on prime-time BBC One.

Earlier on the day of Williams's packed fringe meeting, Tony Benn had been at his oratorical peak. In the conference hall, during a speech of spellbinding resolution – for some at least – Benn had pledged that in its first few days, the next Labour government would nationalize the banks, leave the European Union (or Common Market, as it was known then) and abolish the House of Lords. He argued that the next Labour government would also be accountable to its members, thereby avoiding the 'betrayals' of the administration that had lost in 1979. Parts of the conference roared their approval, while others shook their heads in despair. This was broadcast live on BBC Two. Speaking at several fringe meetings a day, Benn insisted that party members would determine the full policy programme for Labour, and MPs who did not accept the proposals would face deselection. This was part of what Williams meant when she spoke of a fascism of the left. Just over a year earlier, Benn and Williams had been in the same Cabinet. Denis Healey had been Chancellor of the Exchequer and closer to Williams's side of the argument. For Benn's followers, Healey was a much bigger villain than Williams, because of his economic policies when he was chancellor – in particular the spending cuts he had sought.

The autumnal leadership contest that followed the conference and Callaghan's resignation in 1980 was the best chance Healey had to become leader. It was the last in which Labour MPs alone had a vote, which should have been hugely to Healey's advantage; the parliamentary Labour Party was not as left-wing as party members. Yet he did not win. The camera that focused on him portentously at the end of the ITN bulletin at the party conference should instead have turned to another former Cabinet minister, Michael Foot. Healey's formidable record as a minister was a qualification for leadership, but also a towering obstacle.

———

The defining party conference for Healey was not the one in 1980 but the one that was staged four years earlier, when Labour was in government and Jim Callaghan had recently become prime minister. In the autumn of 1976, with the crisis deepening in the

UK to the point where the economy was tottering on another cliff edge, Healey had been about to fly to Manila for an urgent IMF meeting. This was a gathering so vital to the future of the UK economy that Healey was planning to give the Labour conference a miss, highly unusual for a chancellor. Gordon Brown never missed a Labour conference even if he had to leave early for autumnal IMF gatherings. Hearing that the annual Labour gathering was getting ready to vote against his proposed spending cuts, Healey chose not to take his flight. Instead, he dashed to Blackpool to persuade the conference to back his policies. Images shown on TV included Healey's car turning back from the airport. BBC Two also broadcast his speech live as part of its conference coverage.

When Healey finally arrived at the conference, he had to speak from the floor like any other delegate and was strictly limited to a few minutes. Only members of Labour's mighty National Executive Committee were allowed to speak from the platform at greater length. As he delivered his improvised speech with passion, his neatly parted hair became dishevelled and soon the red light intended to signal the end of his slot was flashing. The Labour Party has always known how to cut its senior figures down to size. As he made his case for how to secure the IMF loan, some on the conference floor were cheering. Some were booing. One shouted out 'resign'. Healey carried on making a determined defence of his policy: 'I need your support to negotiate with the IMF... on the basis of existing policies... that means sticking with painful cuts in public spending... sticking to the pay policy...'[6]

The conference supported him in a subsequent vote, even though he made many enemies at that gathering of Labour activists. No potential leader had been tested quite like this – a chancellor taking on his party as sterling tumbled and the UK economy was close to running out of money. When Gordon Brown was under intense pressure during the financial crash of 2008, he was already prime minister. Potential leaders might develop as public figures after fighting epic internal battles, but they also risk alienating those whose support they may later rely on.

The jeering when Healey spoke at the 1976 conference should have been a warning to him and his admirers that his path to leadership would be blocked whenever the vacancy arose. The anger of those who jeered fed on itself and deepened. By 1980, some of his internal opponents would not have been surprised to have discovered Healey had cut spending on the NHS to zero while he was chancellor.

But Healey showed little sign of reflecting on the noisy dissent in the 1970s – or, if he did, he was disinclined to address the implications for his personal ambition. In the mid-1970s, Healey fought not only at party conferences but within the Cabinet. Against him was Tony Benn and his Alternative Economic Strategy, a programme with growing support among Labour members. With energy and charm, Benn put the case for import controls, much greater state ownership and withdrawal from the Common Market, a programme later advocated in only slightly different forms by some on the Tory right during and after the 2016 Brexit referendum. Also opposed to Healey was Tony Crosland, author of *The Future of Socialism*, an intellectual guide for some Labour members.

Healey was so absorbed in the specific task at hand that his future leadership ambitions did not cross his mind. In this respect, he was similar to Rab Butler. This absence of calculating ambition was in marked contrast to Gordon Brown, an even longer-serving chancellor, who was equally committed to policy detail and direction but obsessed with becoming prime minister. When Healey turned away from the hell of managing the economy, he read poetry, played the piano or developed his interest in photography. Though ambitious, he was not tormented by the need to become prime minister. Perhaps torment is a necessary requirement. Although Brown had a wide range of interests, from sport to books, he was impatient about seizing the crown. Brown's unyielding ambition was a virtue; he became prime minister. Healey's indifference to such considerations was a fatal flaw.

Amid terrifying economic fragility, Healey sought to secure a loan from the IMF by implementing cuts, calming the sinking pound, tackling inflation and prevailing in the arguments raging within his party and government. But when he emerged after the 1979 election, battered, bruised and yet still committed, Healey was seen as the personification of 'betrayal' by some MPs, activists and trade union leaders.

Healey's memoir shows the extent to which he prioritized dealing with internal battles over furthering his own ambition. Here is one example of many: 'I made a blistering attack on the trade union leader, Clive Jenkins, at the Party Conference in 1974, which was all the more effective for relying on ridicule rather than abuse. It won me a standing ovation at the time; but another trade union leader warned me that I might live to regret it.'[7]

And he did. In 1980, Jenkins, who relished political intrigue, was one of those who encouraged Michael Foot to stand – not that Foot needed a great deal of encouraging by that point. Healey enjoyed taking on his internal enemies a little too much, without reflecting for long on how his victims might strike back.

There is always a deep connection between party and leader. A newly elected leader is to some extent the personification of a party's mood at the point of a leadership contest. By 1980, Labour had been moving leftwards for a decade, in terms of the greater assertiveness of the membership and the policies that flowed from its new influence. If MPs had elected Healey in 1980, he would not have led a compliant party paying homage to his leadership skills. His election by Labour MPs would have been seen as an act of provocation by a significant section of the wider party.

Healey had shown little interest in party management, an unavoidable qualification of leadership, particularly when the party is as badly divided as Labour was then. It has been said of Healey that he did not suffer fools gladly, and could not hide his disdain for those he thought were advocating policies that were electorally suicidal and would wreck the economy. This was partly a statement of the obvious. Healey certainly showed he could stand up for himself. He was up for a fight with internal colleagues, such as Clive Jenkins, as well as external foes, including Sir Geoffrey Howe, his opposite number on the Conservative frontbench for many years. Healey once described going into debate with Howe as 'like being savaged by a dead sheep'. These were not the words of a shy and self-effacing political figure.

Yet there was also deep restraint within Healey's approach to politics, obscured by the caricature of the battler. He was not someone who schemed against colleagues. He did not have a malevolent bone in his body, and had no time for Machiavellian plots. Intellectually confident, he was content to put his case openly and, sometimes, ferociously. That was the limit of his strategic thinking in terms of leadership.

As an advocate, he was very publicly and openly on one side of ideological struggles and showed little willingness to move on the key issues that divided his party. By 1980, when his party's membership, now from the safety of opposition, was calling for huge increases in investment, Healey was still defending the cuts he had imposed as chancellor. There was a widening gap between the direction of the party and Healey's place within it.

Polls suggested that Healey was the most popular candidate in the 1980 leadership election, at least among the wider electorate. Newspapers with no intention of endorsing Labour under any circumstances published leaders insisting Healey should be elected or the party would cease to be taken seriously. But much of the party disagreed with what Healey had come to represent, even though this representation was an absurd oversimplification. Healey had been far from just an advocate of unpopular public spending cuts when chancellor: in impossibly constrained circumstances, he found the money for expensive and wide-ranging social reforms. But it was Healey's fault that the caricature formed in the first place. He was openly disdainful of the Bennite left and could not disguise it. If he had wanted to become leader, he would have needed to at least woo some of the so-called soft left that was wary of Benn. He did not do so.

There is also evidence to suggest that his internal opponents had a case in arguing that Healey cut spending too indiscriminately when he was chancellor. That evidence comes from Healey himself. In his autobiography, he acknowledged that the Treasury had been far too pessimistic in its forecasts. Public spending did not have to be cut on the scale he had called for when the IMF was making its demands in return for a loan: 'Long before any of the measures imposed by the IMF had any chance to take effect, our balance of payments in 1977 was in equilibrium, compared with the heavy deficit originally forecast. If I had been given accurate forecasts in 1976, I would never have needed to go to the IMF at all.'[8]

But, at the time, Healey had little else to go on but the gloomy Treasury forecasts. The left's argument was that the forecasts should be ignored, not that the forecasts were wrong. Even so, Labour's dividing lines were drawn in the mid-1970s, and Healey was unambiguously on one side.

Another reason why the left's caricature of Healey stuck was that his politics were hard to pin down. It is sometimes easier to loathe figures who seem politically shapeless. They can assume any form, flattering or unflattering. Healey's apparent or perceived rootlessness was not a consequence of calculated evasiveness in the manner of the wily Harold Wilson. Of the two prime ministers he served, Healey was disdainful of Wilson and an admirer of Callaghan, who he regarded as more reliable and honest to deal with. Healey was not an admirer of wiliness as a political skill, but he might have benefited at times from being more devious in a Wilson-like manner. The explanation for Healey being harder to pin down than figures such as Tony Benn, Roy Jenkins and Tony Crosland was a simple one. From 1974 to 1979, he got caught up in so many economic storms that he had little time or space to fully define himself. Staying afloat was his creed; less ideologically glamorous than being a Bennite or a Croslandite, but a mighty task nonetheless.

Healey had been a communist at Oxford, although he put his allegiance down to the Communist Party's unequivocal opposition to appeasement in the 1930s rather than a broader commitment. Still, there were faint echoes in the 1970s of that ideological muscularity. In office, he raised the top rate of tax on high earners to unprecedented levels. But in his attempts to get a grip on inflation, the balance of payments deficit, the related issue of public spending, and industrial turmoil, he could not step aside for a day or two to outline his vision for the future. By the time of Labour's 1979 election defeat, he was not entirely sure what form his vision took or whether visionary politics were even what was required. His pitch as a counter to the crusading Benn was that of a grounded heavyweight.

Later, Healey was an admirer of Gordon Brown, although capable of the occasional barbed criticism. Brown admired Healey too. Brown's senior adviser, Ed Balls, could not disguise his excitement when he was taken to visit Healey at his home in Sussex by the *Observer* commentator William Keegan. Much drink was consumed. Keegan, who has known every chancellor since the early 1950s, believes that if Balls had been a chancellor he would have been 'in the mould of Denis Healey'.[9] Instead, Balls lost his seat in the 2015 election and became a celebrity after his appearance on *Strictly Come Dancing*, a move that Healey would have fully endorsed. While Brown reigned at the Treasury, Balls was seen as a Brownite. Healey had many admirers, but no Healeyites.

Jenkins, Crosland and Healey were the leading social democrats in the 1960s and early 1970s. Many years later, the former Labour MP Giles Radice wrote an illuminating book arguing that if only one of them had been seen as a future leader, and the other two had coalesced around the chosen one, the future of their party would have been very different.[10] One of the three perhaps could have succeeded Harold Wilson in 1976, or moved against Wilson much earlier.[11] The thesis is compelling and provides another reason why Healey never became leader. Three big figures cancelled each other out.

Yet the thesis is also flawed. The three differed greatly in their political personalities and political outlook. They were social democrats united in their opposition to the Bennite left, but the term 'social democrat' was almost as imprecise then as 'centrist' became in the first two decades of the twenty-first century.

As we have seen, Jenkins was closer to the liberal tradition and had far fewer problems working with the Liberal Party when he left Labour than did some of his fellow defectors. In *The Future of Socialism*, Crosland put more focus on social equality than public ownership, a distinction that placed him beyond the pale of what became the Bennite left. His arguments that equality could be achieved within a capitalist economy greatly interested Ed Miliband when he was Labour leader. Miliband cited Crosland regularly.[12] He did not quote Healey often, partly because there is not a great deal to quote. Healey did not write about political philosophy or economics at great length, before or after he became chancellor.

Crosland died while Foreign Secretary in 1977. Jenkins was making early moves to form a new political party soon after that. Healey was still active in Labour – indeed by 1980 the only one of the three to be so. There were limits to the ideas and interests that bound the trio.

But evidently they reduced each other's chances by contemplating their own leadership ambitions simultaneously. All three stood in the 1976 leadership contest when Wilson resigned. None of them did especially well. Whether the Labour Party was in any state of mind to accept one of them with the backing of the other two we will never know. What we do know is that when Healey had the field to himself in 1980, with Crosland dead and Jenkins preparing to form the SDP, he did not win.

Instead, in November 1980, weeks after that stormy party conference when Healey was widely seen as the obvious successor to Callaghan, Labour MPs elected Foot to be their new leader. Healey won the first ballot with 112 votes and Foot came second with 83, at which point the other two candidates, John Silkin and Peter Shore, withdrew. Foot beat Healey in the final round, winning 139 votes to Healey's 129. There was disbelief in much of the media that Labour MPs could commit what it saw as an act of reckless folly. Conspiracy theorists suggested that several MPs planning to defect to the embryonic SDP voted for Foot in the hope of encouraging more defections. There is evidence that a handful did so, but the choice of Foot was not as perverse as it seemed. His elevation could only be baffling to those who ignored the importance of the connection between party and leader. In 1980, Labour MPs were looking to a figure from the left who might unite them.

But there was cause to regard Foot as a strange choice. He had never shown great interest in being a leader. Indeed, like Healey, Jenkins and Crosland, he derived pleasure from writing and reading; he was a more elegant writer than any of them, and a better stylist. Shortly before Foot became leader, he published a collection of essays, *Debts of Honour*, that reflected his range of interests and his eclectic heroes, from his father to William Hazlitt and on to Lord Beaverbrook.[13] For much of his career, he would have been as content reading, writing and campaigning as he would leading the Labour Party. As it turned out, he would have been much happier in the final phase of his political career if he had not been cursed with the burden of leading Labour at its most unleadable.

Debts of Honour provides one clue as to why he was a more logical choice as Labour leader in 1980 than was recognized at the time or since. Most leaders are more rounded and interesting than their cartoon-like portrayals in the media. Healey was burdened by being seen as a stereotype, the miserly right-wing chancellor who betrayed Labour voters. Foot was burdened too, albeit in a different way.

In some respects, Foot's political leanings were less rigid than those of Healey's. One of Foot's heroes in *Debts of Honour* is Disraeli. He even named his beloved dog 'Dizzy', the ultimate tribute to the Tory prime minister. In his chapter on Disraeli, Foot challenged the critical portrayal of the former prime minister in Robert Blake's biography. This is part of a counter-intuitive sequence. Blake was a high Tory who took the Conservative whip when he was made a peer. His gracefully written biography of Disraeli was highly praised, but Foot felt the need to come to the defence of the Conservative prime minister. Foot argued that Blake played down Disraeli's principles and underestimated his commitment to social reform, a consistent conviction that, in Foot's view, defined his career. Blake highlighted Disraeli the game-playing performer. Foot hailed a social champion.

In the same book of essays, Foot wrote of his admiration for Lord Beaverbrook, the Tory press baron. The admiration was mutual. Beaverbrook adored Foot and made him editor of the *Evening Standard*. It would be unheard of in modern times for a right-wing proprietor to make a left-winger the editor of the *Evening Standard*. A former Conservative chancellor is a more likely appointment in the modern era. But Beaverbrook was a big figure on the right who valued the friendship not only of Foot but of the left-wing historian A. J. P. Taylor, who wrote a flattering biography of the press baron.

While wholly committed to Labour, Foot was not tribal; in his own unique way, he was a 'big tent' politician. Another Tory with whom he worked was Enoch Powell. The two were united in their opposition to the Common Market and in their interest in related constitutional issues. Both were orators, and much in demand on TV and radio. This took on an irony when Foot became Labour leader many years later: he was regarded as a poor media performer, even though he had done more broadcasting and journalism than any Labour leader before or since.

More significantly, Foot had been a pragmatic deputy to Jim Callaghan during the torrid period between 1976 and the 1979 election. Foot's pragmatism was such that he began to fall out with old friends like Tony Benn. Callaghan often acknowledged that Foot helped to keep the show on the road, working tirelessly to win votes in the Commons on contentious legislation, and trying his best with his friends in the unions to get some cooperation.[14] To the end of his life, Foot would remain proud of the 1970s Labour government. It was his belatedly discovered expediency as much as other, more well-known, aspects of his political personality that had contributed to that government's successes.

Given that, by the autumn of 1980, the Labour Party had lapsed into civil war, Foot was seen as the unity candidate, unlike Healey. The outcome of the 1980 leadership contest was based on misjudged hope but also sound reason.

After he became leader, Foot was again more expedient than the media caricature suggested. He had no time for Militant Tendency, the far-left force infiltrating some local Labour parties, and he began the process of expelling those associated with the group. He also spent pointless hours trying to persuade the likes of Shirley Williams, David Owen and Bill Rodgers to remain in the Labour Party, only to see them leave and form the SDP.

In a long and varied career, Foot had given little thought to leadership. Yet in 1980 he won a leadership contest, only to face dark onslaughts and dilemmas wherever he turned. He sought to keep the show on the road. Such was the scale of the divisions, the show remained wild. Foot was widely blamed for being ineffectual, but Labour would almost certainly have been as unruly – in different ways – if Healey had won in 1980.

———

Inevitably, Healey was frustrated as he saw Foot struggle as leader, even if he was too loyal to hint publicly at any doubts. As Foot's deputy, Healey appeared to be stronger physically – a commanding figure in the Commons and on TV, seemingly the equal to Thatcher's strident, energized presence. While Thatcher was apparently a superwoman, Foot seemed old and weak. But once more, stereotypes were distorting reality, and the truth was more complex and interesting. Thatcher was not quite the sleepless heroine and Foot was fitter than he seemed, starting his long days early with a walk on Hampstead Heath with Dizzy, during which he often reflected on how his heroes would deal with the challenges he was facing. During one interview with Brian Walden on *Weekend World*, Foot was asked whether, like Hamlet's Denmark, there was 'something rotten in the state of the Labour Party'. Without hesitation, Foot responded with the appropriate quote from *Hamlet*, 'Cursed spite that ever I was born to set it right.'[15]

Foot's leadership was an unavoidable consequence of a Labour Party moving leftward. Healey had more obvious leadership qualities, but they were of no use to Labour in 1980. His unsuitability for the task of leading Labour was highlighted in the most vivid way the following year. In the spring of 1981, Benn announced he would challenge him in the deputy leadership contest, the first to be conducted under the new rules for electing the party leadership. Unions wielded 40 per cent of the vote, and constituency Labour parties and MPs had 30 per cent each. It was a huge change from the year before, when Foot was elected by MPs alone.

The intensity of the battle to be Labour's deputy leader was at odds with the prize. Being deputy was often a thankless role without clearly defined powers or influence. Healey had been performing the task out of a sense of duty since Foot was made leader. Later, Roy Hattersley played the role under Neil Kinnock and could not hide his frustration. John Prescott was deputy leader under Tony Blair and yet still found to his fury that he was excluded from some key strategic meetings in the build-up to the 1997 election. But the limits of the role were obscured by the symbolism of the fight in 1981 – particularly the significance that victory would bring to either the left or right wing of the party. Some of the TV programmes reporting the 1981 contest are on YouTube. They include reports from union conferences that were closer to the mood of a football match, in which half the crowd are shouting noisily for Benn and the other for Healey. Was Labour moving even more towards the ideas of Benn, or did it still seek to be what Harold Wilson had described as a 'broad church', with Healey complementing Foot's position as a figure of the left?

The personalities of the two contenders heightened the drama. Benn was the best orator of his generation, a better speaker even than the more mannered Enoch Powell or the sparkling but less flowing Foot and Kinnock. He was also a fluent and compelling interviewee, witty and a powerful advocate of his chosen theme. In 1981, his main theme was 'accountability', the need for the leadership to be held accountable by members and trade unions. Unsurprisingly, the message went down well with a lot of members and trade unionists.

Away from such audiences, Benn's ideas were derided as dangerous nonsense until the same themes became fashionable in the Conservative Party years later. Influential Tories came to agree with Benn about the EU, accountability and the importance of party members having a bigger say. Some Tory MPs became more loyal to their activists than to their increasingly exasperated leadership. In one of the great ironic twists, they became Bennites.

Healey was the target of heckling at some of his public meetings during the 1981 contest but he kept going, as he always did. His commitment to his party was unqualified, whatever the scale of his frustration. After the 1979 election, or following his defeat in the 1980 leadership contest, Healey could have taken a step back and made a fortune in the City or as a media performer. He did not contemplate such a move.

Instead, there he was in the awkward role of deputy leader, only to be challenged for the post. He was in the undignified position of having to defend his position even if his role as deputy to Foot was not one he had actively sought. No ambitious Labour politician starts a career with the ultimate aim of being a deputy. Healey faced the fight of his life to keep the title. When he was heckled, he gave as good as he got. But the venomous mood throughout the contest was further evidence that Healey would have struggled as leader. The media would have broadly supported his election, and then in the light of subsequent unavoidable confrontations with the left would have concluded that the party was unelectable.

The result of the deputy leadership contest was further confirmation that Healey could not have been a unifying figure as prime minister. The outcome was announced on the early Sunday evening of Labour's annual conference, held that year in Brighton. Healey secured 50.4 per cent of the vote compared with Benn's 49.6

per cent. There could be no more tangible example of a divided party than the percentages for each candidate. Once again, Healey was the most prominent figure on one half of the divide, just as he had been when he was chancellor a few years earlier.

The 1981 contest had many consequences. On one level, Benn's performance was remarkable – coming so close to victory when most Labour MPs and all the significant newspapers were passionately opposed to him. Yet the campaign was the high point in this phase of his career. His failure to win marked the beginning of the end for Benn as the driving force on the left and in the wider Labour Party. He lost his seat in the 1983 general election and, although he returned to the Commons soon after, he was no longer the focus of so much attention. From the 1979 election to September 1981, Benn had commanded as much media attention as the new prime minister, Margaret Thatcher.[16] He never did again.

A third candidate from the so-called soft left, John Silkin, stood in that contest to stop Benn from winning. The influential Neil Kinnock, once a Benn admirer, declared he would be voting for Silkin, a move that infuriated Benn's supporters and yet positioned Kinnock as a potential leader who might be able to bring different parts of the party together, or at least those who supported Healey and elements of the left who had their doubts about Benn. Silkin's candidacy and support from Kinnock were key factors that stopped Benn from winning.

The newly formed SDP, enjoying stratospheric poll ratings in 1981, had hoped to attract many significant defectors if Healey lost the deputy leadership. Although this was not clear at the time, Healey's victory marked the beginning of the end for the SDP. If the likes of Healey still had senior roles in the Labour Party and were winning internal contests, albeit by less than 1 per cent, there would be no permanent space for another party espousing views similar to Healey's.

———

After the dramas whirling around that contest, Healey's admirers did not give up hope that he might still become prime minister one day. The door was seemingly not closed as Labour staggered towards the next general election. At the end of 1982 and the beginning of 1983, Foot was in deep trouble on several fronts, attacked by Thatcher in her post-Falklands pomp and also by the stars of the SDP who were more clearly defined as an anti-Labour Party at this point than as an anti-Conservative one. There were endless internal crises within the Labour Party. They led to cries in the media and within the parliamentary Labour Party that Foot was 'weak', even if a God-like figure would have struggled to appear 'strong' in the same circumstances.

In February 1983, the year of an expected general election, Labour lost Bermondsey – previously a safe seat – in a by-election. Foot had behaved erratically, originally refusing to endorse Peter Tatchell, the local party's chosen candidate, and then allowing his candidacy to go ahead. Labour's campaign was a shambles, and the SDP–Liberal Alliance candidate, Simon Hughes, won by a huge majority. Hughes held his seat until 2015.

Some Labour MPs were in despair and began to plan for Healey to replace Foot in time for the expected general election. One of those scheming was Gerald Kaufman. Unlike Healey, Kaufman was an instinctive plotter and he often manoeuvred successfully. Later, as shadow Foreign Secretary, he helped Neil Kinnock drop the party's support for unilateral nuclear disarmament after the

1987 election. He had also worked with Harold Wilson when Wilson was at his wily best. After the Bermondsey disaster, Kaufman noted that there was another by-election looming in Darlington. He and several other Labour MPs indicated that they would call for the removal of Foot and the installation of Healey if Labour lost that seat too. On the basis of what happened in Bermondsey, a Labour defeat seemed highly probable. Here was another opening for Healey.

The Darlington by-election in March 1983 was a contest with historic consequences, one of the last by-elections in modern times – along with Eastbourne a few years later – to make waves long-term. The Conservatives' loss of Eastbourne in 1990 triggered a sequence that led to the fall of Margaret Thatcher. In Darlington in 1983, Labour won against expectation. As we have seen, the outcome halted the intimidating momentum of the SDP–Liberal Alliance in the build-up to the 1983 election. Any hopes Roy Jenkins had of becoming prime minister were dashed at Darlington. Labour's candidate, Ossie O'Brien, was a popular and reassuring local figure. The party's campaign was slick and its big names rallied around O'Brien, including Healey. After the result, dissenting Labour MPs did not have the ammunition they needed to attempt a coup. Such a coup would almost certainly have failed anyway, and Healey had too much integrity to be directly involved, but if Labour had lost the by-election there was a small possibility he would have led Labour into the 1983 election. Labour won Darlington only to lose it again in the general election a few months later. For Healey, another door had closed.

Once again, Healey kept going. During the 1983 general election he played his part. After Foot, he was Labour's most prominent advocate in a chaotic campaign. Kaufman described the party's

1983 manifesto as 'the longest suicide note in history'. The quote has been cited approvingly many times since, although the most contentious proposals in the manifesto were implemented in future decades. The UK is out of the EU, as the manifesto advocated. The arguments to borrow in order to generate growth and improve productivity, the heart of Labour's 1983 pitch, were deployed with great verve when the Conservative chancellor Rishi Sunak presented his first budget in the spring of 2020.

The shambolic organization of Labour's 1983 campaign was at least as big a problem as the manifesto, however. Healey describes the chaos in his memoir, but his willing participation shows his commitment to the cause. Healey was not a stroppy prima donna:

> Michael Foot and I were given ridiculously heavy programmes and were foolish enough to accept them without protest. For almost four weeks we would start the morning at seven, with a meeting of our Campaign Committee in London, followed by a press conference which relieved lazy journalists of the need to follow us around. Then we would leave London for a series of meetings... Many of our meetings were a complete waste of time; on one housing estate in the Midlands I was made to visit three old people's homes in succession, on the grounds that if I visited one, jealousy from the others would cost us votes.[17]

During the night of the 1983 election, as the scale of Thatcher's landslide became clear, union leaders appeared on TV to declare it was time for Labour to 'leap a generation' when choosing its next leader. Healey knew that meant there was no point in standing in the contest that was bound to follow, although for a moment he dared to wonder whether this time he could win. Once again, in the aftermath of another defeat, Healey was not interested in taking well-paid outside posts, accepting the role of shadow Foreign Secretary under Neil Kinnock instead. There was never a moment again when Healey was spoken of credibly as either a future leader or a prime minister.

Would Healey have done any better than Foot in 1980 or Kinnock in 1983? Would he have beaten Thatcher and been a prime minister rather than one we never had? He possessed the intellect, energy, thick skin, verve and charm to have been a formidable prime minister, but that is an answer to a different question. For Healey, the route was not available to him, because his party was in a different place and because of his indifference to managing a party that was divided on all the big issues. His preference was to seek to prevail over the side he disagreed with, and then to serve as loyally as he could under leaders to the left of him. In serving in this manner, Healey did as much as anyone else to save the party he never led, but he also blew his chances of being a leader and prime minister.

———

After the 1983 election it was Neil Kinnock who had the chance of being a Labour prime minister. As leader of the Opposition, he was the alternative prime minister. Given the electoral defeat in 1983, a loss that propelled him to the party leadership, he faced a long haul. That juxtaposition of defeat and the prospect of a long journey in opposition provide a clue as to why Kinnock, after nine wearying years punctuated by bleak despair and great hope, became another prime minister we never had.

5

NEIL KINNOCK

Neil Kinnock was at the centre of more highly charged political dramas than any of the other prime ministers we never had. He is in a competitive field on this front. It takes a lot to beat the likes of Roy Jenkins, Denis Healey and Michael Heseltine in terms of epic theatrical episodes. Jenkins left Labour and set up a new party; Healey was chancellor when the UK economy was constantly in crisis; and Heseltine challenged a three-times election-winning prime minister. All three were at the heart of historically significant spectacles as they made their moves. The difference is that Kinnock always seemed to be at the centre of political battles too. He never got a break from the fight.

In the mid-1970s, he was often a rebel Labour MP voting against the government from the left. In the early 1980s, his battles took a different form. He was a close ally and friend of Michael Foot, the party's leader. He felt the need to challenge passionately the section of the left that regarded Tony Benn as its hero. Coming from the left and then taking on parts of this wing of the party is unavoidably highly charged and draining. Finally, from 1983 he was Labour's leader at war on many fronts. He took on Militant Tendency, a group that had successfully infiltrated Labour in some parts of the country. He was in a battle with Arthur Scargill, the president of the National Union of Mineworkers (NUM). He was in endless ferocious disputes with his party over policy changes. His main external opponent was Margaret Thatcher, a tough foe against whom he fought with tireless energy and limited results. Most newspapers were on her side, and their doting support for her triggered further confrontations between Kinnock and the media. For a time, even political journalists who had regarded Kinnock as a friend found they were cut off from a leader in despair at the way he was being projected.

Kinnock's personality was a key ingredient in all the dramas played out over the wearying years. He was energetic, charismatic, funny and yet had an introverted melancholic streak. He conveyed at times authentic anger and at others a joyful euphoria. The sense of Kinnock being in permanent combat reflects a personality that had a pugilistic streak, but he was not fighting for fun. In the same way that Harold Wilson was paranoid because he had a lot to be paranoid about, Kinnock had no choice but to go to battle on many fronts.

His reward for energy-sapping perseverance was two election defeats. Nearly all the prime ministers we never had could at least look back to long, fulfilling service at the heart of government, as Cabinet ministers and in some cases also as influential advisers. Although he later became a respected European Commissioner, Kinnock was never a Cabinet minister. The only other political figure in this book not to have held sway in government is Jeremy Corbyn. But the two could not have been more different. Corbyn never sought high office until he accidentally won the Labour leadership. He remained rooted on the left and had opted enthusiastically for the politics of protest and campaigns throughout his long career as a backbench MP. Kinnock saw such a stance as a lazy betrayal of those who most needed a Labour government. He sought power to bring about change. Yet he never became a ruler.

There were times when he hoped he was close to achieving his goal of winning a general election, especially in the second half of his long leadership, when Labour was often miles ahead in the polls. In the 1989 European elections, Labour came first and the Conservatives were well behind in terms of the popular vote, quite a leap after the party's big general election defeat two years earlier. In the build-up to the 1992 election, Kinnock was the favourite to win. As the respected Tory pollster Rob Hayward reflected more than a decade later: 'They said Neil Kinnock would be Britain's next prime minister. That was in 1992, when the BBC's poll of polls gave Labour a two per cent lead in the run-up to the election, and some even suggested they would be seven points ahead.'[1]

Although Hayward was never convinced that such an outcome was likely, a lot of senior Conservatives were extremely worried that they were about to lose the election. A sign of John Major's nervousness could be discerned from his decision to delay the election until the last possible moment. Prime ministers announce elections when they assume they can win, and avoid them if they fear they will lose. In the long build-up to the 1992 election, Kinnock was widely seen as the next prime minister.

Even on the evening of the election he retained some hope he would be moving into Number Ten. The BBC exit poll broadcast at 10 p.m. wrongly forecast a hung parliament. Briefly, Kinnock prepared to be leader of a minority Labour government. Within hours, a distraught Kinnock recognized he was facing another terrible defeat. The exit poll was wrong. A few days later, he announced he would be resigning when a successor was in place. He looked utterly drained and exhausted as he made his statement:

The government elected on 9 April 1992 does not have and will not develop the policies necessary to strengthen the British economy and will not try to address the injustices in British society. My great regret is that I failed to ensure that enough people understood that and the implications which it has for the future. My sorrow is that millions, particularly those who do not have the strength to defend themselves, will suffer because of the election of another Conservative government.[2]

In that bleak resignation statement, he blamed the media for its relentless bias. During the years that followed, he also openly reflected on his own culpability. He never fully recovered from the deep sense of personal rejection or the personal sacrifices he had made leading an unleadable party. As he exclaimed to his biographer on reading a draft of the book: 'Christ! What a way to spend my forties.'[3]

———

By April 1992, Kinnock was almost unrecognizable from the exuberant performer in the years before he became Labour leader. During the 1970s and early 1980s, when both frontbenches were crammed with charismatic personalities, Kinnock had been a star. As a mere shadow Education Secretary under Michael Foot, he was invited to appear on the Michael Parkinson chat show on BBC One, a rare honour for a politician and unique for a middle-ranking opposition frontbencher. Parkinson was not alone in playing host to the shadow Education Secretary. Kinnock was a regular on Clive James's TV chat show on ITV. On BBC One's *Question Time*, back when the programme still hosted scintillating, unpredictable debate rather than unsubtle, choreographed anger, Kinnock was a highly effective participant, taking on heavyweights such as Roy Jenkins and Michael Heseltine. He was even invited to write occasionally for *The Sun*, ironic given how that particular relationship turned out. Kinnock was also an orator – the star turn at by-elections when halls were so crammed that spillover venues were required.

During this pre-leadership phase, Kinnock was also tested politically, much more so than many other future leaders of the Opposition who went on to become prime minister. He became a key figure in Labour's civil war that erupted after the party's defeat in the 1979 election. Kinnock was devoted to Michael Foot and he helped his friend win the leadership against Denis Healey in 1980, even if he feared that victory might prove to be hellish for Foot. Then he became involved in a much bigger battle. Both Foot and Kinnock were from the left of the party but despaired of Tony Benn, who had decided not to join the shadow Cabinet and was touring the country outlining his own vision from the left. They agreed with some of Benn's policy agenda, but not the way Benn presented his programme as an easily achievable wish list and one that was made urgently necessary partly by the 'betrayal' of the previous Labour government. Benn had been a Cabinet minister in that government, when Kinnock was on the backbenches and quite often voting against its policies. But Kinnock fumed against the language of betrayal and saw Benn as a threat to the leadership of Foot.

When Benn stood against Denis Healey for the deputy leadership in 1981, Kinnock made a big call when he backed the third candidate, John Silkin, who had no chance of winning but could attract enough votes to block Benn. For Kinnock, the decision was a formative moment. He had chosen his path, the route of the pragmatic left that recognized the need to work with the so-called right of the party, including the likes of Healey. Kinnock was attacked by Benn's supporters for this; the future Cabinet minister and deputy leader Margaret Beckett, then a Bennite, threw silver coins over Kinnock at a fringe meeting to symbolize his betrayal. From September 1981, Kinnock became a ruthless pragmatist as much as a romantic orator. Later, Beckett became at least as pragmatic as Kinnock. She was a Cabinet minister under Tony Blair, rising to the elevated post of Foreign Secretary.

Still, after opting expediently for the third, less glamorous candidate in the deputy leadership contest, Kinnock packed out halls around the country, the party's uplifting orator. During the crucial Darlington by-election shortly before the 1983 election, Kinnock paid a visit. The stakes were high. As the writer Francis Beckett later recalled, Kinnock arrived and held court. Beckett worked for Labour at the time, and was assigned the role of meeting Kinnock at the town's station:

> He stepped smartly off the London train, borrowed £5 from me and took everyone he found in the nearby party headquarters to the pub. In Darlington in 1983 you could buy a substantial round of drinks with £5.
>
> He did not stop talking for a moment in the pub. As a stream of ideas tumbled out of him, each one perfectly wrapped in an evocative phrase, the ageing Labour grandee Barbara Castle listened in uncharacteristic silence. She seemed to be seeing the reincarnation of her dead hero, Aneurin Bevan.
>
> Eventually we dragged Kinnock across to the biggest hall in town, which seated hundreds and was packed out. He spoke for a full hour, making his audience laugh and cry in turn at his attacks on Margaret Thatcher's government. 'Now, the cabinet wets – By the way, do you know why they call them that? It's because that's what they do when she shouts at them.'[4]

Here Beckett captures Kinnock's mesmerizing energy. He was fun to be with on the campaign trail before he acquired the burden of leadership. But there was no fun to be had by the end of the 1983 election campaign, one in which he worked tirelessly while knowing that Labour was doomed. At his final meeting of the campaign, Kinnock spoke in Glamorgan with a voice hoarse with exhaustion. His vivid words about the next Conservative government were broadcast on TV that evening, not bad for a shadow Education Secretary representing a party about to be defeated heavily:

> I warn you that you will have pain when healing and relief depends upon payment. I warn you that you will have ignorance when talents are untended and wits are wasted, when learning is a privilege and not a right. I warn you that you will have poverty when pensions slip and benefits are whittled away by a government that won't pay in an economy that can't pay. I warn you that you will be cold when fuel charges are used as a tax system that the rich don't notice and the poor can't afford. I warn you that you must not expect work – when many cannot spend, more will not be able to earn. When they don't earn, they don't spend. When they don't spend, work dies... If Margaret Thatcher wins on Thursday, I warn you not to be ordinary; I warn you not to be young; I warn you not to fall ill; I warn you not to get old.[5]

Kinnock could be a poetic speaker, close to his and Foot's hero, Aneurin Bevan, in style. At his best he could deliver speeches with a symphonic quality. On the eve of the election in 1983, he was still a star and hadn't yet been dubbed 'the Welsh windbag' by *The Sun*. Such insults were still to come. He was a media favourite until he became leader.

When Benn lost his seat in Bristol, Kinnock knew he was more than likely to become the next leader. He had a lot going for him: Foot wanted Kinnock to succeed him, and most union leaders supported him. Without Benn as an option, a lot of party members, voting for a leader for the first time in Labour's history, also backed him.

During the leadership contest in the summer of 1983, Kinnock displayed what were to become two of his strengths. Although favourite to win from the beginning, he was never complacent. He toured the country, speaking at meeting after meeting. As leader, he was to show the same relentless energy. He was also far from dewy-eyed about the challenges ahead for Labour. This was a leadership contest, and no candidate wanting to win would be wise to lecture party members in too much detail about how they needed to change. Nonetheless, during the campaign Kinnock did warn of the thorny path ahead.

Take this example from his John P. Mackintosh Memorial Lecture, delivered in Edinburgh at the height of the leadership contest. By the time of the lecture, Kinnock had lost his voice, so one of his supporters, Robin Cook, had to read his speech for him. There was a theatrical quality to the event: the aspiring leader couldn't speak, and had to be replaced by Cook, who would become one of the most significant figures in the Cabinet when Labour finally returned to power many years later. Kinnock's words, spoken by another ambitious politican, were stark: 'If the Labour Party goes down the wrong path it courts disaster, for no political institution has a divine right to exist... and as Isaiah Berlin pointed out, those who have ceased to perform any useful historic functions soon fade into insignificance.'[6]

Here was an early example of a constant motif during Kinnock's leadership. He was constantly alerting his party to what was at stake if it failed to learn lessons from terrible election defeats. His warnings were both brave and problematic. They did give him space ultimately to change Labour, but also signalled to a wary electorate that even its leader was far from thrilled with the state of his party.

Yet the assessment on the eve of his leadership is revealing. Kinnock was more than aware of the mountainous task, but he was unwilling to specify what the wrong path would be and what form a more propitious alternative might take. Or, at the very least, he did not spell out his thinking at a point when he sought to maximize his vote in a leadership contest.

In the end, he won easily against Roy Hattersley, who stood from what was then regarded as the right of the party. Given the scale of Labour's election defeat, Kinnock and Hattersley were two formidable candidates seeking to lead. Hattersley had Cabinet experience and was the closest to a political thinker on Labour's frontbench. Kinnock was the star from the left with a ruthless pragmatic streak. Hattersley became Kinnock's deputy, a role he performed dutifully but grumpily at times. Later, Kinnock gave him the senior role of shadow chancellor, one that was not entirely to Hattersley's liking although he was keen at first. His grumpiness was more down to the imprecision of the deputy's role and working with Kinnock, who could irritate him. Hattersley had many positive qualities, but he was easily irritated.

The strengths and weaknesses of the duo did not matter anywhere near as much as the scale of Labour's defeat in 1983. The Conservatives won an overall majority of 144 seats, not that far behind Labour's overwhelming victory in 1997. Like quite a few other new elected leaders of the Opposition, Kinnock was in an odd position. He had triumphed in a leadership contest, but in the darkest of contexts. William Hague was another such leader, after the Conservatives' defeat in 1997.

Up until this point, Kinnock had been a winner, from becoming president of the student union at Cardiff University to being selected for a safe seat in Wales, to being a star in the Commons, turning down some jobs while choosing other posts such as shadow Education Secretary, to backing Michael Foot, the winner of the 1980 leadership contest, and then beating the more experienced Hattersley himself in 1983. Hours before the party leadership result was formally announced at Labour's October conference, Kinnock took a walk along Brighton beach with his wife, Glenys. He slipped and got a bit of a soaking from the sea. The image featured often in the years that followed, as a supposed symbol of Kinnock's fragility. Yet few saw Kinnock as weak at the time. He was the new Labour leader at the age of forty-one. Only as the tragedy took shape in the years to come did the image seem to fit.

Kinnock became fragile largely because of the dark context of his victory. Labour was far behind the Conservatives in terms of seats, and against Margaret Thatcher the party was losing the wider ideological battle decisively. In his victory speech at Labour's conference in Brighton, Kinnock urged his audience to remember how they had felt on election night as the party lost one seat after another. With a characteristic flourish, he looked up and declared: 'June 9th 1983... never, ever again.' The hall cheered wildly, but some of those applauding did not reflect on the implications of the message. As with illness and long journeys, the horror of election nights can be quickly forgotten.

Labour was also split on all the key issues of that era: nuclear disarmament, the role of the state, Europe (although that was to change), and its verdict on the Labour government of the 1970s. As an additional obstacle, the SDP was being given renewed life under the leadership of David Owen, a leader much admired by those parts of the media that also revered Thatcher. Kinnock faced the toughest inheritance of any Labour leader since the 1930s. Keir Starmer had daunting challenges when he was elected in 2020, but also some advantages compared with Kinnock: there was no formidable third UK-wide party, and the government's majority was smaller than Thatcher's in 1983.

In retrospect, it was a great tribute to Kinnock's leadership that he was ever seen as a possible next prime minister, in a way that William Hague never was after the 1997 election. Yet, like Hague, Kinnock was doomed from the beginning. Thatcher's electoral triumph in 1983 was so great there was virtually no chance of Kinnock overturning her majority after a single term, and yet in the modern era two terms is too long for anyone to be leader of the Opposition. At best, many voters get bored with powerless leaders. At worst, they view them with growing impatience and disdain.

By 1992, Kinnock had been leader of the Opposition for nine years. He could not win in 1987 because Thatcher's majority was so big, and by 1992 he had been there for far too long, which is why William Hague and Ed Miliband were wise to leave after their respective defeats in 2001 and 2015. Edward Heath did win an election in 1970 after losing one badly in 1966, but he had been leader for only one year when he lost and for a total of six by the time of his victory – a relatively short period during an era when media scrutiny was less intense. Nowadays, a leader of the Opposition typically only ever contests one election in that role.

The long haul from 1983 would have been enough to seal Kinnock's fate even if all had gone well for him. And all did not go well for him. As he reflected years later, 'I did not even have a honeymoon as leader. All leaders are meant to get a honeymoon.'[7] For understandable reasons, Kinnock's memory of what happened is darker than the reality. When looking back, he knew how the story ended. At the time of his leadership, with no one knowing the denouement, Labour was often ahead in the polls. William Hague and his party were rarely ahead after 1997. Hague had no space to hope, in some ways a less cruel place to be than Kinnock's. The Labour leader could read the opinion polls and dare to hope.

This was the case even during his troubled first term, but the leads were erratic and there was no clean start because of the miners' strike, an industrial dispute of epic significance that became a crisis for Kinnock. The president of the NUM, Arthur Scargill, called a strike in the spring of 1984 – less than a year after Kinnock had become leader. Scargill did so without the NUM calling a ballot of its members.

From every perspective, this was also a crisis of nuanced complexity. Thatcher's predecessor, Edward Heath, had fallen from power in 1974 because of the miners' strike then, and its many consequences. Meanwhile, Thatcher had constrained the unions from 1979 with a combination of legislation and high unemployment that meant, for many, being in some form of work trumped the desire for higher wages. Even so, Thatcher had not challenged the miners during her first term, conceding to them in pay disputes when coal stocks were relatively low. In 1984, however, stocks were high, and she was ready to take them on.

Kinnock was in anguish about the miners' strike for several reasons. This was the worst possible crisis for him personally. He loathed Scargill and had supported holding a ballot of miners before the strike. He was also uneasy about the timing. Kinnock was painfully aware that Thatcher had been waiting for this confrontation. Yet he came from a mining family and represented a mining constituency. There was no way he could or would side with Thatcher against the striking miners, and he felt empathy for miners and their families losing income. Still, he despaired of Scargill's tactics.

Rarely acknowledged at the time or since is the fact that Scargill had a case in 1984. He was not on this occasion campaigning for big pay rises, but arguing against pit closures and challenging the government's argument that many mines had become 'uneconomic'. Scargill was taking a longer-term approach than Thatcher. Cheap energy imports might have been an alternative option in the mid-1980s, but there was no guarantee that importing sources of energy would always be the economic choice. The striking miners' cause also had a noble dimension in that it was a campaign for an industry, a vocation and the communities formed around the threatened pits. In some respects, Scargill was vindicated. Cheap energy imports became more expensive, and communities based around the pits were ghostly after the closures.

Kinnock faced other difficulties in relation to the seemingly endless dispute – he was a new leader seeking to appear 'prime ministerial', a daunting test not least when some powerful newspapers had decided he had already failed.[8] He wanted a deal – one that would not lead to a terrible defeat for the miners. Kinnock was also desperate to end the need for him to equivocate about where he stood, supporting and yet not wholly supporting the strike.

There were moments when a deal appeared to be possible. Thatcher was never as certain as she appeared to be on any front, and wobbled occasionally in relation to the strike. To Kinnock's understandable fury, Scargill would not concede a millimetre in the negotiations with ministers and the National Coal Board. Instead, Scargill persisted – rejecting any compromise – and led his followers to a terrible defeat. As Thatcher put it in a crude characterization of the striking miners, she had defeated 'the enemy within'.[9]

There were many consequences. The NUM never held sway again as it had done in the past. The pits under threat closed and the jobs went. Thatcher did not believe the state should intervene to revive areas dependent on mining, a neglect condemned by even her close ally Norman Tebbit when he wrote his sensitive and illuminating memoir in 1988.[10]

New to leadership, Kinnock could not hide the degree to which he was tormented by the strategic and moral dilemmas triggered by the strike, and the sense that he felt trapped. He visited striking miners one cold winter morning, and looked deeply troubled as he did so. But his ambiguity was seen in a partisan media and by some voters as weakness. This was calamitous for a leader in the Thatcher era, where she contrived always to appear strong. The adjectives 'weak' and 'strong' are far too simplistic and applied too casually, but once the term 'weak' sticks to a leader they are in trouble.

Much later, Kinnock reflected candidly on his torment during the strike:

> I was absolutely helpless. So helpless that I couldn't convey my helplessness... But all the time, it was churning within me because of what was happening in the coalfields and the mining communities... I did everything I could, but I was certain that without a ballot the strike, however long it lasted, could not result in the saving of the coal industry and everything that went with it. I never felt so helpless in my life but I couldn't afford to despair.[11]

He might not have been able to afford to despair, but he came close to deep despondency. The consequences of the strike and the way Kinnock's near impotence was perceived during the saga were profound. Kinnock, with a well-developed streak of machismo, resolved to be 'strong' or at least to appear strong, the appearance being an art of leadership. He always knew he had to take on his party after the 1983 election defeat and change it. After the miners' strike, the stakes were even higher. He needed to be seen as a strong leader while prevailing over noisy internal dissenters.

Ultimately, the task involved Kinnock looking inwards, and reforming a deeply divided and vote-losing party. Yet he wanted to show the wider electorate that he was acting in a way that proved he was a tough leader. He was looking outwards too. At times, and unavoidably, the divisions within Labour were bound to intensify as Kinnock made his moves.

He made some changes quickly and without a fuss. Almost immediately after his election, he announced that Labour would no longer seek to leave the Common Market – a development of historic significance. Labour became a pro-European party as the Conservatives moved towards intense Euroscepticism. The parties swapped sides.

As the Conservatives tend to win general elections, the Conservative shift was even more historic than Labour's. But it took a bit of time to happen, and for a few years from the start of Kinnock's leadership there was a near consensus between the two main parties that the UK would be better off in what became the European Union. Kinnock won his only national election in the contest for the European Parliament in 1989, with Labour fighting an openly pro-European campaign. The Conservatives warned crudely of a 'diet of Brussels' and lost. Of course, that dynamic was to change. Anti-European populism would win in the end. But for a time from the late 1980s on, it seemed as if being pro-European would help Labour electorally.

Kinnock's fundamental dilemma – the need to change his party while also appearing prime ministerial to the electorate – was most vividly highlighted in his 1985 party conference speech. His address became one of the most lauded speeches since 1945, and continues to be viewed regularly on YouTube by new, youthful admirers. This was the speech in which Kinnock attacked Militant Tendency, specifically targeting those Militants holding senior positions on Liverpool City Council. His onslaught was a sensational moment of unanticipated political theatre, another drama in which Kinnock was centre-stage. He had a great sense of the dramatic, partly because he was an avid theatre- and opera-goer. He understood the art of performance.

Halfway through his speech Kinnock spoke directly to his startled audience:

> Implausible promises don't win victories. I'll tell you what happens with impossible promises. You start with far-fetched resolutions. They are then pickled into a rigid dogma, a code, and you go through the years sticking to that, outdated, misplaced, irrelevant to the real needs, and you end up in the grotesque chaos of a Labour council hiring taxis to scuttle round a city handing out redundancy notices to its own workers. [Applause] I am telling you, no matter how entertaining, how fulfilling to short-term egos – [Continuing applause] – you can't play politics with people's jobs and with people's services or with their homes. [Applause and some boos][12]

At this point, the left-wing MP Eric Heffer walked off the platform in protest, immediately behind Kinnock. The deputy leader of Liverpool council, Derek Hatton, started to protest from his seat in the hall. Others cheered in rapturous disbelief at the cathartic eruption. The media loved it. Kinnock got the best press he had received since becoming leader. Commentators hailed his courage and concluded that he was no longer weak. He was strong.

On one level, Kinnock deserved the approbation from the fickle media. His intervention was indeed an act of courage. He had chosen to take his stand not in the cocooned comfort of a studio or a controlled newspaper article, but in the middle of his annual make-or-break conference speech where he could not be in control of what might happen in response. That courage was not shallow. A confrontation was required. Labour had lost the last two elections, and yet not a great deal had changed in ways that were perceptible to the wider electorate beyond some presentational improvements. This was the definition of accessible politics: a leader on his pulpit berating a section of his tribe. Labour secured an immediate rise in the polls. But there were downsides to Kinnock's historic confrontation that were overlooked at the time and since. And there are lessons here for Labour leaders in opposition.

Most immediately, the rest of his speech was ignored, to Kinnock's considerable long-term detriment. Inevitably, the only words reported, analysed and remembered were his attack on Militant. Yet the same speech contained Kinnock's best attempt to challenge the wider right-wing ideological tide, which was ultimately a much greater threat to Labour than Militant was.

Since Thatcher's victory in 1979, Labour had been on the defensive in the most fundamental debate of all: the role of the state and its relationship with voters. During the election that year, the outgoing prime minister, Jim Callaghan, had referred in a private conversation with his adviser Bernard Donoghue to an unstoppable 'sea change' moving in Thatcher's direction. The chaos of 1970s 'corporatism', during which the state had, in some respects, fuelled crises rather than addressed them, was the perfect context for Thatcher's pitch. According to her, the state was often stifling, inefficient and sinister. A smaller state was a form of liberation. She wanted 'freedom' for the people.

It was not easy to argue against 'freedom' for the people. In successfully framing arguments about the limited role of government, she had won the space for tax cuts, rigid limits on public spending, and a greater involvement for the private sector and non-elected quangos in the delivery of services. Labour's response was easily pitched by opponents as a return to the failed excesses of the past, in which hard work would be punished by high taxes and the people would lose 'freedom'. As long as this was the juxtaposition, Labour was doomed to lose.

Kinnock's 1985 conference speech was a heroic attempt to turn the argument on its head, by suggesting it was Thatcher and her government that had made the state inefficient, whereas in its support for a benevolent and efficient state a Labour government would be the agent of freedom. The following section of the speech is quoted here at length, because at the time the argument became obscured within seconds. It has rarely been highlighted since.

How is it that the party that promised to roll back the state has arrived at the situation where 1,700,000 more people are entirely dependent on the state because of their poverty during the time the Tories have been in government? How can the party of freedom, the friends of freedom, illegalise trade unionism in GCHQ Cheltenham? How can the party of freedom abolish the right to vote in the Greater London and metropolitan county councils? [Applause] How can the party of freedom prosecute Sarah Tisdall and Clive Ponting [two civil servants at the Ministry of Defence prosecuted for leaking secrets]? How can the party of freedom make secret plans to surrender completely the sovereignty of the British people in the event of war? How can the party of freedom do that? [Applause] That did not happen when the Panzer divisions were at the

French coast, when this country was in its most dire jeopardy. The institutions of freedom in this country were maintained. We insist that at all times of national gravity, at any time of public jeopardy, there is all the more reason for us to sustain the values and the institutions of our democracy in this country. That is what we tell the party of freedom. [Applause][13]

This was a clever inversion by Kinnock: the small-state government had made people dependent on the state; the governing party that hailed freedom had taken away liberties. Here was a way for Kinnock to engage with Thatcher's populism, by challenging the election-winning prime minister on her terms. He went on to argue why Labour and its values were better placed to deliver what Thatcher had claimed to seek:

Change has to be organised. It has to be shaped to the benefit of a society, deliberately, by those who have democratic power in that society; and the democratic instrument of the people who exist for that purpose is the state – yes, the state. To us that means a particular kind of state – an opportunity state, which exists to assist in nourishing talent and rewarding merit; a productive state, which exists to encourage investment and to help expand output; an enabling state, which is at the disposal of the people instead of being dominant over the people. In a word, we want a servant state, which respects those who work for it and reminds them that they work for the people of the country, a state which will give support to the voluntary efforts of those who, in their own time and from their own inspiration, will help the old, the sick, the needy, the young, the ill-housed and the hopeless. We are democratic socialists. We want to put the state where it belongs in a democracy – under the feet of the people, not over the heads of the people. That is where the state belongs in a democracy.

With considerable force, Kinnock made the case for what

good government can do (a phrase featured prominently in the Conservatives' 2017 election manifesto), and showed that the state can be the agent of freedom and not its enemy. But no one noticed. Instead, all media outlets focused on his challenge to Militant.

This was one downside. Another was that commentators could not get enough of the internal confrontations, and constantly urged Kinnock to take on his party again and again. Looking back, Kinnock noted that the media wanted a 'shoot-out at the O.K. Corral' virtually every week. The Labour leader had quite an appetite for the bloody internal clash, but even he wondered about the benefits of constant battle. While he knew Labour required sweeping change – including the expulsion of Militant, which had infiltrated the party from the outside – he also became aware that the voters' reaction to internal confrontation was not reliably positive. Over time, voters formed an impression of Kinnock as a leader at war with his party, rather than one planning to be prime minister of the wider country. This impression was unfair, as Kinnock and others in a series of substantial shadow Cabinets had immersed themselves in policy reform and detail. At least, they had done so by 1992. Members of Kinnock's final shadow Cabinet included John Smith, Roy Hattersley, Margaret Beckett, Bryan Gould, Gordon Brown, Tony Blair, Robin Cook and Jack Straw.

So here was a terrible trap, and one that several Labour leaders have fallen for. Most newspapers hailed Kinnock for his courage in taking on his party, and then later told their readers that he was not ready to be prime minister partly because he had spent too much time looking inwards rather than focusing on the country. Yet as the names from his 1992 shadow Cabinet show, his claims of leading an alternative government were more than credible.

By the general election of 1987, there had been only limited policy change. In his four years as leader, Kinnock had worked tirelessly – taking on extremists in his party, seeking to address the threat still posed by the SDP–Liberal Alliance, and navigating the multi-layered hell of the miners' strike. He had also changed the projection of Labour with the help of Peter Mandelson, with slicker presentation, the red rose replacing the red flag, and more coherent communication of messages. Labour fought a campaign in 1987 that was so much more polished compared with four years earlier that it felt in some ways like a different party. Yet in policy terms, there were still echoes of 1983.

During the 1987 campaign, there were also cock-ups over an issue that tormented Labour in previous elections and some that were to follow: the farcical policy area of 'tax and spend', one in which the media treated Labour's policy programme for five years as if it were a detailed budget for the coming few months. Labour was reliably ill-prepared for the hostile scrutiny at every election before 1997.

During one weekend in the middle of the 1987 campaign, Hattersley, as shadow chancellor, gave a live interview on Labour's tax plans that appeared to contradict what Kinnock had pledged a few hours earlier. Such slips can be fatal in front of a hostile media. When challenged about the discrepancy, Hattersley later wrote in his memoir that he took the only option available to him: 'I attacked the interviewer.' Afterwards, Hattersley phoned his friend and colleague John Smith, and asked him how bad the exchange had been. Smith replied, 'Even worse than you think.'[14]

Kinnock struggled with the details of economic policy throughout his leadership. Arguably, he tried too hard to show he was in full command of the details, sometimes getting lost in interviews as the focus of the exchange moved to a small element of an obscure tax proposal. The stress of leadership had already started to undermine Kinnock's once robust self-confidence. In 1987, he was trying to be what he was not, speaking at times in interviews as if he were an accountant or local bank manager in an attempt to prove he was economically 'competent'.

Yet the 1987 campaign was a huge leap forward. As Mandelson reflected in the immediate aftermath, 'We won the campaign and lost the election.' During the campaign, the director of the Oscar-winning *Chariots of Fire*, Hugh Hudson, produced a glossy election broadcast that focused solely on Kinnock. It showed clips from his best speeches, Kinnock walking on a cliff top with a renewed romantic sense of destiny, and him meeting voters with a level of authentic engagement at odds with the media caricature. In each elegantly lit location, Kinnock looked leader-like, compassionate and determined. The broadcast was such a hit that Labour repeated it a few nights later. This was an era when party political broadcasts got big TV audiences.

Kinnock made another of his most famous speeches during the 1987 campaign, the one that Joe Biden lifted from as he sought to become president in the United States for the first time a year later. The crude copying of Kinnock's words was the ultimate form of flattery. Kinnock and Biden became friends as a result. The speech illustrates even more forcefully than the one in 1985 Kinnock's hunt for a way of showing how the state could be an enabler:

> Why am I the first Kinnock in a thousand generations to be able to get to university? Why is my wife, Glenys, the first woman in her family in a thousand generations to be able to get to university? Was it because all our predecessors were 'thick'? Did they lack talent – those people who could sing, and play, and recite and write poetry; those people who could make wonderful, beautiful things with their

hands; those people who could dream dreams, see visions; those people who had such a sense of perception as to know in times so brutal, so oppressive, that they could win their way out of that by coming together? Were those people not university material? Couldn't they have knocked off all their A-levels in an afternoon?

But why didn't they get it? Was it because they were weak? Those people who could work eight hours underground and then come up and play football? Weak? Those women who could survive eleven child bearings, were they weak? Those people who could stand with their backs and their legs straight and face the people who had control over their lives, the ones who owned their workplaces and tried to own them, and tell them, 'No. I won't take your orders.' Were they weak? Does anybody really think that they didn't get what we had because they didn't have the talent, or the strength, or the endurance, or the commitment? Of course not. It was because there was no platform upon which they could stand; no arrangement for their neighbours to subscribe to their welfare; no method by which the communities could translate their desires for those individuals into provision for those individuals.[15]

Once again, Kinnock's speech has a poetic quality and makes a powerful argument about the state helping all voters fulfil their potential. There is, though, a problem with it. In the UK, elections focus on distorted arguments about specific policies. The media gets caught, often willingly and sometimes inadvertently, in a fantasy world based on misleading facts and figures. 'The Conservatives claim Labour will pay for its programme by increasing taxes on all those earning around £12,756.32' is a typical opening line of an election report. There may then be a denial: 'Labour denies its tax plans will hit low earners and states that anyone earning under £21,568.14 will be better off.' And on it goes. By the time leaders are out on the campaign trail, it's too late for an argument about the role of the state.

Rightly, Kinnock framed his argument about the state in 1985, around two years ahead of the election, but because no one noticed he was still making the case during the campaign in 1987. Most London-based newspapers reported the Conservative claims about how they intended to tax and spend as fact, and Labour's equivalent propositions as incoherent, preposterous economic illiteracy. Although sincerely seeking impartiality, broadcasters are greatly influenced by at least the tone and quite often the substance of the newspaper reporting. Biden might have been wowed by Kinnock's speech, but it was too late for the Labour leader to make much impact on voters worrying about Labour's economic and defence policies as projected by opponents.

For Kinnock, the 1987 election result was not wholly unexpected but it was still a disappointment. The Conservatives had won another landslide, with a majority of 102 – Thatcher's third successive victory. The outcome meant that Labour faced yet another mountain at the next election. Kinnock had already been leader of the Opposition for four long, troubled years. Now he faced a second intimidating ascent in the same job. But at least he was free to make the attempt. In spite of the heavy defeat, there were no significant calls for him to stand down as leader. Although sensitive enough to suffer periods of intense self-doubt, he did not for a second consider resigning.

He stayed on with good cause. Even his critics in the media and the party acknowledged Kinnock had fought a successful personal campaign in the 1987 election, by far the most dominant Labour figure even though he led what even then was a strong shadow Cabinet. Following the election, the party was moving at least in the right direction, having made a few gains. Crucially, the SDP began to implode, having failed to make a breakthrough for the second successive election. For Kinnock and Labour, the path to power seemed much clearer with the removal of this obstruction. In the build-up to the 1987 election there was some speculation that the SDP–Liberal Alliance might come second in terms of the popular vote and gain seats. This did not happen: Kinnock had seen off the formidable David Owen and the SDP was soon to disappear. There was a widely held sense in Labour, one that Kinnock shared, that he deserved another go.

Kinnock immediately sought to make the most of the enhanced but fragile authority of a second term as leader of the Opposition. He announced a policy review with a fairly clear idea of what he wanted the outcome to be. This was a big test of leadership, and one that he passed. No leader should announce a review without already having decided on its conclusions. From the two defeats in 1983 and 1987, Kinnock decided Labour could not win an election advocating unilateral nuclear disarmament. And in spite of his occasional valiant attempts to reframe an argument about the role of the state, he sensed that this was an argument difficult to win in England with its tendency to elect Conservative governments. Thus the review was instigated with the intention to scrap Labour's support for unilateralism and for the party to take a more modest approach to state intervention and to the thorny issue of 'tax and spend'.

Although Kinnock had a sense of direction, he still led a resistant party. In particular, the battle over changing defence policy was almost impossibly stressful and draining for him, even with the assistance of his wily shadow Foreign Secretary, Gerald Kaufman. For Kinnock, the trauma was deep on many levels. He had to come to terms with a personal change of mind, concluding that his passionate commitment to unilateralism was wrong, at least in the context of the late 1980s. Then he had to convince his party, including powerful trade union leaders who continued at first to support the policy of unilateralism. His shadow Defence Secretary, Denzil Davies, an old friend, resigned during the sequence.

Kinnock lost lots of old friends while he was leader. In some cases, as with Davies, they turned away from him. With others, echoing Shakespeare's Prince Hal, Kinnock felt the need to turn away from them to become electorally acceptable. He even kept clear of Michael Foot in public, although he and Glenys remained devoted to the Foots in private. Foot had been an election-loser. Kinnock needed to seem like a winner by symbolizing distance. Leadership made many brutal demands.

After endless stressful twists and turns, Kinnock secured a lot of the policy changes he had sought but, as in the first term, there were still many internal battles to be fought. Once again, large parts of the media praised him for leading from the front. Then they attacked both Labour and its leader for being too divided and weak. Even so, it was in his second term as leader of the Opposition that Kinnock began to be seen as a likely next prime minister. In the late 1980s and early 1990s, Labour was often substantially ahead in the polls and made some seemingly significant gains in by-elections. The party gained the Vale of Glamorgan, Mid-Staffordshire and Monmouth from the Conservatives, in some cases with big swings. And there was no longer any threat from the SDP. The newly merged party, the Liberal Democrats, hardly registered in some opinion polls. Labour came first in the 1989 European elections.

The swings were largely explained by disillusionment with the long-serving Conservative government rather than sustained enthusiasm for Labour. By that time, Margaret Thatcher had lost one of her earlier skills as a leader. From her election as Conservative leader in 1975 to her third general election victory in 1987, Thatcher had the knack of looking at the crowded political stage and assessing how far she could push her radical instincts. Sometimes she was cautious, sensing too much opposition within her party or beyond. Other times she instinctively saw swathes of space, such as in 1981 when the Labour Party formally split, and she became more daring. But she lost her powerful sense of what was possible after 1987.

Her flagship policy for the third term, the 'Community Charge', commonly known as the poll tax, took the bizarre form of flat tax to raise cash for councils. All local residents would pay the same, irrespective of income or wealth. Thatcher assumed the policy would be popular, holding to account profligate councils in a way that would keep bills relatively low. The opposite happened. Planned bills in the first year of the tax were much higher than anticipated. The policy was deeply unpopular, not least with lots of Conservative voters.

Nonetheless, Thatcher pressed on. But she did so as the economy was tottering on the brink of recession and her government was visibly divided. Her chancellor, Nigel Lawson, resigned in 1989 after disagreements over exchange rate policy. Lawson had also been a fervent opponent of the poll tax from the beginning. Not long after Lawson's departure Sir Geoffrey Howe resigned, triggering Thatcher's sensational fall.

For Kinnock, the unpopularity of the Conservative government had a single consequence: his party raced ahead in the polls. With Owen no longer a force as SDP leader and the government in deep trouble, Kinnock dared to hope that he could be the next prime minister.

The hope was often stifled by despair. Labour remained a difficult party to lead, with noisy dissenters willing to speak out on any available broadcasting outlet. Sometimes the dissent was justified. Occasionally Kinnock appeared to be taking on the left without a clear sense of what Labour's subsequent purpose would be. In addition, he could be at least as provocative as his internal critics, too often deploying metaphors about shooting anyone who got in his way in a desperate attempt to appear strong.

His efforts partly reflected a determined and courageous approach to leadership. Some leaders hail their own boldness, when they are in reality tamely taking the safest political routes. Kinnock was unceasingly brave. But the pressures of reforming his party while trying to appear 'prime ministerial' had tragically ironic consequences. The vivacious rising star with an effervescent zest for life had gone. Now he appeared wooden and humourless, largely in response to the endless attacks from newspapers. The media onslaught formed a pattern: Kinnock was not very bright; he was not remotely prime ministerial; he was the Welsh windbag; he was dangerously left-wing. They were crude and wildly overstated, but also effective. Kinnock found them painful, as any human being would.

In an attempt to command wider respect, he changed his appearance – brushing his sparse red hair back instead of across his balding head. He virtually stopped using wit. He suppressed his exuberance. There was one sad, emblematic example of this. During the 1992 election campaign, various cultural figures hosted an event supporting Labour in the restaurant at 4 Millbank in Westminster, where the broadcasters are based. Kinnock was the star guest. At one point, a band played and Kinnock instinctively started to tap his feet. Naturally musical, he almost began to clap too but he stopped himself – he suppressed the urge to be himself, fearing it would not appear prime ministerial.[16]

By 1992, Kinnock was not entirely sure who he was as a leader and aspiring prime minister. He knew better than anyone how and why Labour lost elections. But what did he and Labour need to do to win them? In his attempts to answer, Kinnock faced yet another obstacle: his shadow chancellor, John Smith. Smith was well ahead of him in terms of personal ratings. Whereas Kinnock could not hide his insecurities when talking in detail about economic policy, Smith had a natural authority. He had been a Cabinet minister, and exuded the easy confidence of one who knew what government was like. Kinnock had never been in government, even turning down the offer of being Michael Foot's Parliamentary Private Secretary in the 1970s.

For those who have not been a Cabinet minister, there is almost an intimidating mystery about power. Smith had been there in the late 1970s, and showed no sign of being worried about returning to government. The senior Labour official David Hill, who worked for Hattersley and later Tony Blair, was Smith's senior media adviser when he replaced Kinnock. Hill described Smith as the most self-confident politician he had known.[17]

In the build-up to the 1992 election, Smith was cautious in some respects about economic policy and yet overconfident about his persuasive powers. The caution stifled Kinnock's already more muted attempts to put the case for the potential benevolence of the state. With the National Health Service underfunded, Kinnock wanted to argue for a tax to pay for a much-needed increased investment in the NHS. Kinnock believed that such a tax would be popular with the wider electorate. It was not a Labour plan to spend 'recklessly', as the Conservatives tended to claim in elections, but one that would raise money for a single specific purpose.

In spite of all the pressures to be safely technocratic, Kinnock still yearned to be a radical change-maker. He was often asked in the 1992 election about whether or not he had a 'big idea', and he struggled to find a convincing answer. His NHS proposition would have been that big idea, but Smith vetoed it out of fear that a specific tax rise might be unpopular. With a lower personal rating and burdened by the perception that Smith was more economically competent, Kinnock was not in a strong enough position to prevail.

Instead, Smith went ahead with an 'alternative budget' that still proposed tax rises for higher earners, but without the increases being connected to a cause as popular as the NHS. The move was seized on by the Conservatives to show that Labour was planning punitive tax increases. Smith's plans, as presented and distorted, were as unpopular as any policy that Kinnock might have advanced.

There is a theory that Kinnock blew the 1992 election by becoming his old exuberant self during the rally staged by Labour in Sheffield at the climax of the campaign. On the day of the rally, several polls had suggested Labour was significantly ahead. That made the event seem triumphalist when the aim had been to convey a team ready for government in a slick, modern US-style setting.

Kinnock opened his speech by shouting 'We're all right! We're all right! We're all right!' to the cheering crowds. Reporting live from the event, the BBC's political editor, John Cole, was impressed, comparing the mood to John Kennedy's big rallies in the early 1960s. There was no suggestion that Kinnock had made a terrible blunder. But after Labour's defeat, the rally acquired a mythological status as a fatal event, one in which Kinnock proved he lacked the discipline required of leadership. From being 'Kennedy like', the image of Kinnock onstage in an arena eventually fuelled the simplistic narrative that he was not 'prime ministerial'. Retrospectively, it appeared that he had mistakenly believed the hype triggered by opinion poll leads and become transparently overconfident and cocky.

The Sheffield rally saga is a red herring, however. Kinnock and his party would still have lost if the rally had never been held. No single event determines an election. Voters had seen Kinnock battling away for nine years. Some had read in the newspapers how useless he was for virtually all that time. Labour's message in the campaign had been that it was time for a change. This was also problematic: Kinnock had been around for a long time. It was his opponent who seemed fresher. The Conservatives had replaced Thatcher with John Major, who was a different type of leader from Thatcher in many respects: calmer, more modest, and to her left politically. Major's party chairman and closest ally was Chris Patten, even more clearly defined as a Conservative to the left of Thatcher. Briefly, the Conservatives appeared to be moving on from hard-line Thatcherism, although after the general election the lure of her intoxicating spell proved to be as strong as ever.

Before 1992, Major had scrapped the poll tax and adopted a more emollient tone. More fundamentally, the Conservatives were still winning the battle of ideas in relation to the role of the state and related arguments about 'tax and spend'. Kinnock had tried to engage in the battle, and so had his deputy, Roy Hattersley, who in 1987 had written a largely ignored but well-argued book called *Choose Freedom*. Kinnock and Hattersley did not get on particularly well, but both grappled persistently with a key question for the left in England: how to put the case for the state.

Kinnock took responsibility for his failure to become prime minister, shrugging off the praise he received subsequently from Tony Blair, Gordon Brown and others for saving Labour. He wanted to be a winner and prime minister, not merely a leader who lost while saving his party. As he became less confident as a public figure during his leadership, his projection was less convincing. He stopped addressing the all-important 'why' questions in the way that he had in those dazzling speeches about the state in 1985 and 1987, fearing any hint of ideological fervour. But without saying why policies are being proposed, a manifesto emerges from an ideological vacuum and suffers accordingly. Instead of linking the 'why' to the policies, Kinnock sought by 1992 to reassure voters with long technocratic answers in interviews. Having purged Labour of its fatal flaws that doomed the party in 1979, 1983 and 1987, he lost his own sense of mission – at least as a public communicator.

After 1987, Kinnock had been seen as a likely next prime minister, but it was John Major who became the occupant of Number Ten after Margaret Thatcher stepped down in 1990. In the build-up to the 1992 election, Kinnock was again seen as a likely next prime minister, the replacement for Major. Instead, he was soon sitting on the opposition backbenches, nursing a sense of unbearable disappointment while waiting uneasily for Major to propose him to be an EU commissioner.

Many lessons were learned from the Kinnock era, some of them applied to excess. Blair and Brown concluded it was impossible for Labour to win an election with a relentlessly hostile media. They also decided that there was no space for Labour to propose income tax rises, and that the issue of nationalization and state ownership – which had framed much thinking on the left after 1945, and from a different perspective on the right after 1983 – was more or less closed. For the time being, the right had won the ideological battle on state versus private ownership.

There was one lesson from Kinnock's leadership Blair did not have to act on, as he contested only one election as leader of the

Opposition and won. Longevity in that role was Kinnock's fatal problem. A leader of the Opposition has only one chance. If they lose an election they should not seek to stay on to contest another in four or five years' time.

Kinnock could look back on some historic achievements: seeing off the SDP, transforming Labour from a shambles to a modern political party, laying the framework for power with sweeping policy changes on a scale that no Conservative Opposition leader attempted between 1997 and 2010. Comparing Kinnock's reforms of the Labour Party after 1983 with those of William Hague, Michael Howard and David Cameron after the Conservatives' defeat in 1997 is illuminating. Kinnock's reforms were on an incomparably bigger scale. In difficult circumstances, by 1992, he had nearly wiped out the Conservatives' overall majority. Yet the intensity of the effort and the length of time he was leader of the Opposition meant he was never going to be prime minister even if he was perceived as a likely one.

———

Kinnock had briefly been the beneficiary of Thatcher's tumbling poll ratings when she got in deep trouble soon after her 1987 election triumph. Yet Kinnock had to wait for another general election before taking his chance. Within Thatcher's own party, there were those who aspired to seize the crown long before then – and they did not have to wait for a general election to make their moves. In particular, the former minister Michael Heseltine had been aspiring to do exactly this since his dramatic Cabinet resignation in January 1986. He took his chance in the autumn of 1990.

6

MICHAEL HESELTINE

While still a student at Oxford, Michael Heseltine famously had a clear plan to be prime minister, or so it seemed. One of Heseltine's few close friends in the parliamentary Conservative Party, Julian Critchley, regularly recalled an exchange that took place when the two of them were students together in the early 1950s. Critchley spoke of a youthful Heseltine sketching out his life's mission on the back of an envelope. By twenty-five, he would be a millionaire; by thirty-five he would be an MP, and a minister by the time he was forty-five. He would be in Downing Street by the age of fifty-five.[1] The precision of the chronology signalled bold ambition. For Heseltine, there was to be no hanging around. He wanted to be in Number Ten by his mid-fifties, having been hyperactive in his previous decades.

Of all the prime ministers we never had, Heseltine suffered most from perceptions of transparent ambition. Critchley's legendary envelope seemed to symbolize a restless figure driven by egotism. Heseltine had looked ahead and could only see the path that he would take to the top. The writings on the envelope contained no reflections on how Heseltine hoped to change the world nor his ideological inclinations. It was solely about him. And this was as a student, when ideas about changing the world are often at their most optimistically prevalent.

Yet there was a twist, as there often was when a caricature of Heseltine started to form. In an interview in 2012, Heseltine denied the envelope and the words written on it ever existed: 'Well it's so uncharacteristic of me that I don't believe it. I've no recollection of it, and it just doesn't ring true... And Julian was a good friend of mine, and he said this and wrote about it many times, but I've never accepted it. I just don't think it sounds like me. I'm too cautious.'[2] Critchley's anecdote, the denial, and the specific reason given for why the story did not ring true highlight the wider contradictions of Heseltine's complex personality, one that brought him so close to the top and yet prevented him from seizing the crown.

Heseltine did not believe the story, because he was 'cautious'. That explanation is illuminating. Caution was not a characteristic often associated with him. The images that helped to define him convey more of a flamboyant risk-taker: the grabbing of the mace in the Commons to protest at Labour MPs singing 'The Red Flag'; the marching across Greenham Common in a flak jacket as a defiant Defence Secretary; storming out of Margaret Thatcher's Cabinet in a row over helicopters; standing against Thatcher in a leadership contest. These various acts of assertiveness did not suggest that caution was part of Heseltine's armoury.

Yet there he was, reflecting on Critchley's anecdote decades later, self-aware enough to note an underlying tentativeness. He did so with good cause. In government he was a careful reformer, taking his time to make his moves. Out of government he was a patient dissenter – perhaps too patient. Heseltine was a cautious showman. Much of what he did as a minister, and in his attempt to replace Margaret Thatcher, was carefully calculated and incremental. But he was also theatrical. His flamboyance gave him a rare form of political fame and yet triggered mistrust. His caution enabled him to carry colleagues with him as he became a reformer in the governments of Thatcher and Major, but held him back from rising to the very top. His actorly incrementalism both made and hindered him.

Whether or not Critchley misremembered is irrelevant. As Heseltine noted in that interview, given long after his ambitions for leadership had passed, Critchley repeated the anecdote often enough for it to become part of Heseltine's story, not least because the reminiscence rang true even if it was not. He did become a millionaire, MP and minister within the time span alleged to have been outlined on the back of the envelope. And two prime ministers, Margaret Thatcher and John Major, were more than aware of the envelope. Both wondered neurotically about when Heseltine would attempt the final leap. They were not alone in wondering.

This was not solely because Heseltine was obviously ambitious. He also had some of the most important qualifications for leadership. Of all the prime ministers we never had, Heseltine was the closest to a presidential candidate in the US. He always looked elegant, slim and well-dressed, with swept-back hair that never seemed to go noticeably grey. He was commanding as a solo performer, and distinctive in his approach to government.

———

After Margaret Thatcher's election victory in 1979, most Cabinet ministers either tried to please her or, at the other extreme, dissented with barely concealed disdain. The so-called wets in her Cabinet who disagreed with her early monetarist economic policies were fairly open in their opposition. Thatcher knew Ian Gilmour, James Prior and Peter Walker opposed what she was doing, because they made speeches or gave interviews that did not take much decoding. After he was sacked from the Cabinet in 1981, Gilmour wrote a brilliant book that was as scathing of early Thatcherism as were the onslaughts at the time from the Labour Party. He titled the book *Dancing with Dogma*. The front-cover photograph showed Gilmour and Thatcher dancing awkwardly at a Conservative ball, mischievously giving a visual image to accompany the damning metaphor. One of Gilmour's themes was that the policies aimed at curbing inflation were having precisely the opposite effect. He argued in *Dancing with Dogma* that North Sea oil revenue was being squandered on welfare benefits, and that monetarism in its purest form was being applied to a weak economy with an indifference to the economic and social consequences.[3] In slightly more restrained ways, the other wets also described their various dances with dogma, hinting at their concerns about severe spending cuts and an overly rigid attachment to monetarist policies.

Heseltine took a different path from them, and in policy terms a more constructive one. The wets were dismissed or marginalized, and therefore had little or no impact on policymaking. Heseltine, however, kept close to the heart of the Thatcher government. She appointed him as her Environment Secretary after the 1979 election. Instead of complaining about her economic policy, he persuaded her to adapt her theological inflexibility to his more interventionist crusade. This was a much harder task than criticizing her from the safety of the backbenches or in coded speeches. Heseltine partially agreed with the internal critics of Thatcherism, but he had no intention at this early stage of risking a place in the Cabinet to express his doubts.

In the summer of 1981, there were riots in several cities. The most noteworthy were in Liverpool, London, Leeds, Birmingham and Manchester. As Gilmour noted in his book, Thatcher's economic policies were leading to unemployment levels not experienced since the 1930s. The inner-city riots were one of many consequences arising from an economic experiment conducted at first with ruthless rigidity.

Reactions to the riots from within the government were mixed. The chancellor, Geoffrey Howe – at this point largely in step with Thatcher – assumed that the best some of these poor areas could hope for was managed decline. Heseltine took the opposite view. His favoured stance was the political crusade, and in the immediate aftermath of the riots he saw his role as leader of a revival of neglected urban areas. Liverpool and the Docklands in East London became emblems of his campaign, but other cities were also included. He began with Liverpool, courageously persuading Thatcher to part with additional public money to assist in urban regeneration.

The persuasion was close to miraculous. This was 1981, when Thatcher and Howe were following the monetarist creed in its purest form. On the whole, they regarded public spending beyond what they deemed to be essential or politically necessary as almost sinful. Most Cabinet ministers sought to impress Thatcher and Howe, by showing how they could control spending in their departments. Heseltine was subtler. He also sought savings, but he dared to put the case for higher public spending for specific purposes.

In a letter to Thatcher written in July 1981, Heseltine told her that he planned to spend a fortnight in Liverpool and that it would be 'disastrous' if he were not 'empowered' to make some speedy decisions. Astutely, he argued that the private sector would be instrumental in the city's revival, but this would have to be backed up by 'public sector resources to do land clearance, reclamation and necessary infrastructure'. He added: 'I would need to rely very much on your personal support.'[4] That last sentence was clever, a form of flattery and also a challenge that was almost a threat. He wanted Thatcher bound to his cause.

Heseltine had written the letter in a way that made it difficult for Thatcher to refuse his request. He was genuinely as much an advocate of private sector involvement as Thatcher was, but unlike her he was a supporter of the state playing a bigger role – at a point when such a view was a form of blasphemy. Heseltine knew she would be more likely to respond if he highlighted the virtues of the private sector, but he was also being sincere. He wanted the private sector to play an instrumental role in the revival of inner cities. He also demanded around £100 million of government spending.

A few weeks later, in September 1981, Thatcher conducted a defining Cabinet reshuffle. Most of the wets were either purged from her government – or, in the case of Jim Prior, moved to Northern Ireland, arguably a bigger punishment than being sacked. Allies such as Norman Tebbit were promoted to key posts. Heseltine had made demands on Thatcher that might have been viewed as provocative. Instead he prevailed and, at least as important, kept his job. While Gilmour was powerlessly writing a book, Heseltine was making a difference in government. The contrivance was typical of Heseltine; he was no fan of Thatcher's, but he stayed put in her Cabinets for more than six years.

Heseltine became a familiar figure in Liverpool, the performer with an interest in detailed policy implementation – an unusual combination. Most political showmen have little time for the hard grind of policy detail. Many years later, when Heseltine became a freeman of the city, he reflected on what happened there:

Day after day we walked the streets of Liverpool. In a hectic series
of visits here and consultations there, we travelled hither and thither
in a blaze of publicity. 'Why do you waste your time there – with
them?' I was asked again and again by Conservative sympathisers
in the prosperous suburbs. 'There are no votes for us.' But within
days a pattern clearly emerged. Put simply, this was a city without
leadership. It was that void it was hoped that I could fill. It was almost
as though, subconsciously, people were waiting for it to happen. The
apparent goodwill for a new direction was expressed on all sides.[5]

Heseltine's energy and flair extended far more widely too. Alastair
Balls was chair of the Tyne and Wear Development Corporation
in Newcastle, and worked with him in Whitehall as a civil servant:

At a time when Margaret Thatcher was seeking to withdraw state
control wherever she could... Michael Heseltine realised that inner
cities were an issue that the government had to tackle head on...
He was an incredibly inspiring leader to work with. Anyone
who knows about urban regeneration will tell you that the centre
of Newcastle Gateshead is far changed from how it was... its
turnaround over the past 20 years began with Michael Heseltine.
And it's not the only city.[6]

Heseltine was one of the few Cabinet ministers in the 1980s to
have made his distinctive mark in policy terms. Most ministers tend
to be technocratic in their approach, above all seeking to please
Number Ten, especially with a leader as dominant as Thatcher.
Heseltine was different. At the Department of the Environment,
he managed to fuse the Thatcherite fashion for the private sector
with his support for an active state. The fusion was a long-running
theme in his career.

———

In policy terms, Heseltine made another historic contribution as a Cabinet minister. Fast-forward from the early 1980s to November 1990, when he returned to the Department of the Environment in John Major's first administration. In between, he had been a Defence Secretary and a prominent backbencher, but after the departure of Margaret Thatcher he was given a daunting ministerial task. The context of his reappearance as Environment Secretary was a dark one for him. A few weeks earlier, he had hoped to be prime minister, having challenged Thatcher for the leadership. Instead he had failed, though his leadership bid brought about Thatcher's fall and cleared a path for John Major. For Heseltine, a return to a middle-ranking department in which he had served nearly a decade earlier was hardly the fulfilment of his political dreams. Yet he accepted the post without a fuss and with another big project: Major tasked Heseltine with abolishing the much-despised poll tax and coming up with a workable, electorally popular alternative.

Heseltine had been largely loyal to Thatcher on the backbenches, supporting most of the government's policies. The poll tax was an exception. He had long ago spotted the dangers of a tax that took no account of ability to pay. Yet the task of scrapping a system that had been introduced at considerable expense was complex and highly charged. Already Heseltine was seen by Thatcher's more doting admirers as the assassin for challenging her. Now he was abolishing her flagship policy for the Conservatives' third term.

This was also Thatcher's view, though she blamed most of her Cabinet and not just Heseltine for what she saw as an act of bloody betrayal. In exile she remained committed to the poll tax, or thought that she did. In office she had revised the policy several times, hoping to appease internal rebels, but out of power she became convinced again of its virtues. She followed the same pattern in relation to Europe – she acted expediently for most of her time as prime minister, more pragmatic than the Tory leaders that followed her, and then became a passionate opponent when out of office.

There are some political sequences that are intense when they are played out and are then more or less forgotten about once the heat has passed. This applied to the scrapping of the poll tax and its replacement with the council tax. Heseltine got to work immediately. Although he applied his familiar verve, the task proved difficult. The media focus was on him more than on any other minister during the early months of Major's administration. Various contentious proposals about an alternative to the poll tax were leaked, each one leading news bulletins and making the front pages. The leaks were greeted with considerable alarm by Tory MPs who feared the poll tax might be replaced by another disastrous vote-loser. For months, the political temperature was extremely high.

In the end, Heseltine concluded that the local property tax that had been in place before the poll tax – the rates – was the best option. But he could not admit this publicly, as the rates had been deeply unpopular within much of the Conservative Party. With the backing of Major and the chancellor, Norman Lamont, Heseltine made an important move: in order to keep the new local property tax relatively low, he significantly increased the subsidy to councils from central government, paid for by a rise in VAT.

The poll tax was supposed to increase accountability of local government by making councils raise most of the money they spent. Heseltine leapt in the opposite direction. In doing so, he neutered the dire impact of the poll tax on the poll ratings of the

Conservative Party. The Conservatives had introduced a tax that triggered riots, and got away with it by scrapping it before the 1992 election. Heseltine called the replacement the 'council tax', hailed the lower bills that were subsidized by the VAT increase, and killed the issue as a source of explosive contention.

After Major, and arguably Lamont, Heseltine was the key figure in bringing about the Conservatives' fourth successive election victory. He was the one who had challenged Thatcher and abolished her most unpopular policy. He was also the most prominent campaigner during the 1992 election, a regular upbeat interviewee and attender of morning press conferences at Conservative Central Office. An observer from Mars might have concluded that the telegenic, articulate Heseltine was prime minister rather than the more reticent Major. Major only came to life on his soapbox, addressing voters with a crackly loudspeaker, an outdated style that was deemed silly until he won the election. Then it was hailed as a triumphantly authentic form of communication.

After his victory, Major made Heseltine president of the Board of Trade, a revival of a grand title for a ministerial post that had become known as the more prosaic Secretary of State for Trade. Major knew how to flatter Heseltine's hunger for elevated titles. After the 1992 election, Heseltine was not prime minister – but he was a president.

In his first party conference speech in the role – at the deeply troubled annual gathering held in October, shortly after the UK was forced to leave the Exchange Rate Mechanism – Heseltine was one of the few Cabinet ministers still in vivacious form. Once again, he put the case for active government as he had dared to do under Thatcher. He told the conference: 'I'll intervene [to help British industry] before breakfast, before lunch, before tea and before dinner, and I'd get up the next morning and I'll start all over again.'[7] Such were his speaking skills that the audience cheered heartily, even though this was a conference that exposed a deep divide within the Conservatives over Europe and connected issues about the role of the state.

Heseltine never held any of the big departmental briefs – the Treasury, the Foreign Office or the Home Office – but in policy terms he made more of an impact than some of those who did. He also became better known than his colleagues in more senior posts.

His story is one of the more puzzling mysteries in the list of prime ministers we never had. Heseltine possessed an impressive array of leadership qualifications. He knew what he believed in: a fusion of free markets and an active state, a philosophy that might have moved the Conservative Party beyond its enduring infatuation with Thatcherism. He had a clearer sense of purpose than David Cameron or Theresa May, two figures who did become prime minister. He was a communicator, a figure that could make sense of what he was doing. Although he was not as effective a political teacher as Margaret Thatcher or Tony Blair, he was a more compelling speaker than John Major, David Cameron, Theresa May or even Boris Johnson, who can rouse an audience with a Heseltine-like flourish but who rarely makes an accessible argument as he excites those who he is addressing.

Above all, Heseltine delivered in government. Neither Blair nor Cameron had been a minister before becoming prime minister. May had been a formidable Home Secretary, but that was a relatively cocooned role compared with Heseltine's range of posts. Johnson was not associated with any significant policy implementation when he became prime minister – beyond the introduction of 'Boris bikes' when he was Mayor of London, a scheme he inherited from his predecessor, Ken Livingstone.

Heseltine was media-savvy and a good interviewee, increasingly important in the 1980s and 1990s when the broadcasting studio replaced the Commons and the political rally as the main stage for ambitious politicians. He generated a frisson of excitement as an interviewee, being mischievous, confident, assertive and evidently enjoying himself. Unlike other great orators such as Tony Benn, Michael Foot and Enoch Powell, Heseltine had a more mannered delivery as a speaker. He was a physical performer, waving his arms, sometimes moving around the stage, not confining himself to the constraints of a podium. At conferences he made his audience of Tory activists laugh, and for much of his career these annual gatherings were not marked by much laughter. His colleagues on the platform with him laughed too. Even Thatcher smiled as he spoke, albeit with a hint of irritation.

Yet Heseltine did not become prime minister while others did. For all the speculation about his aching ambition, he only took part in a single leadership contest – the one held in November 1990. Given that a potential prime minister must win a leadership contest, this was his best chance of seizing the crown. What went wrong for Heseltine, when so much had gone to plan, if his ambitious back-of-an-envelope calculation is to be believed?

————

The way Heseltine was perceived by November 1990 provides most, though not all, of the answers. Much is made of the cliché that the candidate committing an act of regicide will not inherit the crown. John Major, the eventual winner of the contest, was able to enter the ring as an apparent innocent with no blood on his hands. Heseltine had done the dirty work. Yet, whatever the force of the cliché, perhaps a different character to Heseltine might not have been harmed as much as he was by being the direct cause of the leader's fall. Indeed, the party – or at least the parliamentary party with the votes in a leadership contest – might have been grateful for such an act of courage and voted accordingly. Someone other than Heseltine might have committed the deed, taken a bow and been elected prime minister.

The fuller explanation requires a deeper examination of Heseltine's position in November 1990, when the space finally opened up for him to make a bid to become prime minister. By then, he had been perceived by colleagues and the media for years as a figure who was resolutely ambitious. Indeed, if it were possible to do so, Heseltine's colleagues overestimated the scale of his personal ambition.

This was partly Heseltine's fault. He was fascinated by the politics of projection, but was not always very effective at projecting himself – a common flaw in politicians gripped by the artistry of their vocation.[8] Partly because of his love of the political stage, Heseltine's substantial political career was punctuated by a suspicious question, one posed repeatedly by some colleagues, party members and political journalists: what's he up to? Heseltine generated suspicion even when he made his moves innocently.

Fundamentally, Heseltine was a loyalist. He did not like Margaret Thatcher and viewed her much less fearfully than some of his colleagues did, but he served her diligently until his dramatic resignation from her Cabinet in January 1986. When he returned to the Cabinet under John Major, he undertook a series of challenging briefs with his usual energy. He was one of the few to reliably defend Major when the Conservative civil war over Europe reached new heights in the mid-1990s. He was not recklessly disloyal before November 1990, nor afterwards.

Essentially, he was a loyalist with a distinct sense of personal mission, an awkward combination. Yet even when Heseltine was being dutiful as a Cabinet minister, Thatcher and then Major were suspicious of his intentions. When at his most vulnerable several years after the 1990 contest, Major made Heseltine deputy prime minister partly to bind Heseltine to Major's fragile leadership. Thatcher had assumed some of Heseltine's exuberance was a conscious challenge to her when it was not – at least not until the very end of her career.

Here was the situation in the dramatic autumn of 1990: Heseltine had been seen as a leader in waiting, ready to take his chance when it came, for almost as long as Thatcher had been prime minister. He had been seen in these terms when he was a Cabinet minister, and even more so after his resignation. By 1990, quite a lot of Conservative MPs who agreed with Heseltine that Thatcher should be forced out also had another priority: to stop Heseltine. They had become fed up with him; he had been wanting to be prime minister for too long. Heseltine conveyed such dynamism that most Conservative MPs, members and observers overlooked an altogether different characteristic: the caution that he noted in his comments about the Critchley envelope anecdote. In reality, he was too cautious. And so a pattern formed. He was seen as untrustworthy when he was loyal, and a risk-taker when he was cautious.

By the time of Geoffrey Howe's resignation speech in November 1990, the one that famously and calmly tore apart Thatcher's leadership, Heseltine had been on the backbenches for nearly four years. Like Hamlet, he had become a specialist in putting the case for delay; in his case, delaying his move against Thatcher. He had to act after the Howe speech. But he did so after a long wait, during which his role had become ill-defined and aimless: he was the big figure travelling the country meeting Conservative activists, and a powerless backbench MP. This made him seem less prime ministerial. His chances would have been greater if he had stayed in the Cabinet.

If he had done so, Heseltine would have avoided a media trap. From 1986 onwards, he was endlessly asked whether he would stand against Thatcher – or more simply whether he wanted to be leader of his party. He was the only big figure in the years from January 1986 to November 1990 to be asked this persistently. No serving Cabinet minister was asked, for the obvious reason that they could say they were bound by collective responsibility. Heseltine wasn't, and was therefore burdened with the question.

His answer was neatly evasive and clearly thought through. He replied that he could not 'envisage the circumstances' where he would stand for the leadership. He persisted with this reply until he did indeed envisage the circumstances in November 1990.

Heseltine's sudden resignation in January 1986 was a near-spontaneous act, triggered by his fury at what he regarded as Thatcher's mendacity over the negotiations about a contract for Westland Helicopters. Westland was until this point a not particularly well-known company, even though it was the UK's only helicopter manufacturer. By the mid-1980s, it was no longer profitable and was the subject of a rescue bid. In a preview of what was to follow in terms of the Conservatives' split over Europe, Heseltine backed a European consortium, whereas Thatcher supported a bid from the United States. For a short time, Westland Helicopters was on every front page and led most news bulletins. Heseltine felt he had followed the rules strictly in terms of the negotiations and Thatcher had not. He walked out of a Cabinet meeting in January 1986, never to return as a minister under her leadership.

For days following his departure Heseltine was ubiquitous, putting forward his case on every media outlet. On *Channel 4 News* he even became the reporter, putting together a slick film on what he believed to have happened. Thatcher was briefly worried that she might have to resign over the issue, but after a Commons debate in which the leader of the Opposition, Neil Kinnock, missed several open goals, the issue faded and was more or less forgotten.

The Westland saga shows that Heseltine was not as calculating as his reputation suggested. If he had wanted to resign in order to advance his personal cause, he would have chosen a more accessible issue than the fate of an obscure helicopter company. He would also have given some thought to how long it was politically safe for him to be a backbencher before he acquired a reputation for scheming self-interest. Perhaps he had assumed that Thatcher would lose the next election, only eighteen months away, and he would then emerge as the noble new leader untarnished by the election defeat. She and the Conservatives were well behind in the polls when he resigned. However, they were well ahead by the time of the next election. Thatcher won another landslide in 1987, condemning Heseltine to another long period on the backbenches.

On 14 November 1990, in the aftermath of Geoffrey Howe's resignation speech, Heseltine declared his candidacy with a well-pitched statement aimed at the widest possible range of Conservative MPs. He appealed to his colleagues' instinct for survival, an even more developed instinct than loyalty to a leader, by indicating that opinion polls suggested he had the best chance of preventing 'the ultimate calamity of a Labour government'. He pledged an 'immediate and fundamental review' of the poll tax, without stating that such an investigation would inevitably lead to its abolition. He added: 'Mrs Thatcher's outstanding contribution to the politics of our times is not in question… The issue now, however, is how best to protect what we have all achieved under her leadership.' His message to the narrow electorate was that only he could save Thatcherism: the continued leadership of Thatcher would undo all by bringing in a Labour government.

His approach was clever, but not quite clever enough. In the first round of the contest, Thatcher won 204 of the 372 votes available against 152 for Heseltine. This was a pretty good tally for Heseltine given that he was standing against a prime minister who had won a landslide three years earlier, but not enough to propel him to victory in the next round. After Thatcher withdrew, only a few additional MPs came out to declare that while they had voted for her in the first round they were now switching to Heseltine.

The reluctance of more to flock to his cause was partly a consequence of one aspect of Heseltine's personality. He was wholly at ease on a stage, in a studio and on the rubber chicken circuit, but curiously awkward at wooing MPs in the tearooms at Westminster. MPs are flattered when receiving attention from the bigger players in their party, but Heseltine, like many performers, had a reticent streak. He did not like the one-to-one conversations or exchanges in small groups where the focus was on him. Partly because of this awkwardness, he had few devoted followers in the Commons. Those who were his close allies were wholly committed, yet they tended to be figures who for whatever reason had been marginalized in the Thatcher era. The head of his campaign in 1990 was the long-serving MP Michael Mates. Although Mates had the dream background for a Tory MP – a lieutenant colonel in the Queen's Dragoon Guards and a choral scholar at King's College, Cambridge – he had been overlooked by Thatcher and never been a minister. As the columnist and author Alan Watkins noted in his book on the fall of Thatcher, 'his want of preferment could be viewed as a sign of either the injustice of politics or the distrust which the Colonel somehow aroused in some sections of the Conservative party'.[9]

Mates was fairly typical of Heseltine's small parliamentary entourage. They generated a sense of distrust among quite a lot of Conservative MPs, although no one was quite sure why. There was little reason for the suspicion, beyond their attachment to Heseltine, who was also seen by too many as unreliable. During his exile from government, Heseltine had become famous for touring local constituency parties. His tireless visits were a hit because he was a political star, but while the local activists were thrilled at meeting him, they remained largely devoted to Thatcher as their leader. Even if party members came away from an evening with Heseltine convinced he should be the next leader, they did not have a vote in a leadership contest itself.

There is little evidence to suggest that the membership wanted him to succeed Thatcher by November 1990. MPs reported that their party members were deeply uneasy about the removal of Thatcher and this continued to be so for decades – part of the Conservative Party's post-Thatcher trauma about its purpose and definition. Was the party Thatcherite but had needed to remove Thatcher herself? Was it Thatcherite and should have kept Thatcher? Did it need to move on from Thatcherism as well as replace her as leader? Various bewildered Conservative Party leaders answered these questions confusingly. But in 1990, the MPs were asked whether they wanted Heseltine to replace Thatcher, and their answer was 'no'.

In the second round of the 1990 Conservative leadership contest, there was more focus on who would stand against Heseltine. The two candidates that stepped forward were Major and Douglas Hurd. This was the last leadership contest where all three candidates were from the one-nation wing of the Conservative Party and, with varying degrees of enthusiasm, broadly pro-European. Major won on the basis that he appealed to Thatcherites, including Thatcher herself. He also attracted some non-Thatcherites who Heseltine had hoped would back him. Given that Hurd also secured the support of non-Thatcherites, Heseltine did not have a hope. The non-Thatcherites were split between all three candidates, and of the trio Heseltine was least likely to secure the backing of Thatcher's followers.

Tory MPs had other reservations about Heseltine too. Some regarded him as ill-disciplined and impulsive at key moments, likely to blow a fuse in his overexcitement. Potential leaders often acquire greater definition as a result of a single act or statement. Theresa May became famous for warning that the Conservatives were seen as 'the nasty party'. Tony Blair commanded attention as a shadow Home Secretary by suggesting Labour would be 'tough on crime and tough on the causes of crime', even if the soundbite was generously given to him by Gordon Brown. There are many other examples.

Heseltine became famous for grabbing the mace in the Commons at the end of a debate in 1976. He wielded the mace in fury over Labour MPs singing 'The Red Flag' in the chamber. Tory MPs approved of the cause: none of them were fans of 'The Red Flag' being sung anywhere, let alone in the revered chamber. Yet the act suggested a wild streak – not a characteristic associated with leadership until the era of Donald Trump and Boris Johnson, when recklessness became something of a vote-winner. Heseltine was a more substantial figure than either of those two leaders, but at times he seemed to challenge the old-fashioned conservatism that still permeated parts of the party. In the minds of some Conservative MPs, the mace-lifting was linked to Heseltine's walking out of the Cabinet in 1986 and his challenge to the prime minister in 1990. They did not see these as acts of principled integrity, so when they were offered the apparent steadiness of John Major in 1990 they went for him instead. If his challenge to Thatcher had followed a less erratic course, Heseltine might have been more acceptable to more MPs.

———

Obviously, the leadership contest was Heseltine's best chance to become prime minister. He was not going to get to the top without a contest. But a combination of character – or perceived character – and circumstance meant he had little chance of winning even if he was by far the best-qualified candidate for the task ahead. When Major was in trouble soon after his election victory in 1992, he began to worry that Heseltine might make a move against him as he had done against Thatcher. Heseltine was a big enough figure to still be seen as a potential successor.

Major had little cause for anxiety. On the whole, Heseltine admired Major as a leader. Or at least, he saw him as an improvement on Thatcher's final years. Still, Major was wary enough to invite Heseltine to the key meetings in September 1992, along with his chancellor Norman Lamont and Home Secretary Ken Clarke, in order to involve him in the difficult decision to raise interest rates repeatedly over a single day so as to prop up the pound. The desperate measures failed, and the UK left the Exchange Rate Mechanism in humiliating circumstances. Heseltine was loyal throughout, playing a supportive role in the media during the days that followed.

That loyalty extended well beyond the immediate aftermath of the ERM saga. At fringe meetings during the party's 1992 conference, Heseltine passionately made the case for the Maastricht Treaty that was about to begin its difficult legislative journey in Parliament. Some of those attending cheered. Unusually for Conservative conferences, some heckled. The conference, normally staidly loyal, had become similar to Labour's annual gatherings in the early 1980s. Heseltine was on one side of the divide. Along with Ken Clarke, he was the most ardent pro-European in the Cabinet.

Heseltine might have had another chance to be prime minister after 1990, given the travails of Major in the stormy parliament that lasted from the 1992 election to the slaughter of the Conservatives in 1997, but another dramatic event blunted his ambition. In June 1993, he had a heart attack while on a trip to Venice. Alarming photos showed him being carried on a stretcher to the hospital. These were not the images of a potential prime minister, although Heseltine later insisted they had made him seem far more ill than he actually was.

He was barely visible for several months as he took time to recover, giving his first interview to the BBC's *On the Record* programme the following October. Despite the break, the theme of his return interview was the persistent one: his ambition. This time there was an added twist. Would his heart attack have an impact on his desire to be prime minister? His answer was typically evasive:

I've been in the House of Commons now for about a quarter of a century – over a quarter of a century – most of it on the front bench and I like it. But the fact is that you know you do ask these questions, your family make you ask these questions, quite understandably.

There are other things I could do. I am a manic gardener and that's what I've been doing. I could go back to commerce, although that side of my life is some way behind and it's always been very successfully done by my colleagues in the company that I started. So, you know, I've never had a sort of one way track about politics. Although I adore it and I've enjoyed it hugely – am enjoying it.[10]

What did he mean by that? The only interpretation was that he was 'keeping all options open', as Harold Wilson liked to put it when reflecting on thorny paths ahead.

Heseltine returned to the fray with his usual vigour, but his health scare was to play its part in constraining his ambition, although not immediately. Under Major he would not have made a move even if he were fully fit. For Heseltine, there was no legitimate space to challenge him. In order to contemplate or justify an attempt at unseating a second successive prime minister, Heseltine needed to disagree profoundly with Major over direction of policy as he had with Thatcher by the end – on Europe, the poll tax and much more. On the whole, Heseltine agreed with Major's direction of travel. He also thought for a time that the Conservatives had a chance of winning the next election on the basis that governments normally win when the economy is performing well, as it was in the build-up to the 1997 election. Once Major made him deputy prime minister after the whacky Tory leadership contest in 1995, he and Major were bound together until the following election.

Heseltine's optimism about the Tories' chances in the 1997 election were fleetingly genuine, but they were also a noble attempt to keep up the morale of Major and others. His hopes were wholly misplaced and Labour won a historic landslide. The Conservatives secured a mere 165 seats, with many senior figures being defeated. They included Michael Portillo, who had doting fans on the Eurosceptic right of the party and who would not now be able to stand in the inevitable leadership contest. Major resigned immediately and was the only prime minister of modern times who looked relieved rather than tortured on departing Downing Street. He went off to watch cricket at the Oval. Heseltine was one of the few heavyweights who kept his seat.

Here was another potential route to the top for Heseltine. Some Tory MPs urged him to stand as the only candidate who had a hope of taking on a triumphant Tony Blair and turning around the Conservative Party's dire fortunes. He was tempted, but his doctor advised against it. So the heart attack in Venice blocked him from standing in the contest, and he returned to the backbenches. He was never on the frontbench again.

His doctor probably did him a favour. As a pro-European he would have been seeking to lead a party becoming much more anti-European than it had been in 1990 when Heseltine was a candidate. Thatcher intervened in the 1997 contest to endorse William Hague, who she regarded as closest to her politically. She could still cast a spell over parts of her party. Hague, a young, relatively inexperienced figure in the party, went on to win. Years later he would admit he was too young and inexperienced. Neither of those were issues for Heseltine. Nor was his health, as it turned out. He would be robust for decades to come.

Heseltine remained politically active, but he is not an example of a figure who exerted greater influence as a prime minister we never had than he would have done as prime minister. Out of office he was prominent, but he changed very little. From the sidelines he witnessed his party move in what he regarded as a dangerous direction.

———

Heseltine's commitment to Europe raises one of the more tantalizing 'what if' questions: if Heseltine had won the leadership contest in 1990, would he have made the Conservative Party more supportive of the European Union? Would he have neutralized the forces that facilitated the UK's historic departure many years later?

In 1990, the parliamentary Conservative Party had a significant section of Eurosceptics who cheered Thatcher on as she railed against the EU, but at this point there was not a single Conservative MP demanding that the UK should leave the EU. When Major sought to pass the legislation implementing the Maastricht Treaty, he faced one tough rebellion after another – the frustration of which caused him to call three of his own Cabinet members 'bastards'. The 'bastards' and the rebel MPs were tormenting Major, even though he had negotiated opt-outs from the Treaty in relation to the single currency and the social chapter. But they were still a distinct minority in the Cabinet and the parliamentary party. Occupying the top posts in the Cabinet were Clarke, Hurd and Heseltine, all pro-Europeans who were appointed without cries of anguish from Tory MPs. Most of the parliamentary party was content to vote for the Maastricht Treaty. Major's life was made hellish because he had a small majority, not because the majority of his MPs were against Europe.

Major's approach was to equivocate in his fruitless search for unity. He insisted he was not an unambiguous pro-European and constantly sought to appease the Eurosceptics, declaring an absurd 'beef war' on Europe, vetoing a proposed president of the Commission and pledging a referendum on the single currency. Far from being appeased, the rebels came back for more, a pattern that would be repeated in the future. David Cameron would do the same, giving Eurosceptics what they wanted in the forlorn hope of acquiescence. In the end, Cameron was forced to resign, having lost the Brexit referendum – offered to the Eurosceptics as the ultimate form of appeasement. Instead of being grateful, they destroyed him.

Heseltine would have been different to Major or Cameron if he had become prime minister. He was too unambiguously pro-European to equivocate or deliver different messages to different internal audiences. The intensity of his convictions would have given him no choice but to challenge what was then still a minority position in the Conservative Party: a Euroscepticism that had by no means become a full-scale opposition to the UK's membership of the EU.

The confrontation would have been bloody, but if Heseltine had won the 1992 election as Major did, he would have had a mandate and the personal authority to pursue his own agenda. Of all the prime ministers that have never been, Heseltine might have changed the course of British history. Under his leadership, he might have turned the Conservatives into a more pro-European party at a point when Labour had already moved in the same direction. Instead of being isolated internationally following the 2016 Brexit referendum, the UK might have become a bigger, more influential player in the EU. In some interviews following the result of the Brexit referendum, Heseltine was close to tears as he reflected on what had happened and how his party had brought it about. In the European elections held in 2019, while the UK was still an EU member, Heseltine announced he would be voting for the Liberal Democrats.

A few years earlier, during the coalition era, it had appeared as if Heseltine was making a stunning comeback. Cameron and George Osborne commissioned him to produce a report on how to secure economic growth, and he remained an economic adviser to the government. But his advocacy of decentralization, and his recognition that an active state had a legitimate role to play in economic policy, remained largely unfashionable in the Cameron/ Osborne era, even though both were admirers of Heseltine.

It was typical of Cameron to admire a stylish politician and seek to co-opt them in some form or another. In the end, though, Cameron could never escape his Thatcherite upbringing. While he hailed the likes of Heseltine and Tony Blair, he out-Thatchered Margaret Thatcher in his view of the state. Given this context, Heseltine's practical influence was limited. Subsequently, Theresa May sacked Heseltine from his various advisory roles after he rebelled in the Lords over her Brexit plans. Heseltine had never even met her when she dumped him.

———

As deputy prime minister, Heseltine occasionally stood in for John Major at Prime Minister's Questions. Quite a lot of the commentariat assumed he would be more commanding than Major, who was not a natural performer. But on the first such occasion, Heseltine's hands shook visibly. Perhaps the shaking had more to do with his acute self-awareness than nervousness – a sense that here he was at the despatch box during Prime Minister's Questions and yet he had failed to become prime minister. So near and yet so far.

Above left: Home Secretary Rab Butler and Prime Minister Harold Macmillan outside Number Ten, 6 April 1959.

Above right: Chancellor Rab Butler holding the 'budget box' on Budget Day, 14 April 1953.

Below: Roy Jenkins makes a speech from the platform at the Labour Party Conference in Blackpool, September 1970.

Roy Jenkins applauded by fellow Social Democrat Party member David Owen aft
Jenkins' speech on economic policy.

Barbara Castle, then Minister for Transport, speaking at a meeting in 1966.

ove left: Barbara Castle during her time as Secretary of State for Health and
cial Services, 1974.

ove right: Castle with Prime Minister Harold Wilson, 26 April 1975.

low: Denis Healey entertains a crowd while canvassing for the Labour Party in
uddersfield, 21 February 1987.

Above: Denis Healey, Neil Kinnock and Willy Brandt (former Chancellor of West Germany) raise a glass at a press conference, 1984.

Below left: Labour leader Neil Kinnock gives a speech at the 1985 party conference in Blackpool.

Below right: Michael Heseltine in Scotland during his bid to become leader of the Conservative Party, 16 November 1990.

Michael Heseltine speaking as Prime Minister Margaret Thatcher looks on,
0 December 1983.

hadow Chancellor Michael Portillo makes a point at the Conservative Party
onference in Bournemouth, 2000.

Above left: Michael Portillo at work circa 1995.

Above right: Ken Clarke during his time as Chancellor, 1994.

Below: Prime Minister John Major with Ken Clarke at the Conservative Party conference in Bournemouth, 1994.

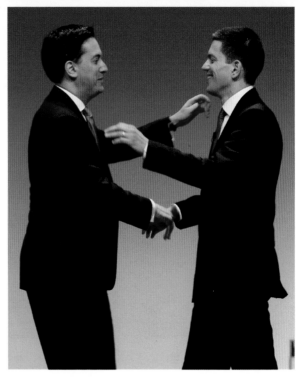

ove left: Ed and David Miliband outside Number Ten the day after
ordon Brown became prime minister, 28 June 2007.

ove right: The Miliband brothers embrace at the Labour Party conference in
anchester soon after Ed became Labour leader, 27 September 2010.

low: Foreign Secretary David Miliband and US Secretary of State Hillary Clinton
a joint press conference in Washington, DC, 29 July 2009.

Labour leader Jeremy Corbyn and former leader Ed Miliband campaigning in Doncaster in the run up to the EU Referendum, 27 May 2016.

Jeremy Corbyn flanked by two former prime ministers, Gordon Brown and Tony Blair, at the annual Remembrance Sunday memorial in London, 11 November 2018.

Heseltine might have been impressively presidential in his demeanour, but the UK has a party-based system and his party would not have him. They moved apart, even though he did not change the political philosophy that had made him one of the most formidable Conservative politicians of the post-war era. It was the party that had changed during the 1980s. Heseltine would have led his party in a fresh post-Thatcher direction. He was the genuine Conservative 'modernizer', not David Cameron and George Osborne. His failure to rise to the top suggests his party did not want to modernize.

Instead there was another Cabinet minister under Major who appeared to be moving with the ideological tide. While Heseltine was fighting losing battles, the committed Thatcherite Michael Portillo was capable of arousing freakish levels of idolatry from those who missed the Iron Lady. Thatcher herself saw Portillo as a Conservative leader, and he certainly had plenty of ambition. In the mid-1990s, he seemed to represent a glittering future for his party and government. But Portillo's ambition was never realized, and those who hailed him fervently were to turn on him with even greater passion.

7

MICHAEL PORTILLO

In the mid-1990s, the Conservative right yearned for a hero or a heroine. They had worshipped Margaret Thatcher and had never fully recovered from her fall; they still ached for an idol to replace her. The need was deeper when they looked at John Major twisting and turning, and saw only pathetic frailty. They recalled a romanticized version of the defiant Iron Lady and sought an equivalent titan to continue her heroic journey to a vaguely defined promised land. Partly in spite of himself, Michael Portillo became their chosen one.

From Portillo's perspective, the role of hero required a degree of reinvention. As a public figure in the 1980s he could be shy and introspective. Even in the 1990s he was as content listening to Wagner as he was being worshipped by Tory activists. Yet he also had a flamboyant side. He relished being a performer at the centre of the political stage, and he had no choice but to let that side take hold. His followers demanded a performance, and fleetingly he delivered for them.

Portillo had always possessed the performer's instinct. At school he wanted to be an actor and directed plays. At Cambridge he grew his hair and wore exuberant clothes. Working at the Conservative

Research Department, the starting place for the most ambitious in the party, he was 'the golden boy… He used to drive around in a black Citroen and eat steak and kidney pie at the pub. He was charming, clever and manipulative.'[1] By the time Portillo was forty, the biggest stars were paying homage to the enigmatic political star. His fortieth birthday party was held at the Spanish Club in Cavendish Square, where politicians and celebrities crammed in to hear Margaret Thatcher hail Portillo as a future leader. To ecstatic cheers, Thatcher declared: 'We brought you up, we expect great things of you, you will not disappoint us.'[2] This was May 1993, as the troubles whirling around Major and his government were intensifying. Those cheering assumed they were raising a glass to a future prime minister. Portillo was in the Cabinet and yet managed to convey a lofty distance from the darkness engulfing Major. Indeed, he was part of Major's dilemma, in that he was already seen by his admirers as a preferable leader.

From the annual party gathering in the autumn of 1992 onwards, fringe meetings at Conservative conferences were closer to those that had defined Labour in the 1970s and 1980s, as Michael Heseltine had discovered when he made the case for the Maastricht Treaty. In September 1992, the UK had been forced out of the Exchange Rate Mechanism, stirring an already forceful Euroscepticism. Portillo, on the other side to Heseltine, was the hero of the Eurosceptic fringe. The Bruges Group held events at the 1992 conference and those that followed, at which Portillo's pamphlets were on sale – along with Portillo posters and anthologies of Portillo's speeches. He aroused passion on the right as Tony Benn had done on the left.

The comparison is revealing. Benn was a natural orator and there was no need to wonder why he was adored: he held an audience like a magician. Portillo was less compelling as a speaker, but he looked good. There was an air of intrigue about his public personality that heightened the sense of anticipation at Tory fringe gatherings. He conveyed a sense that he knew more than his audience, but that they could rely on him to deal with the unrevealed challenges. Even so, he was not dazzling, and beyond the issue of Europe – where he connected with his fans' growing hostility – he did not have a great deal that was distinctive to say at this stage. The flip side to his flamboyance was his shyness. Benn was wholly at ease in any public forum. Portillo was less so.

The result was an occasional discordance between Portillo's projection as a public figure and the intensity of his followers' admiration. In 1995, Portillo addressed his party's conference as Defence Secretary. The speech was misjudged on every level, and even the Tory hawks in the audience were a bit taken aback. Periodically waving his hands above his head almost as a visual punctuation mark, Portillo delivered a speech of jingoistic aggression. He cited Nelson, Wellington and Churchill, and declared with a flourish: 'We are not ashamed to celebrate Britain's military prowess… We are Conservatives. We will speak of pride, of honour, of valour in battle and yes, of glory. The SAS have a famous motto: who dares, wins. We dare. We will win.' It was as if Portillo was leading his country into war, except that he was not. He was making a speech at a party conference.

In the same speech, he had declared a metaphorical war on the EU, but those 'battles' with Brussels had little to do with the SAS. He was talking nonsense, although the tone was in some respects ahead of its time. In the early decades of the twenty-first century, nationalist populism took hold in the UK and the US. Boris Johnson, with his sense of 'British exceptionalism', could happily have made such a speech and flourished.

But, in 1995, Portillo looked as if he was trying too hard to please. The act was clumsily transparent. The best potential leaders are able to hide their actorly skills and convey sincerity. Portillo conveyed little more than a hunger to lead, even if he was not as reliably extrovert on the public stage as Heseltine. John Major was sitting next to Portillo on the podium during the SAS speech. Major tried to look on approvingly, but he could not act either. He was unable to disguise his unease. John Redwood, the right-winger who had stood against Major that summer, when the prime minister briefly resigned as Conservative leader, was waiting to reflect on the day's events in a radio studio near the conference hall. He was not impressed with Portillo's speech, even though he shared Portillo's ideas on Europe and economic policy.[3] Not being a politician who even attempted to act, Redwood saw through the clunkiness of Portillo's performance.

There was too much excitement around Portillo in the mid-1990s – a danger for a potential leader. Excitement is difficult to control, even if anti-climactic disappointment lurks. A potential leader that excites is not even sure whether they want to dampen the anticipatory fervour. Portillo did not do so. Amid the frenzy, Michael Gove, then a journalist, published a biography with the flattering title *Michael Portillo: The Future of the Right.* This was fairly unusual. Portillo had only been in the Cabinet for a few years, and yet here was an influential Tory journalist deciding his life so far was worthy of a book, and one that implied the future was his. Glittering birthday celebrations, cheering crowds, the subject of a biography, over-the-top speeches: Portillo was becoming a ministerial rock star.

Yet arguably he was already passing his peak when Gove's book came out. Earlier in 1995, a few months before his speech at the party conference, Portillo was seen as a possible candidate in the Conservatives' bizarre leadership contest, challenging Major to become prime minister. That internal battle was the most vivid sign yet that the Conservative Party was changing from one that was relatively easy to lead – at least compared to the challenge of leading Labour – to one that was becoming far more insurrectionary. As part of the rebellious mood, some of Portillo's ardent supporters ostentatiously installed phone lines at an embryonic Westminster HQ. In the era before mobile phones, there could be no clearer statement: Portillo's aides were planning to make contact speedily with every Tory MP and influential activist. Yet Portillo's real intent was vague. He did not stop the phone lines from being installed, but he was wary of seizing the moment. He saw what had happened to Michael Heseltine when he stood against Thatcher in 1990. In the end, Portillo did not dare stand. Redwood stood against Major and lost. But Portillo's apparent hesitation did not dampen the ardour of his admirers, at least for a time.

Perhaps the failure to strike strengthened Portillo's desire to be seen as 'strong' subsequently, hence the SAS speech a few months later. The desire of potential prime ministers to be seen as strong tends to arise from a sense of weakness. Portillo was a textured politician: the mix of introspection and flamboyance – laced with a commitment to Thatcher and Thatcherism – was part of his appeal. But the nuanced layers of his political character were partly lost in an attempt to portray strength.

Portillo had qualities as a potential leader that had little to do with going to war with an SAS-style zeal. He had been a politics addict from an early age. His bedroom wall had posters of Harold Wilson, a sign that already he had a youthful interest in the art of politics. At Cambridge, he studied at Peterhouse under the supervision of the conservative historian Maurice Cowling. Although a wholly different personality and never a politician, Cowling had a Portillo-like capacity to entrance. Portillo spoke at Cowling's memorial service in October 2005, and revealed that as a student Portillo's heroes had been Harold Macmillan and President John F. Kennedy. When Cowling discovered this, his response had been direct: 'Kennedy was a liberal shit.'[4] Cowling guided Portillo towards the politics of Thatcherism, but by the time of Cowling's memorial, Portillo was closer to Macmillan's one-nation approach once more.

His political journey – beginning with a teenage admiration for Wilson, moving on to Kennedy and Macmillan as a student, switching to ardent Thatcherite as a minister and then back towards one-nation Toryism – shows that Portillo had an unusual capacity for reinvention. He was the David Bowie of politics. Each change was deeply felt, and yet was executed with a slight air of doubt. Famously, Portillo lost his seat in the 1997 election, a defeat that changed him and his party. He had assumed that, after the Conservatives' inevitable defeat, Major would resign and he would be the candidate of the right and win. He probably would have become leader in such circumstances, given that the parliamentary party looked rightwards when it elected William Hague. However, Portillo could not stand because he was not in the House of Commons. And for Portillo, the lost opportunity to become leader disturbed him least.

Portillo's defeat came to define the historic election night. *Were You Still Up for Portillo?* was the title of a book about the 1997 election, reflecting a gleeful joy that the right's hero had been humiliated. Portillo had not anticipated the tingling euphoria that his loss generated.

Part of the reason he lost was that he had become a caricature. His performance as the SAS-cheerleading Defence Secretary might have been wildly over the top, but this was how he had chosen to be seen. Deep down, he knew it was partly an act to woo party activists. As he performed preposterously, Portillo did not fully recognize that voters beyond his core support in the Conservative Party would not fall for his jingoistic projection in the same way.

The shock of defeat was deep and immediate. When Tony Benn lost his Bristol seat in the 1983 election, he carried on as before partly because that was who he was. He could not change, and did not consider doing so. Also, Benn's defeat did not trigger the same sense of nationwide excitement. Instead there was much reflection across the political spectrum about how a great parliamentarian would be missed. Benn was back in the Commons by 1984, having won a by-election in Chesterfield.

In contrast, Portillo responded to defeat by changing in ways that made him unrecognizable from the Defence Secretary who delivered the conference speech in 1995. Even by the time of the Conservative conference, a few months after the 1997 election, Portillo had begun his next political journey. No longer an MP, he was only a brief attendee at the conference in Blackpool. He was still capable of generating the same level of excitement among activists, but already he was showing signs of becoming a reluctant right-wing populist – moving away from the Portillo who had thrilled party members and alienated those who raised a glass or two when he lost his seat.

His speech at a fringe meeting in Blackpool in the autumn of 1997 is illuminating and worth analysing in detail. It shows a figure who recognized there must be change, but who was unsure what form it should take. Several prime ministers we never had wrestled with this dilemma. They include Neil Kinnock and Ed Miliband, but at least these two figures got over the first hurdle: they became leaders. Portillo never led, although at this point he still had ambition to do so. In his Blackpool speech, Portillo sought to reframe the recent past by arguing not that the long-serving Conservative government had been wrong, but that it had been misunderstood. This kind of assertion is often the beginning of a journey that leads to the conclusion that a government was wrong as well as misunderstood.

In the years that followed, Portillo moved close to such a dramatic judgement in some respects, but at this point he was only setting off on that path. He told his doting yet slightly confused audience:

We never argued that free markets were everything. We increased sharply spending on social security (not because of unemployment, but to help more people and pay higher benefits) and on health and education. We were determined to modernise our economy and to make Britain competitive, but we softened the effects of industrial change with policies to help the inner cities, with regional aid and training programmes for those without work. Ministers fought successfully to attract inward investment and to win contracts abroad. We were anything but laissez-faire.

There had been little of this from Portillo when the Conservatives were in power.

He then went on to make a point about projection: it was not the policies, but the presentation. Neil Kinnock had adopted this approach when contesting the Labour leadership in 1983. Here was Portillo's version: 'That common sense approach must not mask the fact that concern for others and magnanimity are important qualities of Conservatism, and the instinct for social cohesion transcends the nation.'

Significantly, Portillo then made a leap towards policy, always the most difficult element of the sequence when a potential leader wants his party to change. In the 1997 election, the Conservatives had passionately opposed the establishment of a Scottish Parliament. Since there had been a referendum in Scotland backing one, Portillo argued that the party must move on:

> The Conservative party is not an organisation for the turning back of clocks. For example, the Scots are to have a parliament. That is their choice, and we must accept it, unless and until experience leads them to a change of mood. Our interest and duty is clear. We must offer effective participation in the new chamber. We must ensure as best we can that the government of Scotland is carried on well.

Finally, he nodded towards a new, more liberal approach to single-parent households:

> We admire those many people who are doing an excellent job raising children on their own. The important thing is that people recognise the responsibility they have when they conceive children and do all they can to provide a warm, caring and balanced home for them. Our society has changed. For good or ill, many people nowadays do not marry and yet head stable families with children. For a younger generation, in particular, old taboos have given way to less judgemental attitudes to the span of human relationships. There remain many other people to whom the new norms seem all wrong. The Tory party is conservative and not given to political correctness. Still the party never rejects the world that is. Tolerance is a part of the Tory tradition. I believe that the Conservative party in its quiet way is as capable as any other of comprehending the diversity of human nature. That must go hand-in-hand with policies

that reinforce the responsibilities that every parent has for his or her children. That is an area of proper concern for politicians representing the legitimate interests of our society.[5]

These words do not seem especially contentious in the twenty-first century after a Conservative prime minister legislated in favour of gay marriage, several Conservative MPs have come out as gay, and quite a few are single parents. But in 1997, in front of Portillo's fan club, this was a message from an idol who was beginning to leave his followers behind.

His speech was also noteworthy for one omission. Europe was the raging issue that autumn, specifically whether or not the UK should join the single currency. But the Eurosceptics' great champion did not address the issue. Portillo had not changed his mind on the EU or the euro, but he had come to realize that the way he had framed his anti-European arguments – the nonsense about the SAS, the tub-thumping nationalism – had made him a hate figure in parts of the country. The loss of his seat had made a decisive impact on him.

Yet it's worth noting the limit of Portillo's change at this stage. Rather like David Cameron years later, he was making only a little noise about Europe (when he did address the issue), without challenging his party over the substance. Social liberalism, though a source of horror to some of his ageing admirers, was not that daring. This was not the equivalent of Kinnock taking on his party over its policies on Europe, defence and state ownership; the move was relatively tentative. The personal ambition, so intense between 1992 and 1997, was still there. By implication, Portillo was placing himself in the position of leader in exile, reflecting on why the party had lost and how it could win again. There was little reference to William Hague, the new leader, just as there had been virtually no praise of John Major in the addresses that had wowed the party in the mid-1990s.

Nonetheless, there was a Shakespearean quality to Portillo's intervention at the traumatized party's conference in Blackpool. He was Prince Hal alerting his old friends that he was moving on, that he had a duty and a desire to do so. The speech gave the Tory right wing little to cheer about. Some had gathered expecting to hear a rousing denunciation of Tony Blair's approach to the EU. They wanted to be told that Thatcher was the model and he was the new Thatcher waiting to return. Instead, the parts of the Thatcher legacy Portillo chose to cite were the inner-city initiatives driven by Michael Heseltine and the generous benefit payments, not the policies Thatcher chose to highlight when she herself looked back. He spoke of compassion and the need to respect single parents. On his way back to Blackpool station, Portillo bumped into three journalists from the *Guardian* and the *New Statesman*. He spent around twenty minutes talking with them about the need for the party to change and asked several questions about the new Blair government.[6] Portillo had leadership qualities, and he also had a curiosity about his opponents that went beyond the superficial.

He was back in the Commons by November 1999, easily winning a by-election in Kensington and Chelsea. By then he had made further strides away from the figure he'd been when he lost his Enfield seat more than two years earlier. That summer he had given an interview in which he confirmed that while at Cambridge he had homosexual affairs. The limited revelation was a sign that he wanted to clear the way for his return to frontline politics, but also that on returning he would be a different figure – one who had reflected on defeat, the success of Tony Blair, and his own sexuality. In an interview, he put it this way: 'I will say what I want to say. I had some homosexual experiences as a young person.'[7]

The first sentence was as important as the second; Portillo sought to control the narrative. There had been rumours for years about Portillo and gay affairs. Now he would say what he wanted to say. Yet Portillo failed to limit the media's attention solely to his own recollections. Within days, newspapers were reporting further memories of Portillo's past:

> Nigel Hart, who conducted an eight-year affair intermittently with Mr Portillo in the 1970s, accuses him of 'being somewhat economical with the actualité' for describing his homosexuality as youthful experimentation.
>
> His outburst will irritate Mr Portillo who is attempting a political comeback in the Kensington and Chelsea byelection. The former defence secretary said his homosexuality had ceased long before he was elected as an MP in 1984.
>
> 'When Michael came out in the [half-hearted] fashion... he tried to pave his way to power by a cowardly and misleadingly meagre version of what actually happened,' writes Mr Hart, who met Mr Portillo in 1971. Their affair ended when Mr Portillo decided to marry.[8]

Portillo's own disputed memories still bewildered some of his dedicated supporters. His hard-line Eurosceptic followers tended to be the more socially conservative activists. Some Tory MPs predicted that the revelation might prevent Portillo from being selected in Kensington, but this was a local party of more metropolitan types, dazzled by the Portillo enigma and not bothered about his sexuality. Portillo became their candidate and MP.

William Hague paid wary homage to Portillo's stardom, making him shadow chancellor on his return to the Commons. In his first Treasury Questions against the mighty Gordon

THE PRIME MINISTERS WE NEVER HAD

Brown, Portillo made two dramatic and headline-grabbing policy announcements: he declared that the party now supported the minimum wage and the independence of the Bank of England. Until then, the Conservative leadership had opposed both. This marked a further leap for Portillo. As early as that fringe meeting in the autumn of 1997, he had argued that the party should accept devolution having previously opposed it. Now he was endorsing two of the Labour government's biggest policy initiatives since the election.

In the two years that followed, Portillo did not disguise his disdain when Hague announced unfunded tax cuts. Hague called one of his more desperate propositions a 'tax guarantee', in which he pledged tax cuts without making clear how they would be funded. His shadow chancellor was not party to the guarantee, and feared with good cause that Hague was walking into a trap set by Blair and Brown. His unfunded tax cuts enabled Labour to argue that the Conservatives were the same old nasty party planning big reductions in spending. Although still a deep Eurosceptic, Portillo was uneasy about Hague's stridency on that issue too.

Evidently, the new-look Portillo was in a different place to Hague. And some of Hague's close advisers viewed Portillo with outright suspicion. Hague's devoted press secretary, Amanda Platell, was especially uneasy, sensing potential leadership bids in most of Portillo's utterances. Another pattern was forming: leaders did not trust Portillo. Major assumed a knife might be inserted into his back at any moment. He was more worried about the scheming ambition of Portillo than he was about Michael Heseltine's still-unfulfilled hopes.

Major had cause for concern. Hague had less justification to be nervy, as far as his near-Buddhist calm could have been undermined by nerves. Portillo was not a fan of Hague's leadership, but he was not ready to strike and did not consider doing so in the build-up to the 2001 election. The wariness of leaders was both flattering and problematic for Portillo. On one level, their suspicions showed that he was seen as a potential leader. On another, Portillo was generating multi-layered degrees of mistrust – more so than Heseltine had done at his peak.

The distrust went further: his supporters no longer felt they knew what he was up to. Potential leaders become leaders if they are trusted by their parties and can build up a big tent of enthusiastic support. In the 1990s, Portillo had support from the right. By 2001, the right was looking for a new candidate while Portillo was being hailed as a Tory modernizer who had left the right behind. He had attracted interest from both wings of the party, but never from the two sides at the same time.

Nonetheless, after the Conservatives had been beaten in the 2001 election – another landslide defeat – Hague resigned immediately and Portillo was favourite to become the new leader. The Conservatives had thus staged three contests in six years. Lots of leadership contests are a symptom of a party in deep crisis, unclear about direction and who might be in a position to take them to an unspecified destination. They are almost a form of therapy for MPs who sense they are about to lose power or are far from returning to government.

Portillo's glitzy and yet tentative candidacy in 2001 reflected the uncertainties within both the Conservative Party and himself. Here, finally, he was battling for the leadership, after years of speculation. In the end, he had made no highly charged attempt to remove a sitting leader, even if Major and Hague had feared he would. Instead, wholly legitimately, he put his name forward when a vacancy arose. Yet from the beginning he did not appear up for the fight or even sure of what form the fight would take. For all the speculation around him, this was the only leadership contest he fought. Heseltine also only fought one such campaign. Quite a lot of those viewed as potential leaders rarely stand in leadership contests, or they do not stand in many. Ken Clarke is an exception to this rule.

The launch of Portillo's campaign was away from the usual Westminster locations, staged instead at a trendy restaurant near Piccadilly Circus. At first he appeared to speak with Blair-like candour about the state of his party: 'Our party has suffered two stunning defeats and I believe our party is now in grave peril, in grave danger of what may happen next… The duty that falls upon those of us at the top of the Conservative party is that we rebuild the party that we pass on to future generations.'

There were few hints of what that might mean in terms of a policy agenda beyond now-familiar nods towards social liberalism, sincerely felt and unavoidable in the light of his revelation a few years earlier about gay relationships:

I am a person of strong views and firm positions. I have had my ups and downs, I have lived my life and I have made mistakes. In the process I have learnt to respect the sincerity of those who hold different views, and to learn that we do not live in a world of black and white. I now believe that strong opinions gain in strength if they are put forward with reason, moderation and tolerance for opposing views. The Conservative Party that I would like to lead would extend a welcome to everyone living in Britain. We will be a party in favour of things rather than against things and in favour of people rather than against them. Every human being is entitled to equal respect. In particular as Conservatives we should celebrate diversity, not be suspicious of it.[9]

In fairness to Portillo, Cameron did not say much more when he affected to be a modernizing candidate in his successful 2005 leadership contest. The difference was that Cameron had come from nowhere. He appeared 'new' and had made no enemies in the party. Cameron managed to create a big internal tent by claiming to be progressive while also reassuring hard-line Eurosceptics that he would take Conservative MEPs out of the centre-right grouping of the European Parliament. He also managed to convince an admittedly sympathetic media that he was serious about changing his party. Even some BBC correspondents referred to Cameron as a 'modernizer' and a 'centrist', as if these terms were objective and beyond dispute when applied to his leadership. In the end, Cameron's easy ride with parts of the media led to his doom: he held a Brexit referendum he thought he would win.

In 2001, Portillo did not get an easy ride. He had been the star of the Thatcherites in the 1990s, and had courted the various Thatcherite groups in the party. He had been the Defence Secretary of proud, jingoistic machismo. He had been the Eurosceptic who proclaimed his hostility towards the European Union. Now he was the contemplative reformer, urging fellow Conservatives to be more emollient and open. Like the more fresh-faced Cameron after 2005, Portillo was still a Eurosceptic and broadly supported Thatcherite economic policies, but he was less keen to focus on Europe and wanted to stress how the party must change to reflect modern and progressive attitudes. But the move from one Portillo to the next, although in some ways subtle and nuanced, was too much for his old followers. Thatcher disowned him, urging her party in the 2001 contest to back Iain Duncan Smith, a backbench rebel against the Maastricht Treaty who was more than content to talk about Europe during the campaign in a way that Portillo no longer did.

Enjoying campaigns is a test of leadership, as a leader faces the unavoidable prospect of several campaigns. Leaders that find the scrutiny of campaigns a problem are inevitably doomed. He had a sensitive streak that was an awkward counter to his ambition. The years between 1997 and 2001 had been draining for him – losing his seat to the sound of jubilant cheers, revealing his gay affairs as a way of clearing the ground for a return to politics, being disowned by Thatcher and others as he embarked on the next phase of his political journey – and he must have wondered what would happen next in terms of stressful twists and turns, not wholly sure if he was up for nine or ten years as leader of the Opposition, the time it would take to overturn Labour's latest landslide majority.

Portillo was not that good a political actor, and he could not disguise his doubts. In the leadership contest he got through to the third ballot of MPs, but in that one he came last, behind Duncan Smith and Ken Clarke. On the same day, he announced he would be leaving front-line politics, and spent that evening at the opera.

———

Rab Butler had a greater number of chances of becoming Tory prime minister than Michael Portillo did. Nonetheless, there are more lessons arising from Portillo's failure to make it to the very top than there are to be found in Butler's almost-stratospheric political career.

In the mid-1990s, when quite a lot of Portillo's party and an influential section of the media hoped he would be a prime minister, there was too much popstar-like hysteria around him. There was a gap between the drooling fandom and the ambivalence of his personality. Overexcitement can lead to disillusionment. By the time he stood for the leadership, Portillo had disappointed too many of those who had inflated hopes of him.

Most leaders do not generate idolatry in advance. Some do when they become leader, but at that point they have cleared a hurdle to becoming prime minister. Margaret Thatcher and Tony Blair both triggered forms of idolatry in their different ways, but only after they had secured the leadership of their respective parties. Before they were leaders, they were viewed with varying degrees of interest, wariness, admiration and respect – all more controllable emotions.

To add to the overwrought atmosphere, Portillo was a bad judge of character. One of his advisers in the mid-1990s, David Hart, was a curious character: a right-wing libertarian who was involved in various projects close to Thatcher. Hart had some input in Portillo's misjudged SAS speech. He encouraged Portillo to be an aggressive public character, when even at his most ambitious Portillo was a more complex figure. During the Major era, if the pro-European chancellor, Ken Clarke, uttered any words on Europe, Hart phoned the BBC political correspondent, Nick Jones. Hart and Jones had met during the miners' strike in the 1980s, when Hart had found a role working informally for Thatcher. Jones was the BBC's tireless Labour correspondent, reporting every second of the strike and its consequences. Hart renewed contact when Jones became political correspondent, alerting him that Portillo could be doorstepped with TV cameras in response to any utterances about Europe from Clarke. Portillo would then deliver a soundbite that implicitly challenged Clarke. The dance on TV bulletins might have fleetingly delighted the Tory right, but it engendered widespread suspicion too – that Portillo was not a team player. These impressions are not a fruitful context in which to become a leader.

Prime ministers tend to know who they are as public figures – or they can at least pretend that they do. David Cameron was as confused as Portillo but he was a better actor. Other prime ministers gave the impression of being fully developed public figures. Some even were fully developed. Portillo was never wholly sure who he was as a politician, and could not pretend that he was.

Although he reflected later that there was not a single day that passed when he did not observe and envy the prime minister at the time, Portillo seemed more content in his post-politics career.[10] The BBC came to his rescue, giving him some dream series on travel, trains and politics. He became a regular pundit on the BBC's current affairs programme *The Week*, in which he shared a sofa with the left-wing MP Diane Abbott. Both were capable of being cold with those they were wary of. On the sofa they exuded an unexpected mutual warmth, based partly on the fact that in their youth they had gone to neighbouring schools and had taken part in the same school plays. No longer even a member of the Conservative Party, Portillo could surprise with his observations – sometimes critical and at other times supportive of his former colleagues. At a time when politics and current affairs coverage was becoming increasingly dull and formulaic, the discussions involving Portillo were the exception. He was no longer bound to stick to a single line and, as a result, he was far more interesting than he had been in the mid-1990s. Younger audiences who watched his travel programmes would only have had a vague idea of the Defence Secretary Portillo, the one idolized by some and loathed by others.

Perhaps this later Portillo, the final metamorphosis, would have had more chance of being prime minister in the sense that he had wider appeal. But he was not ready in the early to mid-1990s. And the Conservative Party then was not ready to revere the character

Portillo became either. By the time he discovered the virtues of being a more mellow public figure, the Tory Party had turned away and he had moved on from it too.

———

Even at the height of the idolatry of Portillo, he was nowhere near the most popular minister in John Major's government. The chancellor, Ken Clarke, was way ahead of anyone else. Polls suggested the wider electorate approved of Clarke, while Portillo at his peak appealed to a narrower section of Tory support. As Major struggled to lead, there was persistent speculation that Clarke might become prime minister. When the Conservatives were in opposition, the speculation intensified.

Clarke was perceived as the potential leader who could make the Conservatives an electoral force once more. Even more committed to politics than Heseltine and Portillo, and just as ambitious, he still never became prime minister.

8

KEN CLARKE

When looking back on his long political career, Ken Clarke would often joke that he had acquired a favourite hobby: fighting and losing Conservative leadership contests. The joke conveyed self-deprecation, while also highlighting his insatiable desire to be leader of the Conservative Party. Nothing could stop him from trying when the opportunity arose.

All the chances for Clarke opened up relatively late in his stellar career. He fought three leadership elections between 1997 and 2005, a relatively short time span. Each time he announced his candidacy there was a wave of excitement in the media. Would this change the contest? Might he win? How would a Clarke victory change the dynamic of British politics? Clarke would make a bit of a splash and then lose.

The defeats revealed much about Clarke and his party. The campaign polls always suggested that the former Cabinet minister was the most popular candidate with the wider electorate. Tony Blair was prime minister at the time the three leadership contests took place. He and his senior advisers watched the Conservatives obsessively, their own party having lost so many elections before winning big in 1997. They agreed that the candidate they feared most was Clarke, and they were relieved each time he was defeated. The Conservative Party kept rejecting the chance to elect a leader who was popular, knew how to govern, and who worried a Labour prime minister who had won landslide majorities.

The Conservatives were in opposition when Clarke pursued his 'hobby', but such was his distinct longevity he had also been seen as a possible prime minister while the party was still in power. He was close to the top of government for a long time. Clarke's range of ministerial posts was up there with that of Rab Butler, the original prime minister we never had. His approach to governing had echoes of Butler too.[1] Clarke was a determined reformer in the four Cabinet posts he held under Margaret Thatcher and John Major. He went on to secure a fifth Cabinet post in the coalition when David Cameron made him Justice Secretary, but by then his chances of becoming prime minister were nil. Cameron liked having senior ministers who had purged themselves of all further personal ambition. William Hague was his Foreign Secretary, a wholly reliable ally in that Hague had lost all interest in leadership and was even ambiguous about his return to a senior post in Cameron's team. Clarke had given up all hope of being leader or going near another leadership contest by the time he served in Cameron's Cabinet.

But Clarke had been hugely ambitious under Thatcher and Major, in relation to both his policy and his hopes to become leader at some point. His first significant Cabinet post was as Health Secretary, a difficult position for an ambitious Conservative politician. Thatcher gave him the brief in 1988 when she was still on a high from winning a third election victory the year before. Yet her third-term honeymoon was short. By 1988, she was in trouble over contentious policies such as the poll tax and the direction of her public service reforms. She sensed Clarke was a big enough bruiser to pioneer changes to the NHS without wrecking himself or her government. One of her previous favourites, John Moore, had never recovered from his spell as Health Secretary. Until Moore's failure to make a mark, he had been seen as one of the Cabinet's stars – at least by Thatcher, who was not an especially good judge of character. She was more perceptive on some levels about Clarke. She respected him, and he was robust enough to deliver for her.

Clarke did not always deliver what Thatcher had originally wanted when he was part of her Cabinet, and yet he still managed to please her, making a positive impression without trying particularly hard to do so. This was in striking contrast to some of Clarke's colleagues, who tried around the clock to please Thatcher and failed. Clarke was wholly comfortable in his own skin, and one of the few ministers who were not remotely intimidated by her. She respected his casual, unaffected toughness.

As far as she was concerned, Clarke rose to the demands of being Health Secretary even though the reforms he pursued were not the ones she had been exploring with the unassertive Moore. She was interested in some form of US-style insurance policy to pay for additional funding. Clarke was confident enough to resist any move in that direction. Instead, he was the first of several Health Secretaries to seek the introduction of an internal market within the NHS, pioneering the concept of self-governing taxpayer-funded NHS trusts with control over their own budgets and independence from regional health authorities. Clarke also proposed that doctors be given the option to become 'GP fundholders', giving local practices control of their own budgets in the belief that they would purchase the most effective services for their patients. Instead of doctors automatically sending patients to the nearest hospital, the patients would be able to choose where they were treated. In this way, the money would follow the patient, and the most efficient hospitals would receive the greatest funding.

All hell broke loose within parts of the NHS as Clarke made his moves. He almost relished the confrontations with the British Medical Association and other unions. Interviewers arrived at his office at the height of the clashes to find him relaxed, smoking a cigar and determined to prevail. This capacity for relaxation when the pressure was intense was both a qualification for leadership and a flaw. Clarke was seemingly bulletproof in his unfazed political personality, but a little too relaxed in his self-confidence.

Clarke's reforms, implemented in limited ways when he was Health Secretary, became a model for future administrations. After his second election victory in 2001, Tony Blair sought to widen and deepen the internal market, along with expanding the theoretical freedom of the more reliable hospitals to be in charge of their own budgets. To a greater extent than Clarke, Blair sought to empower the patient to choose where they wanted to be treated and to expand the role of the private sector.

In a competitive field, it was Blair's focus on the Clarke model that triggered the deepest tensions over policy with his chancellor, Gordon Brown. Brown's analysis exposed the limits of Clarke's vision. As the Labour chancellor argued, there were severe limits to the effectiveness of a 'market' in a taxpayer-funded NHS where services were delivered free of charge. For patients to have genuine choice, there would need to be a significant surplus of hospital places. If there were such a surplus, taxpayers and their newspapers would start to protest about wasted resources. If a self-governing hospital went bust, the government would have to intervene to prevent it from closing. As a result, financial profligacy would not be punished as it would be in a less artificial market. If efficient hospitals were rewarded with more funding, the less efficient ones were likely to become even more hopeless as their funding was cut. Brown recognized there was a need for cooperation between hospitals as well as focused coordination.

Clarke began a fashion for fragmentation within the NHS – moves that ultimately led to more costly and bewildering bureaucracy. Under Cameron, a prime minister more Thatcherite than Thatcher in some senses, the fragmentation model continued to a point where subsequent Tory Health Secretaries despaired about what one of them, Matt Hancock, called the 'atomization of the NHS'.[2] Clarke's path led to a situation where many agencies were theoretically responsible, but none were actually accountable.

Still, as a reforming Health Secretary under a dominant prime minister he had passed some early tests of leadership. He showed strength in sticking to his reforms. At times, Thatcher – supposedly an Iron Lady – looked on nervously. Clarke more than kept calm; he was more iron-like than Thatcher. He enjoyed himself, even as his reforms triggered protest.

Voters approved of him as a public personality. He was too avuncular to dislike. Other ministers might have cracked under the pressure; Clarke was more likely to head off to Ronnie Scott's for some late-night jazz than suffer a bout of nocturnal introspection. He was fearless in a way that was almost damaging: he saw no reason to be anxious even though sometimes in his career there was much cause for concern.

Thatcher was impressed enough to make Clarke Education Secretary, a sideways move but a significant one. This was the other department where she sought contentious reforms. His style was as determinedly unapologetic as it had been at the Health

Department. He began the process that led to the creation of the agency for school inspections, Ofsted. In doing so he sought the advice of the controversial Chris Woodhead, who became the first head of Ofsted. Woodhead was an advocate of so-called traditional teaching methods, and railed against the progressive teaching that began in the 1960s. Like Thatcher, Clarke was a fan of grammar schools and traditional teaching. He briefed that he was bringing back grammar schools stealthily. He called them 'grant-maintained schools', but struggled to introduce many of them. Councils resisted the removal of their control over local schools, and those that challenged Clarke included many local authorities ruled by Conservatives. In spite of considerable opposition, however, Clarke did manage to remove further education and sixth-form colleges from the power of local authorities.

In doing so, his policies were again a partial model for Blair and Cameron. Blair's 'city academies' had some similarities to grant-maintained schools – accountable to central government rather than councils. The expansion of so-called free schools intensified when Michael Gove and his adviser Dominic Cummings were at the Department of Education, during the early years of the coalition government. Their focus on a return to testing and traditional teaching methods earned them a fan in Clarke. He hailed Gove as one of the successes of the coalition era. This was not surprising, as Gove was carrying on where Clarke had left off in the final phase of Thatcher's rule and in the early days of John Major.

The consequences of Gove's attempts to restructure schools were chaotic and contradictory. To which bodies would the self-governing schools be accountable? If local authorities had no role, would the intermediating agencies, ultimately accountable to the distant Education Secretary, be any more effective? Blair and

Cameron liked to hail 'choice' for pupils. But what if the best school in a local area was full because demand was high? Could all parents 'choose' this oversubscribed school? If they could, the school would cease to be so popular because it would quickly become far too big. If they could not, their choice was extremely limited. Gove and Cummings hailed 'freedom' while being prescriptive about what should be taught. Supposedly 'free' teachers were being instructed from the centre as to what they should teach most hours of the day.

For decades, some complacently neglectful local authorities had needed shaking up in relation to schools and other services. The solution was to do the shaking rather than to bypass them entirely. Clarke instigated the bypassing and education became increasingly atomized, just like the NHS. Compared with Clarke, Thatcher had been far more cautious as Education Secretary.

The consequences of Clarke's embryonic NHS reforms only became fully clear as Boris Johnson's government struggled to respond to the pandemic that erupted early in 2020. Who was in charge? No one was entirely sure, including Johnson. In the spring of 2021, the Conservative government published proposals to establish clearer lines of centralized control and command in the NHS, a belated reaction to the fashion for atomization.

In the late 1980s and beyond, Clarke's reforms were widely supported in the Conservative Party. The Conservative-supporting newspapers were even keener. *The Times* in particular often hailed 'reform' while railing against increases in public spending. Tory MPs and the influential newspapers tended to take Clarke's broad view that, if they were 'reformed', public services could manage without the level of funding provided in other equivalent countries. Such support was welcome for an ambitious minister but was not the consequence of crude calculation on his part. Clarke genuinely believed in what he was doing; he was a figure of integrity, and would never do what he did not believe in. Sadly, this principled stance proved to be a fatal disqualification for leadership when the time came for him to make a move to lead his party.

Long before he stood in a leadership contest, Clarke had played a part in removing a leader. He was Education Secretary in the autumn of 1990 when Thatcher fell from power. As Thatcher made only limited headway in the first round of the Conservative leadership contest, Clarke did what he felt he had to do: he told her she would not win and that she should resign immediately rather than face further humiliation. Other Cabinet ministers delivered similar messages to her and left their meeting in tears. But Clarke was not lachrymose. He was never sentimental, and he recognized that politics could be a cruel vocation. The term 'ruthless' does not quite fit Clarke, because he did not plot excessively or plan to be brutal. He did what he felt to be right. Like Denis Healey, he was tough but not a schemer. Yet Clarke did not suffer guilt if colleagues fell by the wayside as a result of him pursuing what he considered to be the correct course. He was not reflective or introspective. Victims licked their wounds, and as they did so he was once again more likely to head for Ronnie Scott's or to light another cigar over a glass of good wine than to contemplate his culpability.

Clarke in one sense passed another test of leadership in his candid exchange with Thatcher in November 1990. Those who tell senior figures what they want to hear are usually nowhere near strong enough to become a leader. Edward Heath acquired some additional steeliness when, as the party's chief whip, he told Rab Butler that Harold Macmillan was the chosen one to be the next prime minister in 1957. Clarke did not tell Thatcher what she wanted to hear. She announced her resignation the next morning.

Clarke's role in Thatcher's downfall was one of the reasons he was widely perceived as a political figure far removed from Thatcherism. That perception was wrong. His public service reforms sometimes went further than she would have dared to go. Later, he would demonstrate that his approach to the economy was fairly close to hers. Followers of Thatcher were to block him becoming leader when he began his hobby of standing in leadership contests. In a sense, they were blocking an ideological soulmate who also had wide electoral appeal.

———

Thatcher's successor, John Major, was an admirer of Clarke's. At first, Major kept him on as Education Secretary, but after his election win in 1992, Major promoted Clarke to the Home Office. As Home Secretary, Clarke proved to be even more brutal than he had been when he was one of many who were instrumental in the fall of Thatcher. The brutality took a precise from. By early 1992, he had established himself as one of the government's most effective media performers. The broadcasting studio was his favourite stage, and no interviewer was able to lay a glove on him at any point in his Cabinet career. He was funny, direct, and gave the appearance of being candid even when he wasn't. Sometimes his apparent candour landed the government in trouble, but he would step aside from any fleeting furore and carry on as if nothing had happened. His confidence was unshakeable.

By September 1992, Major's government was in deep trouble. The UK had fallen out of the Exchange Rate Mechanism in a humiliating manner. Major got quite a lot of the blame, but unfairly the chancellor, Norman Lamont, was seen as most responsible.

Lamont became a target for Conservative-supporting newspapers even though personally he was a Eurosceptic who saw opportunities in the UK's departure from the ERM. Lamont agreed with the Eurosceptic newspapers that were attacking him.

This is what happens in British politics. We choose to see what we want to see and not what is happening in front of our eyes. In the Eurosceptic newspapers, the Eurosceptic Lamont became the villain. For a time at least, the pro-European Clarke's stock rose.

As the media attacks intensified, Lamont lost what little self-confidence he'd had to begin with. He never did many interviews when he was chancellor and he responded to the post-ERM onslaught by hiding away from the broadcast studios. This was a mistake on his part. Becoming ghostly does not enhance the reputation of a chancellor, especially when there is economic turmoil. When he did give interviews, he had the potential to be a good interviewee. A relaxed Lamont was witty and authoritative. After he had ceased to be a minister, he was a regular guest on most of the current affairs programmes. But his few public appearances as chancellor after the ERM saga were mocked or criticized, discouraging him from adopting a higher profile. Lamont was a friend of the columnist Woodrow Wyatt, who wrote for Rupert Murdoch's newspapers. Wyatt's highly readable diaries are punctuated with pleas from Lamont that he use his influence to reduce the hostility. Wyatt failed in this particular mission and the highly sensitive Lamont remained a media target. Unsurprisingly, Lamont became even warier and ineffective as a performer.

Days after delivering his autumn statement in 1991, Lamont gave a rare interview to the BBC's Jonathan Dimbleby. This is how the exchange opened:

Jonathan Dimbleby: Chancellor, the great issue now is confidence, not only in your policies but in you yourself – you'd accept that?

Norman Lamont: I accept that confidence is a vital ingredient for the progress of the economy.

JD: And do you accept that that is confidence both in your policies and in you as Chancellor?

NL: The two go together.

JD: If one falls, the other falls.

NL: Why don't we get on with the interview?[3]

Lamont was not naturally grumpy, but he had become so. The rest of the interview was as bad-tempered. Lamont more or less disappeared again afterwards.

In contrast, Clarke was flourishing. Without a moment's hesitation, he became the government's main interviewee on economic matters. Often a BBC *Today* programme presenter would introduce an item with a cue along these lines: 'Unemployment is rising, interest rates are still high and its expected that more significant job losses will be announced this week… joining me is the Home Secretary, Ken Clarke.'

Attentive listeners might easily come up with an image of a terrified Lamont incarcerated somewhere in the Treasury, fearful of uttering a word. His replacement, the exuberant Clarke, would dance around the issues as if he were the guest at the best party in London. In one interview, he admitted the government was in a 'deep hole' after losing a by-election in Newbury.[4] On a visit to the constituency, Lamont had declared '*Je ne regrette rien*.' He was making a joke, but Lamont was not allowed to make jokes. His Edith Piaf quote made front-page news and was regarded, unfairly, as a 'gaffe'.

Clarke's tone in interviews about the economy was robust but good-humoured. In effect, he would argue with force that economic problems were present but the government was addressing them and the country would get through this to better times, while Labour did not know what they were talking about. He was applying to be the next chancellor in the most public way possible. Clarke and Lamont were old friends, having been students at Cambridge together. Again, without consciously being ruthless, Clarke put several nails in the coffin of Lamont's political career. That is what potential leaders have to do. They cannot agonize about the consequences of their actions on colleagues and friends. They have to go for it. Clarke did so, and in this instance he was triumphant.

An increasingly fraught Major sacked Lamont and replaced him with Clarke. Lamont felt betrayed by the prime minister. He had helped to organize Major's leadership campaign in 1990 and this was his reward. Clarke had backed Douglas Hurd. In Lamont's resignation speech, he argued that the government was 'in office but not in power'.[5] By then, former Conservative senior ministers were becoming specialists in resignation speeches that caused trouble. Lamont's was nowhere near as devastating as Geoffrey Howe's had been, but it did set the stage for Major's final years in Number Ten. As his small majority faded away, rebels became more numerous and Major struggled to exert power, twisting and turning to remain in office. Lamont's words reverberated while the government headed towards its defeat in 1997. It was during this period that Clarke was seen as a possible next prime minister, a replacement for the increasingly besieged Major.

Not that Major regretted making the switch. Clarke flourished in his new role, as he tended to do in whatever post he was given. There was irony in his success as chancellor. The UK economy was picking up outside the ERM. Clarke had been one of the most passionate advocates of ERM membership and continued supporting the cause. He argued that the UK joined at the wrong time and at the wrong rate, but that was a different issue to whether its membership was fundamentally wrong. He believed with unyielding conviction that it was not.

Apart from the tricky issue of Europe, Clarke's approach to economic policy was Thatcherite. Public services were creaking. The NHS in particular was becoming better known for its long waiting lists than the idealism that brought it into being. But it still retained huge support, to the bewilderment of some Conservative MPs. The image of an elderly patient waiting on a trolley in some bleak corridor for eternal hours was becoming familiar and politically awkward for Major's tottering government. Public transport was also an increasingly haphazard experience – underfunded and suffering from the familiar fragmentation that had become the fashion for public services. When some of London's theatres took bookings, their operators were instructed to tell callers that they must leave extra time to get to the venue, such were the delays imposed by unreliable transport. These were small examples of a repetitive theme: the growing private affluence of some, and the public squalor that had an impact on all voters.

Clarke's solution was like Thatcher's in the 1980s. On the whole, he regarded public spending as a problem rather than a means to boost the economy and the UK's low rates of productivity. Obscured by the highly charged debates, Clarke was a passionate supporter of the Maastricht Treaty as originally conceived and the single currency that arose from it. The treaty aimed to impose rigid public spending and borrowing limits on each member state. Later, when there were signs of chronic instability in the Eurozone,

Clarke blamed it on the failure of the participating governments to enforce the Maastricht criteria. If such limits had been applied to the likes of Italy and Greece, their economies would have ceased to function and they would have been forced out of the euro. But the fun-loving Clarke was a puritan in relation to public spending. One of the many ironies of the UK's debate about Europe was that Maastricht was an endorsement of Thatcherite economics – a reason why Clarke was a passionate advocate. In theory, those countries that hoped to join the single currency had to adhere to strict fiscal rules – one of the propositions in the Maastricht Treaty – including tough constraints on borrowing. As chancellor, he applied his own Maastricht criteria to reduce the UK's deficit. In this he was more disciplined than the economically orthodox rulers of Germany. By being tough on public spending and borrowing, Clarke managed to stabilize the UK economy after the ERM crisis. But he pulled this off by largely ignoring the plight of public services. A chancellor can perform miracles with a deficit if they choose not to spend what is so obviously required.

Although they got on well and largely agreed on economic policy, Major was a victim of Clarke's stringency. Major's distinctive innovation had been to propose a Citizen's Charter, theoretically empowering users of public services to demand higher levels of delivery. The Charter became much derided, but the idea was a good one in theory at a time when users of services felt hopelessly disempowered. Under the Charter, for the first time NHS patients were supposed to have guaranteed time limits for all consultations and some treatments. The utilities – including gas and electricity – were also expected to offer and keep appointments for home visits, as part of the attempt to put consumers' rights first. Compensation was in theory to be made available for some delayed and cancelled trains. But there was inadequate funding to make the Charter work effectively. Citizens filled in forms of protest and little improved. Clarke's priority was to balance the books.

Despite all this, Clarke was perceived as one of the most successful chancellors of modern times. After the darkness of 1992, he left an economy that was seemingly booming by 1997. By some margin, he was the most popular minister in the government – so much so that speculation Clarke might replace Major was rife from 1995 onwards, even after Major triggered a leadership contest that he went on to win. During Clarke's speech to the 1996 Conservative party conference, he felt the need to show his support for the prime minister by declaring, 'any enemy of John Major is an enemy of mine'. In the usual awkwardly choreographed way, the two of them appeared together onstage at the end of the speech to symbolize mutual support.

The words were typical of Clarke. They appeared to be supportive of Major while placing the chancellor in the stronger role, even though Clarke was not actively trying to appear stronger. He meant what he said. He liked Major, worked well with him and the two agreed on most issues. Was he going to challenge Major? What would trigger such a challenge? While Major was prime minister and wished to remain in the post, there was no way Clarke could remove him. Political journalists saw the relationship differently. This was the era when Clarke was at his peak. Those who accompanied Major and Clarke on flights to international conferences reported back that it was the chancellor who held the attention of journalists during exchanges on the plane. He was more compelling and charismatic than the fragile and insecure prime minister.

Major and Clarke had one major disagreement. Inevitably, the issue was Europe. Fearing further internal eruptions, Major wanted to pledge a referendum before the government joined the single currency. At this time, the euro was the dominant issue in British politics, wreaking havoc across the political spectrum. At first Clarke resisted. With good cause, he loathed referendums, recognizing them to be a calamitous method for making complex decisions. He also knew the offer was the equivalent of a block on the UK joining the euro. No prime minister would dare to hold the referendum if they feared defeat.

This proved to be the case. Even though Tony Blair also pledged a referendum on the euro, it never happened: the referendum was too big an obstacle, although the prospect of a plebiscite was by no means the only hurdle in the New Labour era.

Clarke succumbed in the end because Major was adamant that only by making such a pledge could he keep his party together in the build-up to the 1997 election. This is the main role of referendum pledges in the UK, though their efficacy is only temporary. Major secured a moment's calm when he made the pledge. But soon enough, the Eurosceptics in his parliamentary party and in the media resumed their role of making his life difficult. They took the referendum and began to make other demands. Clarke had warned Major that the huge concession would only paper over the cracks. David Cameron should have taken note, but chose instead to appease with a referendum on the even bigger issue of the UK's membership of the EU.

A pattern was forming: the Eurosceptics prevailed over Clarke, even when he was a mighty chancellor at the height of his popularity. The fundamental problem was that he was a pro-European in a party growing increasingly hostile to Europe. There was no squaring of this circle. If a potential leader is at odds with their party on an issue of towering significance, leadership becomes impossible. For all the focus on leaders in the media, British politics is party-based. A titan like Clarke will not become leader or prime minister if they are too much at odds with their party, though this is not the fault of party members or the titan that yearns to lead. Understandably, activists are bound to support candidates they agree with on the major issues. Similarly, a principled figure like Clarke won't switch their views purely to win. There is no way round this. The only solution is for the party not to elect the titan.

In the 1997 leadership contest, Clarke tried to square the circle by forming a pact with John Redwood, the right-wing Eurosceptic who had stood against Major in the 1995 battle when Major resigned as party leader while remaining prime minister, a contortion that neatly illuminated the scale of the party's existential crisis. The Clarke/Redwood alliance was not as preposterous as it seemed at the time. On most issues, Clarke and Redwood were at one. Both were fiscal conservatives. Both assumed the key to improved public services was reform rather than increased public spending.

Perceptions of Clarke were partly distorted by his political personality. He was so fun-loving and gregarious that people assumed he must be miles apart from the more humourless and earnest right of his party. Redwood's awkward yet lofty personality seemed to embody the right. Personalities can lead to many misperceptions in politics: because David Cameron chose to dress like Tony Blair – crisp white shirts often worn without a tie, denim shirts while at Chequers or on holiday – there was, in some quarters, an assumption that Cameron must be taking his party to the left in the same way Blair moved his to the right. The same applied to Cameron's friend and early senior adviser Steve Hilton, who often wore a tee-shirt and shorts and walked barefoot around Number Ten. Some of those who assumed that Hilton personified the Tory 'modernization' programme were taken aback when Hilton became a cheerleader for Donald Trump years later. But Hilton had not changed in any way. He had been as much of a right-wing anti-state libertarian in the UK as he was in the US.

Clarke and Redwood were different personalities and had contrasting approaches to the way they projected themselves and their ideas, but they agreed on quite a lot. On Europe, though, there was a huge gap. Clarke had no intention of compromising over his support for Europe. Nor did Redwood in his unyielding criticisms. By now, the issue of Europe alone was shaping the Conservative Party. The Clarke/Redwood double act went nowhere as a result, and William Hague was elected.

Hague's Cabinet experience was limited to a brief spell as Secretary of State for Wales. He was bright and calm, a better orator than Clarke, but nowhere near as developed a public figure. Hague won because he was a Eurosceptic. He had secured Thatcher's endorsement – not insignificant in a party still paying homage nearly seven years after her removal. The vote was confined to MPs for the last time, and in choosing Hague the shrunken parliamentary party signalled that it was hardening its attitude towards the EU.

During the 1997 contest, some of Clarke's allies pleaded with him to tone down his pro-European views in order to win. Clarke realized that to be victorious with a false pitch on the biggest issue of the late 1990s would have neutered him as leader. Anyway, his political style, and a big part of his appeal, was to say what he thought. An attempt to be what he was not would have destroyed his wider character. He went for the dignity and potential potency of authenticity. In doing so he lost, but he might not have won by becoming weirdly inauthentic either.

Clarke returned to the backbenches for the first time in decades, but his profile remained high in a parliamentary party unused to opposition – not least opposing a Labour government with a huge majority. Part of his prominence was down to the matter of Europe. He and Michael Heseltine were scathing about Hague's attempts to form policies around populist slogans. Hague insisted the UK should be 'in Europe but not run by Europe'. He headed to Dover in order to make his pledge to 'save the pound'. In retrospect, these messages were a model of restraint compared with what was to follow. But they showed the direction the party was heading in, more at ease with bashing the EU than being 'at the heart of Europe', as Major had put it in his early phase as prime minister. Revealingly, in the 2001 election such populist sloganizing did not help Hague build up a bigger tent of support. The party lost by almost as wide a margin as in 1997. At this point, Euroscepticism was not a vote-winner in British general elections.

After the election, Hague resigned immediately. His career reveals much about the way politicians are perceived in the UK. When he was Conservative leader, Hague struggled to be heard. After he resigned, companies paid him many thousands of pounds to speak at events and on the after-dinner circuit. Labour's Ed Balls had the same experience. When he was an influential adviser to Gordon Brown and then a Cabinet minister, few voters paid much attention to what he was up to, even though he was at the heart of policy decisions that would impact on their lives. After he appeared on *Strictly Come Dancing*, having lost his seat, he was hugely in demand on the speaking circuit and for TV appearances. But Hague had lost his political ambition. Balls had lost his seat. With a safe seat in Nottingham, Clarke kept going, his obsession with politics as deep as ever.

Clarke stood next in the 2001 leadership contest, the weirdest in a competitive field of whacky Tory leadership campaigns. This was the one in which Michael Portillo began as favourite.[6] Once again, polls suggested that Clarke was the most popular candidate among the wider electorate. As in 1997, Europe was the main issue as far as the party membership was concerned. Although Hague had led the Conservatives to a dark defeat, he had done so by dancing with his party over Europe. The party wanted a similar dance in 2001. This time, members had a vote, and in the final round they selected Iain Duncan Smith, a candidate with less experience and charisma than Hague but who was even more unyielding in his Euroscepticism. Clarke was on the wrong side again.

Unsurprisingly, Duncan Smith did not last long. Another Eurosceptic, Michael Howard, took over halfway through the parliament and in effect saved his party by ensuring it was not as badly defeated in 2005 as it had been in the two previous elections. The Conservatives lost but were still breathing. Howard was an important and underestimated figure in the revival of the Conservative Party at a time when some commentators wondered whether it would ever rule again.[7] He had enough experience to keep the show on the road, and recognized the talents of the younger generation of Tory MPs, including David Cameron and George Osborne.

After Howard announced his resignation following the Conservatives' 2005 election defeat, Clarke declared he would be standing once more. His 'hobby' was taking up much of his post-Cabinet career. In spite of standing on the campaign motto 'It's time to win', this time he did not even make it to the final round in which two candidates would battle it out for the votes of party members. That contest was between the Eurosceptic David Davis and David Cameron, who took an even more hard-line approach on Europe. As leader, Cameron equivocated over Europe, telling his party not to 'bang on' about the issue – an altogether different instruction to suggesting the party might need to change its approach.

Some of Clarke's allies pleaded with him once again to be more flexible on Europe, but the former chancellor came from an era of big political figures who had strongly held beliefs that were not going to be given up in pursuit of personal ambition. For Cameron and Boris Johnson, politics was partly a game in which becoming prime minister was almost an end in itself. Clarke was in a different league in terms of principles and depth. Like them, he loved politics. Indeed, he was far more of an addict, staying in the Commons until the 2019 election when he was seventy-nine. Cameron left Parliament soon after resigning as prime minister. Johnson was not wholly at ease in the Commons even when he became prime minister.

For admirable reasons, Clarke could not dump his convictions on Europe, and equally his party was right from its perspective to reject him as a leader. A growing number of Conservative MPs and members were hostile to the EU and were beginning to contemplate support for leaving altogether. They needed a leader who was at the very least willing to accommodate this stance. Cameron was accommodating. Later, Boris Johnson claimed to share the members' hostility. British politics is not presidential. However popular Clarke was with voters, his party had moved away from him on Europe and he could not lead it.

———

After the last of these leadership contests, there was an unusual development in the governing party. The chancellor, Gordon Brown, widely seen as the next prime minister, succeeded Tony Blair and moved into Number Ten after a leadership contest in which he was the only candidate. Rather than signalling a smooth transition, this suggested there was trouble ahead: Brown's solo contest left questions about the legitimacy of his victory.

The subsequent trouble took the form of a series of attempted coups against Brown. Each time there was an attempt to remove him from Number Ten, the plotters looked to the Foreign Secretary, David Miliband, to take over. There was high excitement in some parts of the Labour Party and the media that David might be the next prime minister. Yet in the 2010 leadership contest after Labour's election defeat, it was David's brother, Ed, who won. Quite often in the years that followed his victory, Ed was favourite to win the next general election. Throughout the period from 2007 to 2015, there was much talk about one or other of the Miliband brothers becoming prime minister. Neither made it to Number Ten.

9

DAVID AND ED MILIBAND

The saga of the Miliband brothers is unique. The two brothers served in the Cabinet together. Before they became Labour MPs, one advised the prime minister. The other was a senior adviser to the chancellor. Quite often, Tony Blair and Gordon Brown were at odds with each other over policy, strategy and when one should leave Number Ten to give the other a chance. David was close to Blair. Ed was a committed ally of Brown. When Blair and then Brown took a bow, the two brothers fought each other in a leadership contest. Only one could win. At different points, both were seen as potential prime ministers. Admirers of Blair ached for David to get the top job. Those to the left of Blair saw Ed as the figure who could guide Labour back to power.

After years of tension between two instinctively decent individuals, not one but both Milibands failed to reach the top. Neither had set out for lofty heights at the start of their careers, but each acquired an appetite for leadership later. This hunger drove them on and ultimately made them miserable. The two brothers and their families were torn apart.

David's big chance appeared to open up in the turbulent politics that erupted between 2007 and 2010. For these three years, David and leadership were a persistent theme. Whenever he spoke or wrote an article, there would be quick analysis of the substance and then a much longer commentary about whether his words were a 'leadership bid', and further noisy talk about where this left his ambitions. Indeed, for a short time there was more intense speculation about David's leadership hopes than was the case with any of the other prime ministers we never had.

From the summer of 2007, David was Foreign Secretary in Gordon Brown's government. Brown had promoted him to one of the most senior posts in the Cabinet in the hope that he would become part of his team, and that his admirers in the party and the media would no longer see him as a prime ministerial alternative. As with quite a lot of Brown's calculations around the time of his accession, this one was misjudged. At moments of maximum vulnerability for Brown, David was the great hope of the internal dissenters. They had been supporters of Blair and could not accept that Brown had finally realized his ambition, seeing only his weaknesses and not his strengths. In their determination to be rid of Brown, they made his weaknesses and insecurities much worse while obscuring his considerable positive qualities. This was the beginning of the era when any leader a millimetre to the left of Blair was briefed against by some Labour MPs. Those doing so were clearing a path for several terms of Conservative rule.

Brown endured more attempts to remove him than any modern prime minister. The plotters hoped each time that David would emerge from the Foreign Office to lead their charge. They assumed that if their hero did so, he would be well placed to win the next general election. These shallow dissenters made far more miscalculations than the increasingly insecure Brown. Although the subject of much flattery and speculation, David did not emerge from the Foreign Office to lead them to their promised land, and he was wise not to make the attempt.

David came to realize that his admirers were making the wrong moves. There was no smooth route to Number Ten for him at such a time. Brown had no intention of standing aside and he had good cause to stay put, being supremely qualified to respond to the global financial crisis that took dramatic form in 2008. Brown was in a curious position: he would speak to world leaders like Barack Obama and Angela Merkel about the need for a coordinated fiscal stimulus and interest rate cuts, then put down the phone and hear that MPs with no known experience of economic policy, or much else, were plotting to bring him down.

The plotters were so obsessed with what they regarded as Brown's inadequacies that they overlooked his role as an authoritative leader in the global emergency. Brown was leading the international response to the financial crash, having been chancellor for ten years and possessing a grasp of every complex detail. David was far less qualified to move in and rise to the task, as part of him knew. He had not held an economic brief in government. Being Foreign Secretary was a senior post, but as Boris Johnson would prove later, it does not necessarily provide the experience to lead in a national emergency. David's only other Cabinet post had been Environment Secretary, again inadequate preparation to lead a response to the biggest global crisis since 1945. Besides, even if David had announced he was challenging Brown, and Brown had stood aside, a bloody leadership contest would have ensued in which his victory was not guaranteed. There would have been other formidable candidates.

Most of David's personality was self-effacing and shrewd enough to appreciate that the Labour MPs and commentators urging him to seize the crown had got it wrong. This was not his moment. But there were times when he could not resist fuelling the fantasies of his fans. He had a vain streak. Perhaps vanity was impossible to resist when, as a senior Cabinet member, David read columnists and heard Labour MPs arguing that he should be prime minister and save his party. Politicians are human beings. Flattery is intoxicating.

In July 2008, David wrote an article for the *Guardian* that caused a considerable stir. In it, he put the case for a 'radical new phase', adding that there was a need to be 'more humble about our shortcomings, but more compelling about our achievements'.[1] The article was characteristically vague and yet its effect was incendiary. Days before, Labour had lost a by-election in Glasgow East, theoretically a safe seat, reinforcing the view of the dissenters that Brown was a vote-loser. There was no mention of Brown in the *Guardian* article, but for twenty-four hours following its publication, David was treated like a rock star, signing autographs as he arrived at Broadcasting House for an interview and facing question after question about his prime ministerial ambitions during a packed press conference with the Italian Foreign Minister. The headlines generated by his intervention included 'David Miliband Lines Up Challenge to Gordon Brown'[2] and 'David Miliband Refuses to Rule Out Leadership Challenge'[3]. They intensified the speculation that he would soon make his move.

He did not do so, even though at the next Labour party conference he was asked endlessly about his leadership plans and at one point was photographed grinning awkwardly with a banana in his hand. The photo captured an ambiguity: David was only being photographed because he was seen as a potential challenger to Brown, but the photo made him look silly rather than prime ministerial, partly because he was not always at ease as a public performer. And perhaps there was a deeper reason for the awkward pose: he was not sure about the wisdom of making a challenge and could not hide his doubts. He was highly articulate, and yet a clunky actor.

The same sequence, in which David's supporters had high hopes he would make a move against Brown, recurred in various forms. The final attempted internal coup occurred in January 2010, the year of the next general election, when several MPs called on the prime minister to stand down and waited yet again for David to emerge from the Foreign Office to declare his candidacy. They waited and waited. Finally, David declared his support for Brown. Throughout this period, David was an unlikely political rock star, the idol of the Blairites. In the same way that Michael Portillo was a prophet for the more ardent Thatcherites in the John Major era, David packed out fringe meetings at party conferences with doting supporters hanging on his every word. Although David enjoyed the adulation, he was becoming trapped as a Blairite figure near the top of the Labour Party, when he was a more complex politician than that. His instincts and ideas were slightly to the left of Blair's, though he was still a long way from Ed's politics.

Each time there was talk of a coup, David's doubts about the wisdom of the challenge were correct. Equally, his willingness to give hope to the dissenters was wholly misjudged. As Peter Mandelson, then back in the government and supporting Brown, observed later, 'The idea that David could be carried aloft in a chariot and moved into Number Ten was absurd. There would have been a civil war.'[4] Brown had many devoted followers, some of whom were in the Cabinet. He would not have gone quietly in January 2010, just as he would not have done earlier. But by occasionally wallowing in the speculation that he should be the next prime minister, David appeared indecisive.

The *Guardian* article written in July 2008 was illuminating. The act of writing the article showed that David wanted to stir the pot and speak on behalf of Brown's despairing critics. But the fact that the article did not say very much of substance and was published at the end of July, when MPs were heading for their holidays, suggested he did not want to cause that much of a stir. The article was as ambiguous as the banana photo. David was far from sure about how to become prime minister or what he would do if he got the job. He was not as flamboyant as Michael Heseltine, who waited several years before making his move against Margaret Thatcher. Heseltine also did not become prime minister. Most routes to Number Ten are blocked.

Even so, from the autumn of 2007, when Brown's honeymoon in Number Ten came to an abrupt end, David was widely regarded as a possible prime minister. His next chance to become leader of his party was in the 2010 leadership contest after Labour had left office. He began as favourite to win. Instead the contest was won by David's younger brother, Ed. David stood for the leadership as a former Foreign Secretary. Ed had been an Environment Secretary, a post David had also held.

Ed qualifies as a prime minister we never had on the basis that he was leader of the Opposition from 2010, quite often ahead in the polls, and was the favourite to be prime minister, perhaps in a hung parliament, up to the night of the 2015 election. In retrospect, given that their party was defeated in 2015, some Labour MPs and commentators wondered why there was not any significant attempt to remove Ed, given the partial attempts against Brown. There were many private whisperings of discontent from dissenters in Ed's shadow Cabinet for much of his leadership. They hoped that the popular former Cabinet minister Alan Johnson might succeed him. Johnson was not interested in doing so, but there was no momentum towards a substantial coup for another reason.

Throughout his leadership, polls suggested Ed might win the next general election. Leaders are not deposed when they look as if they have a chance of winning. Indeed, Labour leaders aren't often removed even if they look like they are about to lose an election. Ed assumed he would be the next prime minister until the exit poll was broadcast at 10 p.m. on the night of the 2015 election, forecasting an overall Conservative majority. Until that brutal moment, Ed had spent the evening composing his Cabinet and wider frontbench.

The Miliband brothers were both prime ministers we never had. The fact that they were brothers shaped their careers and fates, even though in many respects it was their differences, rather than their similarities, that were so striking. Early on, those diverging paths were defined by who they worked for during the New Labour era.

———

Shortly after the 1992 election, David became secretary of the Social Justice Commission, a body established by the then Labour leader, John Smith. David gave his first-ever television interview in his role as secretary, and Tony Blair took note as he saw him on TV.[5] When Blair became leader in July 1994, he appointed David to become head of policy in his office. The appointment meant that David became known as a 'Blairite', thereby highlighting the limits of defining individuals by such terms.

David was committed to Blair, as were all those who worked for the Labour leader. Blair inspired an unyielding and sincere loyalty.

But in some respects David was to the left of Blair, as were quite a few of those who worked for the long-serving prime minister. David could see the case for higher spending and tax rises to pay for them when Blair could not. Although at first a supporter of the war in Iraq, he came to regard the invasion as a 'disaster'.[6] He could be more daring in government, seeking for example a vocational qualification as Schools Minister that Blair vetoed partly on the grounds that the policy risked alienating Middle England and its newspapers.

In other ways, David was close to Blair. He was committed to the 'third way' as an ideological guide, and was the only senior Labour politician other than Blair to cite it with passion. Gordon Brown and his entourage, including Ed Miliband, never used the term. In contrast, David travelled the world attending third-way seminars and regarded the ideas arising from them as a modern form of social democracy. Like Blair, David was a fan of the Clintons, and was excited when they were part of the third-way discussions. Seminars were hosted in cities in a range of countries after Labour's election win in 1997, from Washington to Rio de Janeiro and on to Stockholm. For a time, left-of-centre leaders across the democratic world were fascinated by how New Labour had won a landslide in a country that normally elected Conservative governments. Both Tony Blair and David Miliband continued to believe that the third way was a durable political philosophy, although apart from Bill Clinton few left-of-centre leaders deployed the term then or since. The imprecise ideological guide, the 'third way', captured the cautious, vote-winning expediency of Clinton and then Blair in the 1990s.

When he worked for Blair, David was more involved in policy developments than in the many intense dramas blowing up in

Number Ten – from rows with Brown to what Cherie Blair was up to. David was slightly above the fray, and therefore had not been greatly exposed to the burning heat of politics until he moved quickly to the centre of the public stage after becoming an MP in the 2001 election. As an adviser, he had been largely in the shadows – much talked about at the centre of the Blair wing of New Labour, but not as an advocate on the political stage. Advisers are not required to be public performers.

Very quickly, he became an education minister and was seen as a star in the parliamentary party. From the slight distance of the Number Ten Policy Unit during Labour's first term, naturally he had taken Blair's side in the storms. He continued to do so as an MP. When David stood for the leadership in 2010, he had the full support of Blair and the Blairites.

Ed became an adviser for Gordon Brown in 1994, having briefly worked for Harriet Harman. From the beginning of the New Labour era, it was evident that Ed was to the left of David. He was as committed to Brown as David was to Blair. In some respects, Brown was to the left of Blair and Ed was to the left of Brown. Sometimes, Brown joked 'here's my Tony Benn' when Ed joined him in a meeting.[7] Ed saw his role partly as urging Brown towards a more defiantly left-wing approach. He was on a distinct high after Brown announced a significant tax rise to pay for investment in the NHS in the 2002 budget, a move that had made David more nervously supportive. Ed described the budget as the moment when 'Gordon found his true voice'.[8] Some of Blair's senior advisers, though not David, worried that the tax rise could lose Labour the next election. Ed was also excited when Brown, as prime minister, raised the top rate of income tax on high earners, a move that unnerved Blair's followers.

On the whole, Ed was frustrated by the New Labour era. Even when Brown dared to challenge Blair ideologically by arguing that there were limits to market solutions in the provision of public services, Ed did not believe his boss went anywhere near far enough in explaining why markets often fail. Nonetheless, he saw Brown as a figure of greater depth and substance than Blair. While he and Brown would stay up late into the night discussing the challenges posed by inequality, he wondered whether the dilemmas would even cross Blair's mind.[9]

Ed remained loyal to Brown even when David contemplated making his tentative moves against the prime minister after 2007. Indeed, Ed was one of those seeking to dissuade David from striking while Brown was adapting to his newish role as prime minister. Like others from Brown's senior Treasury team, he was partly disappointed by Brown as a prime minister, but not anywhere near disillusioned enough to support his brother taking over. Almost certainly, Ed would have supported Brown in such circumstances, although he would have found a leadership battle between his brother and Brown a nightmare.

Long before the leadership contest of 2010, there were tensions between the brothers. Ed irritated the older David, following the same paths at Oxford and on to the Labour Party and government. Ed felt a fraternal loyalty, but viewed with some disdain what he saw as his brother's ideological rootlessness. During the leadership contest, Ed reflected to a journalist in private: 'I'm not sure what David's politics are.' In the heat of the battle David wondered whether Ed could take a tough decision or whether he had ever done so in politics. Before one leadership hustings, as the candidates arrived, Ed told David that an old friend of the family had died. David barely responded, too annoyed from his perspective to engage with a brother who was making the leadership contest something of a family psychodrama merely by standing.[10]

During the campaign Ed acted ruthlessly, persuading one newspaper editor who had planned to endorse David not to do so.[11] At one point in the contest, David reflected that their late father, Ralph, would have found the duel utterly bizarre.[12] Their father, a prominent left-wing academic and writer, died in 1994 shortly before the two brothers began their political journeys. Ed was closer to his father politically in that he was more rooted on the left, but Ralph was to the left of the Labour Party. He was not a member, leaving the party in the mid-1960s. He would not have been a cheerleader for New Labour.

In interviews, Ed would refer to his father whereas David rarely did. Ed complained loudly and justifiably when the *Mail on Sunday* described his father as 'the man who hated Britain'.[13] Unusually, the *Mail on Sunday* apologized. David spoke less about his father in a political context, but was as committed to the family. One of his many worries when he left the UK to live in the US in 2013 was the distance from his elderly mother.

As the two brothers moved into the public arena, there were clear ideological differences. But there were similarities too. Obviously, they came from the same family, and family discussions revolved around politics and current affairs. They also had some shared characteristics. Although both were addicted to politics, they could be slightly awkward in public arenas. They were at ease discussing policy and ideas, but less sure of their voices on the political stage. Their public personas in interviews and speeches were similar to Blair's. This might have been subconscious but it was not accidental. They saw at close hand the most polished performer in British politics and, uncertain of their own voices, adopted some of his mannerisms. This gave both of them a degree of inauthenticity as public figures.

Both brothers shared a fascination with ideas and policies that was more intense than Blair's, but they failed by some margin to make their ideas and policies as accessible as Blair did, or to appear as at ease in public. There was David's banana photo. In the build-up to the 2015 election, Ed was photographed eating a bacon sandwich awkwardly. The sandwich image should have been trivial but it fed into a caricature of a leader who was seen by wary voters as geeky and a bit weird.

Most of the time, both David and Ed were decent, humble and modest given their spectacular rises in politics. They engaged with others. They were listeners as well as talkers. They had the gift of genuine curiosity that added to their capacity for depth. There was also self-awareness at times. David joked about his speedy rise, laughing at the grandeur of having breakfast at the White House with Hillary Clinton.[14] When hosting gatherings at Chevening as Foreign Secretary, he could ridicule the grand surroundings rather than wallow in them pompously. His wife, the musician Louise Shackelton, could do so too. They were not lofty or grand. Similarly, at all stages of his career Ed asked for advice from friends and colleagues, not out of politeness but because he was eager to get their sense of the political mood. When reflecting on his new post as Keir Starmer's shadow Business Secretary in June 2020, Ed joked that the headline might be 'Relic or relevant?'[15] This was not the joke of a figure whose position at the top, or close to the top, of his party since the mid-1990s had gone to his head.

This partial modesty is a rare quality in those rising fast in British politics. And at certain times, their ascendancy did challenge their capacity for self-deprecation. When David was spoken of as the next prime minister and he swept through cities in smart cars as Foreign Secretary, he acquired a sense of self-importance and destiny. When Ed came to believe he was Labour's Margaret Thatcher, a left-of-centre figure who would change the country on the scale that she had done, it led to him sometimes conveying a distant grandeur that was not his natural demeanour. He assumed the aloof pose was required to be prime ministerial. But the bigger requirement is at least an appearance of authenticity. How can a potential leader appear to be authentic? Successful leaders manage an answer to that question.

———

The 2010 leadership contest was a complex psychodrama. Months earlier, Ed had decided he would stand in the contest that would inevitably be held if Labour lost the election. Ed had every right to stand. He held a distinct position to the left of New Labour and had been at the heart of government since 1997, although at one point he did take a break from the Treasury to teach at Harvard. He was a great hit with the students and flourished in the academic environment, but his willingness to leave the political arena for even a short time hinted that he perhaps lacked the uncompromising hunger many of those who reach the top possess. At the time, Ed told friends he had to take a break from the relentless demands made by Gordon Brown and his senior adviser, Ed Balls.

David was troubled but not deeply affected when Ed first declared his candidacy. He had lived with his brother following in his footsteps for many years. He also assumed he had a good chance of winning, better than Ed's chances of doing so. The tensions became unbearable only when Ed won. David was devastated – as were some of his supporters, who were fuming publicly on the evening the result was declared at Labour's conference in Manchester. Later, Ed was to admit he was taken aback by the scale of David's sense of betrayal.

Apart from the grim psychodrama, the 2010 leadership contest was a relatively dull affair. Four exhausted former Cabinet ministers – David and Ed, Ed Balls and Andy Burnham – were joined by the left-wing MP Diane Abbott for a series of hustings that rarely came to life. Some of the hustings were chaired by Allegra Stratton, who went on to become Boris Johnson's press secretary briefly at the end of 2020. When the result was declared, David had secured the support of most Labour MPs, but Ed won overall thanks to the backing of the unions. Some of the MPs who voted for David never forgave Ed for winning. This would become a problem for Ed. MPs hate to be on the wrong side of a leadership contest. Leaders that are elected without the support of a majority of Labour MPs tend to be undermined by dissent.

Ed won by recognizing a need for his party to move on from the New Labour era. He could sincerely condemn the war in Iraq, still a totemic issue in the Labour Party. Conveniently, he had been at Harvard when Tony Blair made his moves towards war, but privately he was an unequivocal opponent at the time and could now say so during the campaign. On other matters he was to the left of David in his pitch to the party, and privately even more so.

During the leadership contest, one of David's senior allies, the former Cabinet minister James Purnell, urged him to declare his genuine retrospective view that the war in Iraq had been a disaster. Purnell said to him, 'I still support the war... you don't... tell the party you don't.'[16] David did not do so. Blair was supporting his leadership campaign and he felt a deep loyalty to Blair. In the build-up to the war in Iraq he had been a supporter. But even though David's retrospective opposition to the war might have helped him in the contest, he did not express overt criticism, instead making a contortion about how more should have been done to 'win the peace'.

David was more decent than he was ruthless. In his decency, he became the Blairite candidate in an election where closeness to Blair was not the best positioning. The contest took place at the end of a long period of New Labour rule, and after the trauma of Iraq and the financial crash. If David recognized the risks, he was too loyal to Blair to signal significant distance. If he did not fully see the risks, he was not a sharp enough reader of the political rhythms to reach the very top. Indeed, he had Blair as a model in the need to establish distance. In 1994, on becoming leader, Blair made an overt leap from the party's recent past. Now Labour was 'new'; all that had happened previously was 'old'. David made no such overt leap from the New Labour era during his campaign.

David was as obsessed with politics as Ed. After his defeat in the 2010 leadership contest, he initially resolved to stay on as an MP, alarmed by the direction his brother might take the party, and still hoping he might be called upon to save it. On this he was in denial. If Ed failed, the party was not going to turn to another Miliband, whatever the political differences of the two brothers. Before long, David found his position to be impossible, a backbencher known to be critical of his leader who happened to be his brother. Every time he spoke in public, the words were decoded to examine whether he was attacking Ed. This was a nightmare for a serious thinker who wanted to articulate his ideas about the future.

Soon, David was unable to speak up on very much at all. In March 2013, he announced he would leave the Commons and the UK, an extreme step that pointed to his frustration. I bumped into David and his wife, Louise, on a train from London to his constituency in the north east of England. David was speaking at a farewell dinner for local party members, and they were both close to tears as they reflected on their suddenly changed lives. David was taking up a post as chief executive of the International Rescue Committee, an NGO in New York. It was a prestigious and important role, but he had hoped to be Labour leader and, eventually, prime minister. Instead, he had been forced into exile by his brother – or that was how he saw it at the time.

David had become trapped, first by being seen as the Blairite candidate when Blairism was going out fashion, then by being perceived as the dissenting elder brother. His way of escaping was to move to the US, a considerable upheaval for his family whatever the satisfactions of a new job away from British politics. Louise was a successful and fulfilled musician in London. Although American, she was not sure whether the same opportunities would be available when they moved. During the same train journey, David pointed to recent polls and suggested Labour was not in a good place. He did so without mentioning Ed.

Before David left for the US, and to some extent after, Ed's space to make his moves as leader was constrained by his elder brother. While believing New Labour was nowhere near radical enough, he was as much a product of the Blair/Brown era as David was. Ed's political apprenticeship was another reason why he was cautious in giving room to his radical instincts. He also yearned for media approval in the way that Blair and Brown had. A rare positive word in *The Sun* or *The Times* gave him a thrill. But above all, he was conscious of David and his followers. Having won the contest, he felt the need to appease them.

Immediately, he tried to bind David to his project by making him shadow chancellor. The offer highlighted Ed's confusion. With good cause, Ed did not accept the Cameron/Osborne claims that profligate spending by the last Labour government had been a factor in the global financial crisis of 2008. On the contrary, he envisaged a wider role for the state and regarded the deficit as a consequence of the crash rather than its cause. David viewed matters differently.

In 2011, the *Guardian* secured a copy of the speech David would have made if he had won the leadership contest the previous year. David had planned to argue 'George Osborne says we are in denial about the deficit. Because he wants us to be. So let's not be. It is a test.'[17] The draft speech, leaked by an ally of David's to cause trouble for Ed, is very like a Blair speech in rhythm, tone and message. It was not the speech of a new and distinct leader. David was copying Blair, as David Cameron sought to imitate Labour's election-winning prime minister while struggling to find a substantial public personality of his own. Beyond the inclination to imitate Blair, David was a more substantial figure than Cameron proved to be.

Still, David had planned to walk into Osborne's trap and accept the centrality of the 'deficit' – even though, over the years that followed, the new Conservative chancellor failed to meet his objective of wiping it out in a single parliament. Osborne became widely blamed, not least by Conservative MPs who lost seats in the 2017 election, for taking austerity too far. Before the pandemic struck, Boris Johnson declared that he would not be following austerity economic policies. Johnson appeared to oppose 'austerity' with a vehemence that Ed might have adopted had he felt freer as a leader. Johnson proclaimed he was not even going to utter the word 'austerity'. Ed did not want to accept Osborne's agenda, but he felt constrained. He could not make a clear Keynesian case as he would have liked to have done, partly because he feared the disapproval from those in his shadow Cabinet and beyond who had backed David.

Occasionally, Ed inadvertently revealed his true position. In his pre-election conference speech in 2014 he forgot to mention the deficit, an omission that he was heavily criticized for at the time. Ed learned his speeches off by heart and walked around the stage without notes; when he forgot the section on the deficit, he perhaps revealed a subconscious awareness of its limited significance. After the 2016 Brexit referendum, Osborne, who was still chancellor, announced he was abandoning plans to wipe out the deficit in that parliament, at which point the media and politicians from across the spectrum dropped their preoccupation too. Not for the first time, Ed was ahead of the game in his instincts. The deficit had been elevated out of all proportion, and Osborne's means of addressing it with deep real-terms spending cuts had been widely perceived as the only available route. Now, even Osborne was turning away from his chosen path.

Constantly torn throughout his leadership, Ed at times felt the need to affect the same concern about the deficit as David. At one point, he thought he had no choice but to concede that Labour had overspent in government, as some of David's supporters in the shadow Cabinet were demanding he do – even though he did not believe this was the case. His shadow chancellor, Ed Balls, threatened to resign if he did so. Balls tended to constrain Ed's radical instincts, or at least that was Ed's view. But on refusing to blame the last Labour government for overspending, Balls was more resolute. Balls was right. 'Sorry we overspent and wrecked the economy' is hardly an election-winning slogan, but in effect this is what some of David's allies were arguing the party's position should be.

The degree to which Ed agonized about his radicalism can be highlighted by a single event. In January 2015, the left-wing party Syriza was elected in Greece unexpectedly. The morning after the result, quite a few in Ed's office agreed that they must distance themselves from the Greek radicals, who had been elected on a policy of challenging EU demands for stringent public spending cuts. Ed arrived in the office and declared without equivocation: 'What an exciting result in Greece.'[18] He and his staff spent most of the day working on a statement in which they both welcomed and warned against the outcome of the election. This was Ed's mindset as leader from the beginning: radical yet cautious.

Wisely, David turned down Ed's offers to be in the shadow Cabinet. He would not have been able to put up with sitting there observing his younger brother lead. Also, he knew of their significant political differences. The arrangement would not have worked. But, without his brother, Ed worried about keeping David's wing of the party on board. He yearned to be more radical but he also wanted the Blairites cheering him on. As often happens when leaders make contorted calculations, Ed stifled his own voice – and yet some in the shadow Cabinet were still scathing of his leadership even as he tried to please them.

There were times when Ed broke free of the constraints. In his party conference speech, delivered in September 2013, he caused a stir by pledging to freeze gas and electricity bills. More widely, he argued that some markets were not working effectively due to failures of government:

We need successful energy companies in Britain. We need them
to invest for the future. But you need to get a fair deal and frankly,
there will never be public consent for that investment unless you do
get a fair deal. And the system is broken and we are going to fix it.

If we win the 2015 election, the next Labour government will freeze
gas and electricity prices until the start of 2017. Your bills will not
rise. It will benefit millions of families and millions of businesses.
That's what I mean by a government that fights for you. That's what I
mean when I say Britain can do better than this.

Now the companies aren't going to like this because it will cost
them more, but they have been overcharging people for too long
because of a market that doesn't work. It's time to reset the market.
So we will pass legislation in our first year in office to do that, and
have a regulator that will genuinely be on the customers' side but
also enable the investment we need. That's how Britain will do better
than this.[19]

The political culture in England was not used to this, and it
triggered a furious response. *The Times* led with the clichéd headline
'Back to the 1970s', echoing comments from senior Conservatives
and the private alarm of some in the shadow Cabinet. They were
all unable to cope with the idea that modern governments could
intervene effectively in markets.

The degree to which the media's horror was misplaced was
illustrated when Theresa May became prime minister in 2016. She
began to make precisely the same arguments as Ed, pointing out
that some markets were not working and highlighting the good that
government could do. Under the guidance of her innovative senior
adviser, Nick Timothy, May espoused a blend of Ed's faith in the state
with a hint of Enoch Powell's Midlands nationalism. Submerged
by Brexit and the loss of the Conservatives' majority in the 2017

election, she and Timothy never got the chance to flesh out their agenda but it pointed in interesting directions and marked a move to the left in terms of the Conservatives' approach to economic policy.

Ed's strength was to be ahead of his time, and he was sharper than David in reading the way politics was changing from the assumptions and orthodoxies of the mid-1990s when New Labour took shape. But his foresight was also his fatal flaw. The trouble with being ahead of the game is that voters and the media are still some way behind. He did not have the communication skills or the self-confidence to convince enough voters – or indeed his party – that they should join him in looking ahead. To his detractors, he became 'Red Ed', when in fact he was being relatively modest in his proposals. In most European countries, Ed's ideas were mainstream. Still, in the UK it was David Cameron and George Osborne, implementing economic policies to the right of Margaret Thatcher and proposing a referendum on Brexit, who were regarded by many as 'centrists' and 'modernizers'.

Ed had hit on the worst of all worlds. His radicalism had alienated England's Conservative media. His caution had failed to excite younger radicals who would later hail the leadership of Jeremy Corbyn. After the 2017 election, when Corbyn performed much better than expected, Ed argued that he had been the 'bridgehead' to Corbynism.[20] He was inconsistent in his views on Corbyn, supporting the attempted coup against him in 2016, excited by Labour's gains under Corbyn in the 2017 election, and becoming wholly disillusioned by the time Labour was seen off in the 2019 campaign. In contrast, David had been scathing of the Corbyn project from the beginning.

If Ed had won the 2015 election, there would almost certainly have been no Corbyn leadership and there would not have been a

Brexit referendum. Courageously, he argued against a referendum on the UK's membership of the EU. Cameron had placed the proposition at the heart of his pitch to the electorate. Opposing it was not easy. During the campaign, Cameron and Osborne both argued in interviews that they 'trusted the people' to decide whether the UK should remain in the EU. It is a challenge for an opposition leader to explain why they do not 'trust the people' with a referendum. If Ed had become prime minister in 2015, the UK would have remained a member of the EU, and the energy-draining, costly, divisive Brexit saga would never have happened. He would also have embarked on a domestic agenda that was not far removed from the one Theresa May and Boris Johnson claimed to embrace a few years later. *The Times* did not accuse either of them of going back to the 1970s, not that their advocacy took the form of much policy implementation.

On the journey from his constituency back to London on the night of the 2015 election, Ed collapsed in tears, at one point cursing his fate. The shock of defeat was profoundly disturbing for him. Hours earlier, he had assumed he would be driving to Number Ten via Buckingham Palace. He resigned as leader on the Friday morning. A few days later, David gave an interview from New York arguing vaguely that: 'Over the last few years we turned the page back... Now it's time to turn the page forward.'[21] These were not words of fraternal loyalty. The volume of Alastair Campbell's epic diaries that spans the 2010 leadership contest to the 2015 election defeat ends with a text from David. Campbell asked him how he was feeling. The reply was blunt: 'Gloomy, angry, sorry'.[22]

Even in defeat there was no immediate rapprochement. This was a family tragedy, not least because they were not malevolent schemers by instinct and yet circumstance had led them to scheme against each other. Both would have been more substantial than some who became prime minister. The fact that both sought the crown meant that neither had a chance of wearing it. Two of the most decent people in British politics destroyed each other.

———

Following Ed's resignation, Labour staged another leadership contest. The subdued battle began with echoes of the one Ed and David had fought five years earlier, with weary frontbenchers making a cautious, bland appeal to party activists, all depressed by another election defeat. Then, at the last minute, Jeremy Corbyn became a candidate. To Corbyn's surprise, he not only won the contest but briefly became a possible future prime minister, wiping out the Conservatives' overall majority in the 2017 election.

10

JEREMY CORBYN

Jeremy Corbyn was the least likely leader in the history of modern party politics. Occasionally, he was compared to Labour's early leader George Lansbury, a figure on the left who led his party to electoral doom with a romantic flourish. But Lansbury had served as a minor Cabinet minister, placing him in a different league to Corbyn in terms of experience near the top of politics. Before becoming leader, Corbyn had not been on the frontbench in government or opposition, even though he was first elected to the Commons in 1983. Suddenly, in 2015, he won a landslide in a leadership contest. Some MPs ache to be leader of their party. Corbyn had never wanted to acquire the crown.

He was the equivalent of a tennis player in a local park being transported to Centre Court at Wimbledon. The athletic artistry of tennis at the highest levels and political leadership have a common factor: the skills cannot be suddenly acquired. Leadership involves ruthless focus, discipline, a capacity to explain a message to the electorate, credible policies to back up the message, and an ability to manage a party at every level, from the leader's office downwards. There was no reason why Corbyn should have possessed such skills when he became leader. He showed no inclination to learn speedily.

This was a near-fatal problem, and there was another: some Labour MPs who were shocked by Corbyn's rise behaved appallingly. A few of them tweeted their disdain within minutes of Corbyn being elected leader, and they continued to be noisy dissenters for the duration of his leadership. Not only were they disloyal, they had no coherent strategy for removing Corbyn or replacing him with an alternative left-of-centre project. Feeling besieged, the Corbynites joined the battle. On this basis alone, with both sides culpable, Labour was doomed to lose under Corbyn. Voters do not follow politics closely, but they note when different sections of a party fight each other.

Yet Labour did not lose spectacularly at first. The 2017 election received little media scrutiny subsequently, due to the fact that so many pundits were proved to be spectacularly wrong in forecasting a big defeat under Corbyn's leadership. Normally after an election there is endless analysis about what happened and why. After the 2017 results, the bewildered pundits moved on to other matters.

They misread and then brushed aside a campaign of great significance – the first election since before the Thatcher era that revolved around a debate over the 'good that government can do' (a quote from the Conservative manifesto). The theme worked for Corbyn, a committed statist, more than it did for Theresa May. The Conservative manifesto was incoherent, with half of it making a belated leap away from Thatcherism, and some of it going back in time with a pledge to scrap the ban on fox hunting. At its heart was a plan to pay for social care. The proposals were flawed, but it was at least an attempt to address the thorny question, even if it was bonkers to do so for the first time in the middle of an election.

At the 2017 election, Labour wiped out the Conservatives' overall majority. Corbyn's party gained Canterbury in Kent and

Kensington in the wealthier part of London, neither known for their attachment to revolutionary socialism. Labour came close in many other seats too, suggesting that with one more push the Labour leader could become prime minister at the next election. For a time in the immediate aftermath of 2017, those who assumed Corbyn could be a prime minister before very long included George Osborne and Tony Blair, both critics from what they saw as the centre ground.[1] They regarded their revised view of Corbyn's prospects as a warning as well as an acknowledgement that he had secured a much higher vote in 2017 than either had expected. Labour's former deputy leader Harriet Harman made a more generous observation. She declared that now Corbyn had proved a left-wing manifesto could be a vote-winner, she was content to become an advocate of more radical policies. She had only been reluctant to do so in the past because she assumed the electorate would turn away.[2]

Labour had made significant gains in the toughest of contexts: a prime minister calling an election suddenly and unexpectedly when she was twenty points ahead in the polls. Corbyn's critics pointed out that Labour still lost. Most did not also record that, under Corbyn, Labour had secured a level of support not achieved since Tony Blair in 2001, when he won a landslide.

The 2017 election divides Corbyn's leadership into two parts. The first was up until Theresa May called the election. The second was after the 2017 campaign, when briefly even his severest critics saw him as a potential prime minister. After which, Corbyn descended towards the hell of the December 2019 election when he led his party to a huge defeat. There are overlapping themes, such as the noisy dissent of some Labour MPs; Corbyn's lack of leadership skills and the ineptitude of his office; the initial scorn of the media and then a renewed hostility when it appeared he might be prime minister. Yet, in between, there was the 2017 election, a significant and unexpected peak in Corbyn's leadership.

In the spring of 2021, one of the key strategists and weighty Cabinet ministers from the New Labour era, Peter Mandelson, insisted Corbyn only did relatively well in that election because of Brexit. Remainers wanted to punish Theresa May, who was taking an increasingly hard line: '2017 of course was a Brexit election. It was like a rerun of the referendum the year before, when the Leave half of the country lined up solidly with the Tories, and indeed increased the Tories' vote share, and the Remain vote quit the Lib Dems and swung around behind Labour, raising our vote share too. That's what that was about. It wasn't a vote for socialism. It was actually a vote for Remain.'[3]

That was part of the explanation but not the whole one. Brexit did not feature greatly in the campaign. And even if it were a factor, many commentators argued during the campaign and before that Corbyn was so dangerously calamitous that voters would not vote for him under any circumstances. Yet voters did, in unexpectedly high numbers.

There were other strong currents in the Corbyn era, ones that played their part in his bizarre rise to the top of his party and, briefly, moved him close to Number Ten. Nothing in politics happens by chance. There are reasons why leaders become leaders and potential prime ministers. In Corbyn's case the reasons extend beyond Brexit, an issue which was at all points a nightmare for him rather than an advantage.

———

Labour's 2015 leadership contest had a funereal air during the early stages. The party had lost again, this time unexpectedly. Most party members had assumed that Ed Miliband would be prime minister, in a hung parliament at least.[4] Instead, David Cameron had won a small overall majority. Inevitably, the subsequent Labour leadership hustings were attended without great enthusiasm. The candidates and those with a vote in the contest were exhausted and deflated after the election campaign.

All the early candidates worked on the assumption that because Miliband had lost with a pitch a little to the left of New Labour, they had to move in the opposite direction. The favourite, Andy Burnham, launched his campaign by overtly looking back to 1997: 'Our challenge is not to go left or right, to focus on one part of the country above another, but to rediscover the beating heart of Labour. And that is about the aspirations of everyone, speaking to them like we did in 1997.'[5]

It was as if Burnham was trying to appeal to *Times* columnists and parts of the BBC rather than Labour members. Perhaps he was, hoping the approval of those in the media who regarded Labour's 1997 victory as the eternal model would gush in a way that would impress the membership. Another former Cabinet minister, Yvette Cooper, conveyed a similar message. Cooper wanted to 'move beyond the old labels of left and right' and be 'credible, compassionate, creative and connected to the day-to-day realities of life'.[6]

As the leading candidates projected themselves with an apolitical caution that bordered on the banal, the BBC and the newspapers were setting up a test of credibility: would they agree with the then chancellor, George Osborne, that the Labour government had overspent when it was in power? Towards the end of the 2015 election campaign, Miliband had been asked this question in front of a live audience during a *Question Time* broadcast to millions of viewers. Miliband said 'no' and was jeered by some in the audience. His response was widely regarded as a gaffe by broadcasters and columnists, who had broadly accepted Osborne's deficit narrative.

Journalists persistently posed the same question to Labour's leadership candidates. The media orthodoxy was that the new leader would only have a hope if they accepted, unlike Miliband, that the last Labour government had been culpable by overspending. Burnham sought to pass the media's credibility test by arguing that there was a brief period before the 2008 crash when Labour should have imposed tougher spending constraints. Cooper knew the media narrative was dangerous nonsense, and that Labour's spending had not caused the crash. It was the other way around: the crash had led to the deficit. Equally, she recognized that this was the test that the media had set and she could not avoid it. She spent an entire afternoon with advisers trying to devise an answer that would not condemn the last Labour government, nor constrain what she could then say and do as a leader in relation to economic policy, while also seeking to avoid the 'no' answer that had condemned Miliband to ridicule on *Question Time*.

While these leading candidates were agonizing over how to prove they were economically 'responsible', the contest was punctuated with meaningless statements from other senior figures. David Miliband had led the way with his vague remarks about Labour needing to turn the page forward rather than back. Jon Cruddas, who had thought more deeply than most as to how Labour should respond to David Cameron's leadership, suggested that it was necessary to go to 'some dark places' in order to recover.[7] He did not specify where the darkness lay.

The contest was dull and vague. After five years of the coalition government rushing through ideological and dizzyingly erratic reforms – real-terms spending cuts, the atomization of public services, the weakening of local government, the introduction of fixed-term parliaments and much more – there were only shallow attempts at framing an alternative and little analysis as to what they faced now that Cameron had secured an overall majority.

Later, Burnham was to discover his public voice as a formidable Mayor of Greater Manchester, and Yvette Cooper was one of the few Labour politicians who could unnerve Tory prime ministers as chair of the Home Affairs Committee. Both had leadership qualities, but at this juncture they were trapped by a party membership moving to the left, the media making a key test of their leadership potential that they leap to the right, their own sense that Ed Miliband had lost by being too left-wing, and the sheer exhaustion of following a general election defeat with a leadership contest.

Corbyn entered at the last minute, reluctantly becoming the latest figure from the left to join the contest. He assumed he would be defeated and could return to the relative comfort of the backbenches. His close friend and ally John McDonnell warned Corbyn that the two of them would wander around the country attending near-empty halls like the ageing characters from the TV series *Last of the Summer Wine*.[8] But within days, Corbyn had become the equivalent of a rock star. His first public meeting of the campaign was in Camden, north London. The vast numbers attending meant that Corbyn had to address a spillover meeting. The same pattern applied across the country.

Corbyn's message could not have been more different to the cautiously calibrated words of the other candidates. Did the last Labour government overspend? No, it did not spend enough. The crash was caused by lightly regulated banks – his solution was tougher regulation and state ownership. Corbyn was further strengthened by his opposition to the war in Iraq at the time of the conflict. The new candidate in the contest demanded more power for party members in policymaking, and suggested their input would lead to radical solutions. His campaign was boosted by a new rule that allowed virtually anyone to join and vote for the price of £3, but even a significant number of existing party members were enthused.

Enough of them yearned for a radical change of direction; Tony Blair's third-way politics had led him towards the darkness of Iraq, and Gordon Brown's need to identify with bankers to provide cover for his more stealthy left-wing objectives left him vulnerable after the 2008 crash. Ed Miliband had got trapped in his own third way, seeking to move on from New Labour but too keen to woo the right-wing media and his brother's wing of the Labour Party to make as big a leap as part of him wanted to.

Corbyn had a distinctive appeal that other candidates from the left had lacked. He was polite and driven without appearing to be angry. One admirer, new to politics, said he went to a rally and regarded Corbyn as a 'religious prophet'.[9] For a time at least, before the pressures of leadership started to infuriate him, he came across as a gentle radical. Previous candidates from his wing of the party, such as John McDonnell, had a reputation for a more aggressive form of politics. Corbyn's tone had a wider appeal. He won a landslide.

As leader, Corbyn's personal emollience initially took a generous form. He tried to form a shadow Cabinet of the widest political range, asking the other candidates in the contest to join the frontbench. Most of them declined to do so. Critics condemned his first shadow Cabinet for the preponderance of men. Quite a lot of the women he had asked to join turned him down. His opening attempts to form a frontbench team were haphazard – the first example of Corbyn being like a recreational tennis player who had found himself at Wimbledon. Corbyn had never needed to appoint a team of any sort in his life. Suddenly, he was appointing a shadow Cabinet and wider frontbench as leader of the Opposition. He needed the help and guidance of the chief whip, Rosie Winterton, as he spent the day after his election frantically making appointments.

Inevitably, he alienated more MPs in the process. Even leaders with experience of carrying out reshuffles unavoidably antagonize, and this was all completely new to Corbyn. Chris Leslie, who had been acting shadow chancellor, spent the day of the reshuffle wondering whether or not he should accept an offer from Corbyn to join the shadow Cabinet, until realizing late in the evening that no such invitation was going to be made. The following day, Leslie returned to his office at Westminster to discover that the new shadow chancellor, John McDonnell, had taken it over. No doubt Leslie was always going to be a vocal critic, but such slights fuelled disillusionment when MPs were already feeling stroppy.[10]

The public dissent of Labour MPs had many causes. One of them was trivial but significant: they were in a state of shock. A lot of them had spent their entire careers shifting to a perceived 'centre ground', and they assumed that any leader would see such positioning as a reason to promote them. The left as represented by Corbyn had been a minor irritant. They had never for a second had to contemplate trying to woo the likes of Corbyn to secure advancement. Suddenly, they were the ones on the outside. They struggled to cope with Corbyn's success, but Corbyn was struggling too. For him, spending a Sunday appointing his first shadow Cabinet was a form of political hell. In his past life he would have been out campaigning or perhaps spending a couple of hours on his allotment.

While Corbyn's expedient offers to join the shadow Cabinet were rebuffed by some so-called moderate MPs, he made one defiant stand: he offered senior posts to his allies. Diane Abbott was made shadow Home Secretary. As Leslie discovered, John McDonnell was made shadow chancellor. Once again, disillusioned Labour MPs and much of the media misread the significance of the appointment, and McDonnell's elevation provoked outrage. It turned out to be not just an act of loyalty but an astutely imaginative elevation. From the start, McDonnell displayed a counter-intuitive pragmatism, and conveyed authority based on his many years framing the left's economic policies from the backbenches.

His first act as shadow chancellor was to announce he would comply with Osborne's various gimmicks aimed at constraining spending – or perhaps trapping Labour into appearing profligate. Here McDonnell was displaying pragmatism to the point of naivety; Osborne did not comply with his own constraints and McDonnell had no need to declare that Labour would do so. However, the gesture showed his determination to prove he was economically responsible. He would soon become the most formidable figure on Labour's troubled frontbench.

As Corbyn staggered out of his office on the Sunday evening, having spent his first full day as leader appointing a frontbench, he was doorstepped by Sky News. It is the fate of leaders to be doorstepped, but again this was new to Corbyn. He was incapable of acting, a big drawback for a leader, and he did not disguise his annoyance at being questioned in this way. Corbyn was not an instinctively angry person but he loathed much of the way politics was reported, and he showed it. He was seen on TV bulletins most often leaving his house in the morning trying to get to his car as cameras crowded around him. Miliband and his wife had found the doorstepping outside their house the biggest burden of his leadership, but he knew how to hide his unease. Other leaders loathed the experience but learned to smile. Corbyn could not be other than what he was. He looked thunderous, which reinforced the simplistic caricature of the angry 'hard left' revolutionary.

More significantly, Corbyn had displayed an early lack of strategic coherence in his appointments to the frontbench. Was he seeking to be pragmatic, or ideologically committed? The answer was a bit of both. He wanted to reach out to other parts of the parliamentary Labour Party, not out of a clearly thought-through strategy, but because he was decent. Yet by appointing McDonnell and Abbott, Corbyn showed that he would not curb his radical zeal even as he tried to accommodate those who did not share his convictions.

Corbyn's early confusion over how to manage a team took a dramatic form when in December 2015 the Conservative government sought parliamentary backing for air strikes in Syria. In the Commons debate, Corbyn opened for Labour by opposing the military intervention. His shadow Foreign Secretary, Hilary Benn, closed for Labour by making a speech passionately in favour. Benn's speech was applauded by Conservative MPs and those Labour backbenchers who were taking every opportunity to torment Corbyn in public. There could be no more vivid example of a divided party than a leader and his shadow Foreign Secretary taking opposite positions in the same debate. Even though Corbyn had been elected by a landslide, he had little authority over his own MPs. Dissenters assumed he would be a catastrophic loser. Only leaders seen as potential election-winners can command their parliamentary party.

McDonnell, who did think strategically and did not want to blow this rare opportunity for the left, discussed with Corbyn often how divided parties do not win elections. To some extent, McDonnell's model at this unexpected phase of his career was Harold Wilson, a leader who had sought to bring left and right together.

Within Corbyn's office, the way of avoiding another open division on foreign policy was straightforward: Corbyn needed to sack Benn. His close allies had a point; Corbyn was the leader. He had been elected by a huge mandate and had the right to prevail over key policy disputes. In January 2016, Corbyn met Benn in his office. Corbyn's advisers assumed this would be the meeting in which their leader would tell Benn to leave the frontbench. But Corbyn could not bring himself to do so. He had not only never assembled a team before in his career; he had also never dismissed anyone, and regarded sackings as inhumane. Corbyn and Benn had a convivial conversation. The meeting ended with Benn still in his post.

For Corbyn, there was another issue in relation to Benn. Hilary's father, Tony, had been Corbyn's hero. During his leadership, Corbyn was projected by some critics as a supporter of Putin's Russia. Others suggested Hugo Chávez's Venezuela was his model for government. As with so many public figures, the caricatures made little sense. There was no leader less like Corbyn than Putin, a figure who thrived on machismo and terrorizing opponents internal and external. Corbyn was so lacking in machismo he could not even sack Hilary Benn. His admiration for Chávez's Venezuela was indiscriminate, but of limited use as a guide to what he sought to do in the UK.

As far as Corbyn had a clear idea of what he would do as prime minister, Tony Benn was the guide, not Putin or Chávez. During the first leadership contest, in 2015, Corbyn thought of Benn every day as he tried to discover the strength to make sense of what was happening to him.[11] In the late 1970s and early 1980s, when Benn was at his peak, Corbyn had been a regular attender of rallies in which his hero was the star speaker. Corbyn campaigned for Benn in the 1981 deputy leadership contest. Benn almost won. When Corbyn became an MP in 1983, he was always there when Benn spoke in the chamber, looking on admiringly. He was a regular visitor to Benn's home.

Corbyn had wanted Benn to become leader. It never crossed his mind that he would be leader while Benn never got close. Benn was not only more ambitious, he was far more qualified for leadership. He had been an experienced Cabinet minister, drawing many conclusions from his experience in government about the timidity of Labour in power and the impotence of the membership to inject some more daring radicalism.

After the Labour governments that tottered precariously towards defeat in 1979, Benn announced he would not serve on the frontbench. Instead, as a liberated backbencher but a powerful figure on Labour's National Executive Committee, he argued that the leadership and MPs should be held to account by the membership. Part of his pitch was an 'alternative economic policy' that included import controls to protect jobs, as well as extensive state ownership. Having been a leading advocate in the 1975 referendum for leaving the Common Market, Benn remained a passionate opponent of membership – arguing that the UK Parliament should be the sovereign body and that the European institutions were too disconnected from voters.

Benn's overriding theme was accountability. Who was accountable to whom? In the 1970s, there was a media caricature of Benn that was as distorting as the one that later mis-described Corbyn while he was leader. Benn was portrayed as a threat to democracy – closer to Stalin, according to some newspaper front pages. But while Benn's analysis of what was wrong with the UK and his proposed remedies were flawed, he was an obsessive democrat. While many of his followers on the left were gripped by economic policy, Benn was more interested in themes relating to democracy, constitutions and accountability.

Benn was the best orator of his generation by some margin, witty as well as sweeping in frames of reference and in his attempt to explain why he believed what he did. Benn could move from the miners in the UK to Nelson Mandela and on to the significance of Benson & Hedges sponsoring an event in the span of a few sentences, making connections wherever his speech went next. He admired Margaret Thatcher for being a political teacher. He was one from the left. Benn almost qualifies as a prime minister we never had but fails to do so because, unlike Corbyn, he was never leader of the Opposition and he never had a credible chance of becoming prime minister while Labour was in government. Benn did stand in the 1976 leadership contest when Labour was in power, but made little headway. His high point was the 1981 deputy leadership contest when he came within less than 1 per cent of defeating Denis Healey.[12]

Benn never had the means of becoming prime minister. Even so, he is an example of a politician who exerted enduring influence, arguably more than some former prime ministers. During the second decade of the twenty-first century, senior Tory Cabinet ministers were 'Bennite' in their arguments about sovereignty, support for Brexit and in the way they chose to be held to account by increasingly hard-line party activists. Meanwhile, on the other side, one of Benn's devoted followers had become Labour leader.

In the oddest of twists Corbyn rose to the top of his party in a way that Benn never did. And in doing so, Corbyn resolved broadly to deliver Benn's agenda. Benn might not have become leader, but Corbyn would act on his behalf. Over time, this was reflected in Corbyn's attempts to increase powers for the party membership, his growing domination of the party's institutions, and in two election manifestos with Bennite themes.

Benn was also Corbyn's posthumous guide as crises erupted around his early awkward attempts at leadership. The anti-Semitism saga, a constant dark theme during Corbyn's leadership, erupted when the new leader's ally and former London mayor, Ken Livingstone, defended the Labour MP Naz Shah. In a Facebook post in 2014, before she became an MP, Shah had shared a graphic showing Israel's outline superimposed on a map of the US under the headline 'Solution for Israel-Palestine conflict – relocate Israel into United States', with the comment 'problem solved'. Her posts were reported in April 2016. Shah responded to the furore with sincere proclamations that she would learn from her Facebook provocations. In spite of this, Livingstone took to the airwaves, not only defending Shah without qualification but adding his own theory, based on the work of a historian, that Hitler was a Zionist before he 'went mad'.

This is when anti-Semitism and Labour became front-page news and led TV bulletins. The Labour MP John Mann approached Livingstone in the broadcasting studios at Westminster, accusing him of being a 'Nazi apologist'. Camera crews pursued Livingstone as he rushed to hide in toilets within the building. As he waited with his usual placidity, reporters shouted from outside, 'Ken Livingstone, are you a Nazi?'

Corbyn came under great pressure from within his party and beyond to suspend Livingstone. By then, several months into his leadership, he had been through various dilemmas. This was by far the worst for him. Livingstone was a friend and ally. Amid a crowd of critics, Livingstone had been Corbyn's most prominent and articulate defender in the media. Livingstone was in his seventies, even older than Corbyn. He had been around for decades. It was not as if a new, sinister public figure had surfaced with no past. Livingstone's past was packed with controversy, but also a Corbyn-like willingness to meet those whom other British politicians would not, including the IRA and Hamas representatives.

Was his latest insensitive outburst enough to merit suspension? Corbyn reflected that Livingstone's past was familiar when he stood to be Mayor of London. He was elected by big majorities twice without facing front-page allegations of anti-Semitism on a regular basis. Not for the only time, and with some justification, Corbyn concluded that part of the furore was aimed at undermining his leadership.

As he agonized about what to do, Corbyn reflected on what had happened to Tony Benn. During the 1981 deputy leadership contest, some of Benn's more ardent supporters noisily heckled his opponent, Denis Healey. The abuse was wholly at odds with Benn's own character. Benn was nearly always polite to his internal and external opponents. He used to reduce Harold Wilson to raging paranoia, but Wilson's devoted and loyal senior aide Marcia Williams would not hear a word against Benn. She liked the wit and charm. So did those Conservative MPs fascinated by his ideological journey. Benn got on well with Enoch Powell and Keith Joseph, two figures at the other end of the political spectrum. Nonetheless, Benn never disowned the abusive hecklers, even though he was under huge pressure to do so. Later, he reflected that he'd been attacked ferociously by virtually every media outlet, Conservatives, and quite a lot of the Labour Party. He was being asked to turn on those who were supporting him. He was not going to do so.

To some extent, Corbyn felt the same – about Livingstone, and then later when demands intensified for him to purge other allies who were being accused of anti-Semitism. He regarded his big achievement as generating the biggest membership of any party in Europe. Now that success was being turned into a big problem. Some of those being investigated, though by no means all, were committed supporters of his who had joined Labour when he became leader. Like Benn, vilified wherever he turned, Corbyn was under huge pressure to challenge those who did back him.

Even so, Corbyn had no choice but to suspend Livingstone, who refused to give up his obsession with asserting that Hitler was a Zionist. Corbyn found it painful to reach the decision, and characteristically could not face telling Livingstone that he was being suspended from the party. He asked Livingstone's former senior adviser, Simon Fletcher, to phone him with the news. According to Livingstone, Fletcher was in tears as he delivered the message.[13]

Similar sequences were played out many times in the years that followed, much more vividly after the 2017 election than before. In response to the Livingstone debacle, Corbyn asked the former Liberty director Shami Chakrabarti to chair an inquiry on Labour and anti-Semitism. Chakrabarti was unfairly attacked for taking on the task and then agreeing to a Labour peerage. She had been a hero for many 'liberals' who could not accept that she was now working with Corbyn. They felt betrayed, and yet her support for the Corbyn leadership was sincere. She could have accepted many other less draining roles than moving into his shadow Cabinet. Her report was compiled quickly and with limited recommendations. It neither reassured Corbyn's many critics nor offered much of a practical guide to dealing with the issue. The anti-Semitism crisis deepened and the number of allegations about the conduct of activists soared, even though quite a few of those accused were not party members – one of several nuanced qualifications that were largely ignored.

What was clear is that, for complex reasons, the party machine failed to move speedily in dealing with complaints of anti-Semitism. More fundamentally, Corbyn did not recognize the central importance of showing he was addressing the issue. Leaders often feel a crisis that erupts is in some ways unfair or distorted. The successful ones know that they have to prove that they are addressing a perceived crisis, even if they feel that the furore is partly overblown.

On both sides of Labour's intense divide during the Corbyn era, passions were stirred most about the past. Corbyn's opponents accused him of being too close to Hamas, a militant Islamist group, and Hezbollah, a Lebanese paramilitary group, when he was a backbench MP. Both were widely viewed in the West as terrorist organizations. Corbyn described representatives of Hamas as his 'friends' after inviting them to a meeting in Parliament in 2009. He later said he regretted using this language, but insisted his motivation in talking to enemies of Israel was the promotion of peace in the Middle East. In March 2018, Corbyn was criticized for sending an apparently supportive message to the creator of an allegedly anti-Semitic mural in 2012. In the message, sent via

Facebook, he appeared to question a decision to remove the artist's controversial work from a wall in east London.

Corbyn had explanations or offered apologies for his conduct in previous years when he was a campaigning backbencher with no interest in becoming party leader, but the accumulated examples added to the pressure on him to show that he was displaying resolute and determined leadership in dealing with the current allegations of anti-Semitism within the Labour Party. Evidently, he failed to reassure his critics, as the attacks on him intensified in the second half of his leadership. McDonnell was subtler and sharper from the beginning, expressing unqualified remorse and a determination to speedily address what had gone badly wrong – or what was perceived to have gone wrong.

Tony Benn also hovered over Corbyn's other epic challenge during the first half of his leadership. David Cameron called the Brexit referendum in June 2016, less than a year after Corbyn was elected Labour leader. There could have been no thornier issue to test Corbyn's capacity to lead, especially at a point when he was still struggling to adapt to the unexpected life-changing event of accidentally winning the leadership contest. Like Benn, Corbyn had been an opponent of the UK's membership of the EU. He had been opposed for much longer than Boris Johnson, the chaotic and calculating figure prominent in the pro-Brexit campaign. But Corbyn's party members, even a lot of those who had joined since he became leader, were passionately pro-European.

When faced with dilemmas, most leaders or aspiring leaders ask two separate questions: What do I believe? What do I need to say and do in order to navigate the entire party through difficult terrain? If personal convictions clash with leadership responsibilities, successful leaders ruthlessly focus on the best way to reconcile the conflicting demands. In this case, Corbyn did not want to jettison deeply held beliefs and yet he had a responsibility to keep the party together. Although Corbyn had been personally generous to colleagues from other parts of the party, offering frontbench posts to dissenters and allowing Hilary Benn to speak out on Syria, he was stubborn about his own convictions. As a backbencher for decades, Corbyn had been content to address the first question – about what he believed. He knew what he felt about virtually every issue and had been happy as a backbencher to campaign without compromise.

Now he had no choice but to attempt to answer the second question, given his new elevated role. How might he get the entire Labour Party through the referendum? As a leader, he was trapped. There was no way he could campaign for Brexit. His pro-European party membership would have erupted. But Corbyn could not equivocate convincingly. He had never acted or equivocated throughout his career. He could not learn those arts now. Instead, he sought to convince himself that remaining in the EU was the best course for those on the left. This was difficult for him, partly because he knew Tony Benn, unlike Hilary, had been an opponent largely on the grounds of democratic accountability. Corbyn's ideological solution was to have several conversations with the former Greek Finance Minister, the left-wing radical Yanis Varoufakis. During their meetings, Varoufakis gave him a protective ideological shield, persuading the Labour leader that for all its flaws there was a collective spirit in parts of the European project. Unsurprisingly, when Corbyn made his tentative case for Remain in the referendum, he did so by emphasizing workers' rights and environmental protections, while stressing he would seek reforms in other areas.

Although more ardent Remainers in the shadow Cabinet fumed at Corbyn's limited endorsement of their cause during the referendum, he had moved a long way towards them, leaving behind his career-long opposition to the UK's membership. Indeed, one of the ironies of Corbyn's leadership is that while internal opponents despaired about his unyielding inflexibility, it was he who made the more expedient moves. Within his first year he had suspended his friend, ally and media advocate Livingstone, then for the first time in his life he had put the case for the UK to remain in the EU, and before that he had allowed his shadow Foreign Secretary to put the case for military action in Syria. At times, Corbyn displayed a curious and yet wholly authentic mix of soothing tones, modest humility and rigid attachment to some of his own views. He could not leave his old self behind, and yet was trying to be the leader of a parliamentary party at odds with him.

———

During this first phase of his leadership, Corbyn was never remotely commanding or intimidating in managing his parliamentary party and the largely hostile media. He was not protected by opinion poll leads – the most important factor in bestowing authority on leaders. If polls suggest a leader might win an election, they acquire greater respect among parliamentary colleagues and in much of the media. The opposite also applies. In the case of Corbyn, within months of him becoming leader his many critics assumed Labour was heading for a historic landslide defeat. In this context, when the Brexit referendum was lost in the summer of 2016, despairing pro-Europeans in the shadow Cabinet and beyond were not furious with David Cameron for calling and losing a referendum – they were apoplectic with Corbyn for not being a more enthusiastic Remainer.

What followed showed that the Labour Party was in crisis on many different levels. A significant section of the shadow Cabinet resigned and called on Corbyn to stand down. Those leaving included Hilary Benn, who was sacked after warning in the aftermath of the referendum that 'there is no confidence to win the next election if Jeremy continues as leader'.[14] The departing frontbenchers were supported by many Labour MPs.

Contrary to later mythology, Corbyn was not a narcissist who assumed politics revolved around him; or at least he was not at this stage. He was too besieged to allow vanity to take hold. Faced with the onslaught from his own MPs in the days following the Brexit referendum, Corbyn contemplated giving in to his critics, a part of him yearning for the backbenches and his north London allotment rather than the hell of leading a party. He was talked out of it by his closest supporters. The likes of Seumas Milne from within his office and John McDonnell argued that his leadership was the best chance the left had secured since the formation of the Labour Party, also pointing out that he had won a landslide in the leadership contest less than a year earlier.

Corbyn opted to fight on, and he proved once again to be a more formidable campaigner than the rebels. His critics had a lot going for them. They were hailed by much of the media for their perceived bravery and principled stand. Polls suggested most Labour Party members were passionate Remainers and shared the MPs' despair about the referendum result. But the dissenting MPs were inept strategists, and had no clear sense of an alternative platform in terms of ideas and the policies that arose from them. The rebels were either newish MPs or those who had been brought up subserviently under Blair/Brown's New Labour, where all the big policy and strategic decisions were taken at the very top and their limited role was to carry them out. As a result, they were half-formed campaigners, strategists and policymakers.

When another leadership contest was triggered in the summer of 2016, they had no obvious candidate and had not thought through how they would sway a membership that had elected Corbyn by a huge margin less than a year earlier. In the end they chose Owen Smith to be their candidate; he was a decent and competent politician, but one who had little fresh to say and lacked Corbyn's recently discovered capacity to wow a crowd. The essence of Smith's pitch was that he would more or less adopt the same policies as Corbyn but would be more effective as a leader. This was an anti-climactic message in the context of a seismic move – the attempt to depose a recently elected leader. Corbyn won another landslide, one that made a weak figure much stronger and unassailable in the short term. The rebels had achieved the opposite of what they had set out to do, and had advertised noisily to the wider electorate what they thought of their leader – one who would now be their proposed alternative prime minister at the next election.

While Labour had been preparing for its second whacky leadership contest within a year, the Conservatives had elected Theresa May as their leader and therefore prime minister. Given the nightmare that lay ahead for her, May had a dream start to the job. Like many other prime ministers, while appearing to flourish she was sowing seeds that would eventually lead to her doom. Her decision to appease hard-line Brexiteers when she was in a strong enough position to challenge them, as well as the appointment of a Cabinet that was ready to go for her when it detected weakness, ultimately contributed to her fall. Yet there was little sign of weakness at first. Indeed, senior ministers who betrayed her later were terrified to say a word against her, even in private, during her honeymoon period. She and her Number Ten operation were dominant and intimidating.

Largely down to her joint chief of staff, Nick Timothy, May arrived in Number Ten with a modernizing mission that suggested a commitment to taking the party away from an increasingly outdated Thatcherism. Timothy had convinced May that part of her governing philosophy should recognize the importance of the state, intervening in markets that did not work, and in delivering more widely a competitive economy with fairer outcomes. With Labour fighting another civil war in the summer of 2016, a triumphant May had the stage more or less to herself.

When she called the surprise election outside Number Ten immediately after a sunny Easter weekend in 2017, she was more than twenty points ahead in the polls. The announcement was executed perfectly; there had been no leaks from a disciplined and focused team. Few had expected May to make such a move. She had ruled out an early election several times in interviews, and she was cautious by instinct. Yet her dramatic announcement did not appear to be a risk for her. Corbyn was seen as the ideal opponent. He was hopelessly inexperienced, on the left and had been disowned by many of his MPs. She was apparently strong and stable, and yet a few weeks later May had lost her party's overall majority.

For Corbyn, these few weeks marked the high point of his leadership. He was at ease campaigning. Before he became leader he spoke at endless meetings, protests and rallies. May was not a campaigner. She was shy and awkward, incapable of addressing voters with compelling accessibility. She delivered a radical and candid manifesto and never spoke to it. Instead, she repeated like a machine that her leadership would be 'strong and stable'. The gap between radical intent and bland messaging was absurdly wide. Her manifesto included bold plans to pay for social care that became known as the 'dementia tax'. She should never have launched such a policy in the middle of an election campaign, but she assumed she would win big so her advisers sought a mandate to be radical subsequently. Yet during the campaign May claimed only to be strong and stable.

In contrast, Corbyn had been a statist throughout his political career. In a campaign in which the state had become part of the solution instead of the cause of most problems, he was at ease. Labour's manifesto, portrayed widely as a return to the 1970s by a media struggling to keep up with the changing zeitgeist, was a more confident proclamation than May's about the good that the state could do. There would be a national education plan, extensive state ownership, an ambitious housing programme and much more. Corbyn performed confidently in live TV debates and was relaxed on lighter outlets such as the BBC's *The One Show*, where he arrived with some jars of his homemade jam to give to the charmed presenters. At his rallies, he was greeted once more like a rock star. The packed audiences chanted 'Oh, Jeremy Corbyn' as if they were in the presence of Jesus Christ.

Corbyn was modest enough to be embarrassed by the idolatry at this stage. His friend and shadow Home Secretary, Diane Abbott, joked at the time that 'Jeremy doesn't really like the chanting of his name and all that went with it. He travels to so many rallies because he loves train journeys.'[15] Corbyn was a great train buff, subscribing to various rail magazines. By the end of his leadership there were some signs that the homage had gone to his head, but it took some time.

In the 2017 election, the support for him was partly ideological. Fleetingly, Corbyn appeared to offer hope to parts of an electorate that had felt disconnected from the broad liberal consensus linking the likes of Tony Blair, David Cameron, George Osborne and Nick Clegg. During the campaign, the state was portrayed as an agent that could make connections with those who had been 'left behind', a phrase deployed by Brexiteers even though the UK's fractured society had little to do with the role of the EU. Students, whose first direct connection with the state was being landed with big debts, were part of a wider education plan that included free access to universities. Those fending for themselves in the wild housing market were to be offered help. Commuters dependent on private trains and buses providing erratic services and charging high fares were pointed to new possibilities. For some voters, the vision implicit in the message was uplifting rather than terrifying. Labour made a net gain of thirty seats and the Conservatives a net loss of thirteen. In the most febrile hung parliament for many decades, and with Theresa May struggling to stay afloat, Corbyn was seen for a time as the possible next prime minister.

There were many consequences of this overlooked election. Theresa May was doomed to two years of darkness before her party removed her. Brexit became increasingly fraught as May failed to secure a majority in the Commons for her deal, in spite of making several attempts. In 2019, Boris Johnson became prime minister as Conservatives turned away from May and feared the rise of Nigel Farage's Brexit Party. Johnson was not a natural leader, but this was the tempestuous context that gave him the chance to be prime minister. The campaign also marked a tentative shift leftwards for the Conservative Party which, in terms of language and aspiration, continued under Johnson. The Johnson government pledged to 'level up' while the prime minister hailed President Roosevelt as his model for high levels of investment to revive the economy. In the case of both May and Johnson, the vast majority of their Cabinets remained dry Thatcherites, including their respective chancellors, but still, a leap of sorts was marked by the 2017 election.

Another consequence of the election outcome was that Corbyn became a victim of his own success. He had wiped out May's majority, but a hung parliament with Brexit still to be resolved demanded energetic wiliness from the leader of the Opposition. Corbyn was not especially driven and he certainly was not wily. The second half of his leadership was a disaster. The patterns were the same as in the first half, but the rosier context of the 2017 election result made what followed seem darker still.

———

Predictably, there was little strategic thinking about how to turn the significant 2017 gains into a majority at the next election. Corbyn was not a strategist. He had never had to be one as a backbench rebel and he was not going to discover the skills required at this late phase of his career. His senior aides concluded wrongly that because broadcasters were obliged to give balanced coverage during election campaigns, they could largely keep him away from the 'mainstream media' until the next election, relying on clips on Facebook as the main way for Corbyn to be seen and heard. As a result, he became largely invisible. John McDonnell performed strongly in media outlets. The few others chosen by Corbyn's team to make TV and radio appearances were poor performers, while the leader was a ghostly figure. His main public platform was at Prime Minister's Questions, where he lacked the quick wit and ruthlessness to thrive. Up against an embattled May, an equally poor performer, an Opposition leader should have made hay. But Corbyn made no impact. These were his first years on the frontbench, and he was learning the art of performing at the despatch box as leader of the Opposition. He never mastered it.

Feeling besieged, Corbyn's increasingly neurotic and paranoid office prioritized cocooning its leader over all other matters. There were divisions within the office, and with an increasingly pragmatic McDonnell. Labour MPs were starting to show their disdain publicly again after being muffled briefly by the unexpected outcome of the 2017 election. Columnists who'd misread the last election soon returned to the fray.

Corbyn gave them the space to do so. Unsurprisingly, his response to events lacked guile. His unsubtle and clunky reaction to the Salisbury poisonings in 2018 was typical, allowing a perception to intensify that he was determinedly pro-Russian and therefore pro-Putin. At first, Corbyn would not accept the widely held assumption that the Russian government was directly responsible. But this did not mean Corbyn was 'pro-Putin'; he was close to being a pacifist and had not even a hint of machismo, whereas Putin deployed military forces with zeal and other forms of terror of which the poisonings in Salisbury appeared to be an example. Putin's machismo extended to posing shirtless for photographs, a posture Corbyn would not even contemplate adopting. His naive response to the Salisbury poisonings arose from other, broader judgements. Corbyn was against assuming that the US was always right or innocent and Russia automatically guilty. In this case, however, he was too keen to give Russia the benefit of the doubt.

Meanwhile, crises that had begun to take shape before the 2017 election deepened after the heady summer and early autumn. Even if Corbyn had convinced himself he was taking adequate action to address the anti-Semitism charges, he failed to reassure many others. Part of the art of leadership is to remove as many critics' causes as possible, especially allegations as serious as these ones. A leader attuned to winning elections would ask: Is this issue going to cost us seats? Is this issue going to undermine claims of a wider moral purpose? The answer to both questions in relation to the anti-Semitism charges was 'yes'. The accusations didn't go away. Instead they reached an imprecise but explosive crescendo during the 2019 election, when the UK's Chief Rabbi, Ephraim Mirvis, wrote a *Times* article arguing that 'a new poison – sanctioned from the very top – has taken root' in the Labour Party.[16]

The term 'sanctioned' could not have been stronger, but the Chief Rabbi gave no interviews to explain precisely what he meant, in what was an unprecedented intervention from a religious leader in an election campaign. Corbyn could not hide from the media at such a time in the way a religious leader could. The Chief Rabbi was not questioned on any outlet about his article. In contrast, Corbyn was asked about it constantly, more or less starting with a long BBC interview with Andrew Neil, during which he chose not to issue a cathartic apology. The Chief Rabbi's article shed no light on what Corbyn had or had not done to 'sanction' anti-Semitism, but his anguished, sincere and yet vague cry confirmed that the Labour leader had failed to ensure the allegations did not move centre-stage in a general election campaign.

Much of the policy development fell on the shoulders of John McDonnell from the 2017 election onwards. It was not correct that McDonnell was planning to take the UK 'back to the 1970s' – whatever that superficial analysis had meant. He worked with a range of sectors, businesses and think tanks to develop elements of his economic policies. Even the proposed model for the nationalization of the railways, an echo of the past, was far removed from the old British Rail. But with all the internal rows and crises, none of this was communicated to the wider electorate. When voters sense they are being largely ignored as the internal battles are fought, unsurprisingly they will usually turn away.

In a competitive field, the biggest problem for the inexperienced leader was Brexit. A big majority of Labour MPs and party members saw the hung parliament as an opportunity to stop Brexit one way or another. But significant numbers of Labour voters were Brexiteers. Some Labour MPs became Brexiteers on the basis that their constituents wanted the UK to leave Europe and would never forgive them if their cause was 'betrayed'. For Corbyn, this was a multi-layered nightmare. May was determined to negotiate a deal without working with Labour, even though a significant section of her parliamentary party had lost faith in her ability to do so. Even if she had turned to Labour in the immediate aftermath of the election, Corbyn would not have been able to convince his MPs and members that working with May was the best way forward.

Such a conundrum required the guile, ruthlessness and capacity for flexible conviction of Harold Wilson. Corbyn thought he was being Wilson-like in his approach. Regularly, he would cite Wilson's approach towards Europe in the early and mid-1970s. That would have been quite a metamorphosis if true – the former backbencher of unyielding beliefs becoming closer to the most pragmatic of Labour's leaders. But Corbyn was not in Wilson's league. As a human being, this was partly to his credit. He did not have a devious bone in his body. As a leader of a party navigating the highly charged issue of Europe at its most highly charged, he was doomed.

In the early 1970s, Wilson had faced a similar problem over Europe. Edward Heath signed Britain up to membership of the Common Market with the passionate support of a section of the Labour Party. He did so with the equally intense opposition of a majority in the Labour Party. Both sides of the Europe divide had Labour figures with big followings in the party and charismatic stardust. Wilson saw that a referendum with a 'right to differ' in relation to Labour's frontbench was the only way that he could keep his party united. But crucially, this would be the first referendum on Europe. Wilson was able to argue that Heath had taken the UK into Europe without consulting 'the people'. Corbyn ended up proposing a third referendum a relatively short time after the second in which Brexit secured majority support. This was a very different proposition to Wilson arguing for that first referendum in order to secure voters' approval for the UK's membership of the Common Market.

Wilson used his referendum pledge to help Labour win the election in February 1974. The Tory MP Enoch Powell resigned at the start of the campaign, and urged his followers to vote Labour solely on the basis of the referendum pledge. Wilson's pitch was that he would seek to renegotiate the 'terms of membership' and would decide then whether to recommend the UK should stay or leave. By the time of the referendum in 1975, Wilson urged voters to support staying in the Common Market.

Corbyn got into a mess during the December 2019 election campaign by suggesting that at no point would he declare a view. This was not what Wilson had done. More to the point, in an election campaign triggered by Brexit and facing Boris Johnson, who was sloganizing only about Brexit, Corbyn and his team decided with spectacular naivety to pretend this was not the central issue. There was little done to challenge Johnson's false claims that he had secured an 'oven-ready deal' or that a vote for him would 'get Brexit done'. Instead, Corbyn failed even to explain credibly that he would offer another referendum, even though the pledge was less contentious than some of the claims Johnson was making about Brexit.

The more fundamental error in the run-up to December 2019 was the decision – if 'decision' is not too elevated a term – to cram Labour's manifesto with a mountain of policies. The mountain expanded further during the campaign, with pledges out of the blue to provide free broadband and various other costly measures. The free broadband proposition was an interesting one, but one that required much preparation in advance. Months earlier, Corbyn and McDonnell should have been protesting about the cost of broadband, the iniquities that arise as a result and the innovative, entrepreneurial potential of making broadband free. McDonnell mentioned in passing during the campaign that a similar policy had been successfully implemented in South Korea. In which case McDonnell should have visited South Korea months earlier and built up the case to the point where voters were screaming for free broadband. Then an announcement might have seemed like a thought-through response to growing demand, the end of a case put incrementally over time. Instead, the costly policy came from nowhere and got only fleeting attention because of the need to highlight the rest of the mountain.

Unlike electorally successful leaders, Corbyn failed to address the key 'why?' question when announcing other policies. The most successful leaders are teachers, constantly explaining why they are making propositions or responding to events in a particular way. The teaching is an attempt to persuade the wider electorate to at least engage with the ideas and the policies that arise from them. Corbyn came from a culture where like-minded people on the left gathered at meetings or demonstrations, made assertions and agreed with each other. The art of persuasion was not required, because the audience had been persuaded long ago. Corbyn had not learned the art of convincing a wider audience why he was advocating certain policies, and as a result he tended to announce a policy or a stance and assume that would be sufficient. If the assertion made no impact, he pulled another policy out of the bag. At least, this was the case during the December election. Successful leaders address the 'why' question constantly, guiding voters towards their chosen programme.

There was a final cause of Corbyn's demise. Johnson ached for a December election. He was still a novelty as prime minister, enjoying a honeymoon of sorts. In a hung parliament, it was not in his power to bypass the Fixed Term Parliaments Act and go to the polls on the day he wanted. However, Corbyn granted his wish and gave him the election at the time he sought. In fairness to Corbyn, he was in a hole after the naive and preposterously overconfident Liberal Democrat leader, Jo Swinson, also called for a December election. So did Nicola Sturgeon, but with more self-interested cunning – Sturgeon knew the SNP would flourish. Even so, a more commanding leader of the Opposition, with a Wilsonian wiliness, would have worked with other parties to block Johnson's wish rather than grant it. In a hung parliament, the Opposition wield considerable power. The Conservatives had called the 2017 election, not the opposition parties: they had every right to let the still-young parliament run. They did not do so. Johnson won an overall majority of eighty.

———

The period in which Corbyn was seen as a possible or likely next prime minister seemed like ancient history by December 2019. But it was not that far back. After his semi-triumph in the 2017 election, he was a huge hit at the Glastonbury Festival, the vast crowd chanting his name as if he were a rock star topping the bill.

In the aftermath of the fire at the Grenfell tower block in west London in June 2017, a tragedy that caused seventy-two deaths, Corbyn paid a visit of authentic humanity, comforting distraught residents. May's trip was a public relations disaster. She did not speak directly to those who had survived the trauma. Unintentionally, she conveyed a lofty distance, talking to the emergency services and showing what appeared to be only ritualistic concern rather than outrage and grief.

In the early autumn, Corbyn presided over a successful party conference which was close to a victory celebration at times even though Labour had not won. Over the summer and autumn of 2017 and to some extent as May's Brexit crises deepened, Corbyn was a potential prime minister.

Probably a part of him was relieved he failed to make it. Corbyn never conveyed a hunger for power. In the spring of 2020, during Keir Starmer's first Prime Minister's Questions, Corbyn was one of the few MPs in the chamber, sitting on the near-empty backbenches waiting to ask a question. The Covid-19 pandemic meant that any MP who turned up was conspicuous; most contributed virtually. Many observers thought it odd that Corbyn chose both to be in the Commons and to speak as a backbencher. But for Corbyn it was a return to his natural home.

The freakish aberration in his late sixties had passed and he was doing what he contentedly had done before: seeking to make hay as a near-powerless backbench MP.

CONCLUSION

In the introduction I outlined how each of the prime ministers we never had qualified for inclusion. Now we must conclude our investigations by solving the mysteries as to why none of them got to the very top, even though some may well have flourished there. Quite a few might have changed the course of the UK's history for the better.

The most striking lesson is that prime ministers are much safer than they appear to be. Few politicians get to the top, and when they do succeed they are exposed to many wild storms. Most of the time, there is considerable speculation within governing parties and the media that a prime minister is about to fall and be replaced by a mightier figure. The opposite tends to happen: the tottering prime ministers continue to rule for much longer than assumed or anticipated.

From 1968 to the early 1970s, there was much excited talk that Roy Jenkins would replace Harold Wilson. Instead, Wilson remained in place until 1976, when he resigned voluntarily. Wilson was paranoid at times about Jenkins, and yet it was Wilson who became a long-serving Labour prime minister.

John Major was almost as neurotic about the intentions of Michael Heseltine and Michael Portillo. After the UK fell out of the Exchange Rate Mechanism in September 1992, not a day passed when John Major seemed wholly safe. In the spring of 1994, the BBC's *Newsnight* opened with a shot of Number Ten as the presenter, Jeremy Paxman, boomed: 'Will John Major survive the week?' He survived until the general election of 1997, nearly three years after Paxman posed the question.

Only Margaret Thatcher and Theresa May were forced out by their MPs, but Thatcher had been prime minister for more than eleven years and even May survived longer than most of her colleagues had expected. On the weekend after the 2017 election, when the Conservatives had lost their overall majority, the former chancellor George Osborne described May with some relish as a 'dead woman walking'.[1] She walked for another two long, wearying years.

In spite of the rarity of a prime minister being removed, all the prime ministers we never had were seen as prime ministerial or having a chance of moving into Number Ten. Colleagues and political observers who saw them in this light viewed fragile prime ministers and formidable alternatives. In some cases, those alternatives were dripping with ambition, seemingly ready to make a move.

Yet being ready to make a move is not the same as making a move. Quite a lot of the prime ministers we never had did not want the top job badly enough. Those that reach Number Ten tend to behave with a ruthless focus, at least by the time they sense they have a chance of seizing the crown. This is one of the lessons of leadership: those who succeed are willing to go for it with the stamina and determination of an athlete.

While Rab Butler wanted to be prime minister, he was not obsessed enough about leadership. When he was a reforming Education Secretary and Home Secretary, or when he performed a significant role as a modernizing chairman of the Conservative Research Department after Labour's 1945 landslide victory, he did not ask constantly: 'If I do X or Y, will I alienate so many colleagues my path to the leadership might be blocked?' On the contrary, he made huge strides in each of these posts and others, but in doing so alienated more traditional, right-wing Conservatives. When his chances came, he lacked support precisely because he had been such an effective reforming minister. Some of his colleagues disapproved of the reforms and the way he had gone about implementing them.

In the 1960s, Barbara Castle was flattered by suggestions she might be the UK's first woman prime minister, but she never gave much focus to becoming a leader. Castle was a completely different political personality to Butler, but like him she pursued reforms resolutely without being preoccupied with her own ambitions as she did so. When she proposed *In Place of Strife*, her doomed attempt to place trade unions in a new regulatory framework, her diaries expressed daily frustrations about her colleagues' successful attempts to block the reforms. She chronicled no concern about whether her moves would block her from being prime minister. She did not seek the elevated role, or assume that it was within her grasp.

By the time Michael Portillo stood for leader in 2001, he was deeply ambivalent about winning. He could not altogether hide his doubts. A figure who had previously ached to be leader when he had little chance had lost much of his fire by the time a vacancy arose and he was in a position to be a candidate.

Similarly, after the 2017 election Jeremy Corbyn largely hid from public view, re-emerging to be defeated in the 2019 campaign. Corbyn showed few signs of being desperate to become prime minister, and some indications of relief when he failed to do so. With varying degrees of doubt, Butler, Castle, Portillo and

Corbyn did not want it enough. Of that unlikely quartet, Butler was by far the least doubtful about his desire to be a leader, but he still lacked the ruthless instinct of the more relentlessly ambitious.

The prime ministers we never had were trapped by perceptions about potentially glittering futures and hostile views about their pasts. On the whole, the very few that become prime minister have little or nothing to hide. The past can be a near-fatal obstacle – or, to be more precise, the perceptions of the past that are sometimes wilfully formed. When he became Labour leader, Corbyn was questioned as much about what he got up to in the 1970s and 1980s as about his plans for the future. His meetings with representatives from Sinn Fein and Hamas, held when he was a campaigning MP with no hope of moving anywhere near the top of his party, featured extensively as he contemplated the possibility of Downing Street after the 2017 election. Corbyn had no intention of disowning his past, but his 'failure' to apologize in some instances became big stories that fed on themselves.

Long-serving Cabinet ministers were also tormented by their pasts, however distinguished they seemed from a safe distance. Denis Healey was not forgiven for what he did as Labour chancellor in the 1970s, even when he was seeking to be leader in the changed context of the 1980s. Butler worked beyond party boundaries to secure his reforms as a minister. In doing so he introduced radical change, but he alienated too many that lived within Conservative Party boundaries. Butler also suffered from the fact he had supported appeasement as a youthful minister in the 1930s. Being on the wrong side of a historic policy dispute is never forgotten. As a supporter, at the time, of the war in Iraq, David Miliband discovered the same. Aspiring leaders cannot escape their pasts.

In contrast, Tony Blair and Gordon Brown were broadly recognized to have been on the right side of Labour's internal battles at the time they became leaders in 1994 and 2007, respectively. Margaret Thatcher was a loyal Education Secretary, getting into some trouble only over her decision to scrap free milk for some pupils. John Major had served as both Foreign Secretary and chancellor for such a short time that he could not be defined by a single contentious policy. David Cameron had been shadow Education Secretary for a few months before becoming party leader. Theresa May kept her head down in the Home Office, and again during the Brexit referendum campaign. None of the prime ministers were burdened by their pasts when they climbed to the top. This is a depressing lesson, as it suggests that being an effectively courageous Cabinet minister can prevent aspiring leaders from becoming prime ministers.

Being principled can also be a problem. Possessing deeply held beliefs should be an asset for a prime minister, but they can stop the believers from getting close to Number Ten. On the whole, prime ministers need to be flexible with their convictions, although Thatcher was to some extent an exception to that rule. Roy Jenkins, Michael Heseltine and Ken Clarke were all passionate pro-Europeans at a point when attitudes towards the European Union were defining ones, first in the Labour Party and then the Conservatives. Leaders cannot be fundamentally at odds with their party in their beliefs. To their credit, Jenkins, Heseltine and Clarke were not willing to pretend they had changed their views on Europe in order to have a better chance of becoming leader.

In contrast, Harold Wilson voted against the UK joining the Common Market in 1973 while advocating continued membership in the referendum he called in 1975. In the build-up to the 1997 election, Tony Blair managed to convey the impression that he was keen on joining the single currency while also proclaiming that he 'loved the pound'. David Cameron told his party to 'stop banging on about Europe' while removing Conservatives from the centre-right grouping in the European Parliament, and later calling a referendum on Brexit. Cameron took flexibility to new extremes; but while he became prime minister, the principled trio – Jenkins, Heseltine and Clarke – never did.

There is another problem for the prime ministers we never had to which there is no solution. Successful and ambitious ministers are bound over time to be seen as likely prime ministers. The perception can be the undoing of an aspirant leader. They cannot move without an action or utterance being interpreted through the prism of insatiable personal ambition. If Heseltine gave a rousing party conference speech, as he normally did, his performance would trigger a thousand articles about the chances of him becoming the next leader and the substance of the speech got less attention. As a backbencher, if Heseltine did not support the government in a Commons vote, the rebellious act was viewed almost as a challenge to Thatcher's leadership.

Michael Portillo never recovered from the frenzy of excitement he generated in the mid-1990s as the Thatcherites thought they had discovered a new idol to replace their fallen one. There was too much excitement around him, as there was briefly when Blairites hoped that David Miliband was about to seize the crown. It is best for aspiring prime ministers not to become glittering political stars before they have made it to the leadership. Once they are leaders, a bit of glitter is fine. Before they make it, the idolatry generates suspicion or jealousy among colleagues, or usually both. Their colleagues resolve with even more jealous determination to prevent them from becoming leader or prime minister. Even their adulatory followers can be fickle and turn – as Portillo discovered, although in fairness he moved away from them.

Prime ministers tend to be effective performers without quite becoming the equivalent of rock stars, although Thatcher and Blair could generate responses as if they were pop legends playing to adoring crowds at the O2 Arena. In both cases, they developed their charisma once they had safely become leaders. Until that point, Thatcher had done little to overshadow her leader, Edward Heath, and Blair had been loyal to Neil Kinnock and John Smith. In contrast, Heseltine, Portillo and even to some extent David Miliband were seen as stars as they made their moves towards the top and therefore were mistrusted by some colleagues. Mistrust is a problem for those who want to become leader of their party and then prime minister.

That does not mean aspiring prime ministers should opt for dullness. At key moments, performance is necessary. Some blew it. Butler was a sophisticated performer, especially in the Commons, sometimes deploying wit to good effect. He was not in the same league as Harold Macmillan, who was wittier in public and more wily. At the Conservative party conference in 1963, Butler had the stage to himself, standing in for Macmillan as acting prime minister. There was an unofficial leadership contest taking place. But Butler failed to rise to the occasion, delivering a dull speech that did nothing to excite those gathered in the conference hall on the verge of selecting a new prime minister. At the Labour conference in 2008, David Miliband did little to electrify his dissenting followers as they dared to hope he would replace Gordon Brown. Instead it was Brown who performed, as he could when he was in the mood. As part of his speech, the prime minister declared that this was 'no time for a novice' – a warning to Miliband that this was not the time for an insurrection. David half agreed with the warning.

The fate of David's brother, Ed, highlights another striking lesson from our investigation. In most cases, being leader of the Opposition is a necessary precondition to becoming prime minister, but that is not the remotest guarantee of acquiring the crown. This is especially the case for Labour leaders of the Opposition. In the time span of this book, only Blair and Wilson have won elections for Labour from opposition. The others lost general elections, even when polls suggested they were heading for victory. A still-powerful right-wing media might set a higher bar for Labour leaders, but evidently Labour – and specifically those the party elects to lead it – are not good at winning general elections.

There is a temptation to end with a proposal that would remove the biggest obstacles that prevented some prime ministers we never had from reaching the top. There is such a constitutional reform that would make the difference. The deepest explanation as to why quite a lot of the characters in this book failed to become prime minister is the deep connection between a party and the leader it elects. At key moments, some of the prime ministers we never had were at odds with their parties over the most urgent policies of their times. This was the biggest factor that blocked Butler, Jenkins, Healey, Heseltine and Clarke. They were all capable of being formidable prime ministers, but not as leaders of their respective parties when they sought the crown.

If we seek the best possible leaders, there is a strong case for the UK to elect presidents rather than prime ministers in a party-based system. Given that the UK has a presidential culture, with the relentless focus on the prime minister, perhaps such a major constitutional change would not be too seismic. Some of the prime ministers we never had may well have been elected as a Conservative or Labour president running on their personalities and their own mandate, rather than a programme intimately bound to their parties' demands and wishes. Also, party leaders like Kinnock, Ed Miliband and Corbyn might have had more of a hope in such a context, as so much of their time as leaders was taken up by managing their party and dealing with various forms of dissent.

I am going to resist the temptation to advocate the change. A presidential system might have helped some of the prime ministers we never had but it is not a guarantee of more effective leadership. Take a look at some of the recent presidents elected in other Western democracies.

There is also much to be said for parties, leaders and potential leaders gyrating awkwardly on the same political dance floor. Leadership is not solely about technocratic skills. There is a hugely important ideological dimension. On the big debates at any given time, leaders or potential leaders must sway their parties or move towards the ideological positions of activists. The dynamic changes regularly, but it does so on the basis of ideological arguments.

Margaret Thatcher moved her party rightwards. She and her party did not begin in the same place, but long after her departure as prime minister she was an intoxicating influence on the Conservatives – an astonishing feat. Tony Blair moved his party closer towards his views by being an election-winner. Other leaders adapted to the mood of their party. Harold Wilson recognized the might of the left by appointing the likes of Michael Foot and Tony Benn to key Cabinet positions. Boris Johnson became a hard-line Brexiteer to reflect the mood of his party's members. In British politics, part of a leader's skill is to make the dance more cordial. The prime ministers we never had could not make the dance work.

Though that is not enough of a case to scrap the need for deft footwork.

———

In spite of their doomed moves on the political stage, this book is not a study of failure. Each of the prime ministers we never had achieved more than most who enter British politics with high hopes and steely ambition. Butler was the most successful Tory Cabinet minister of his generation in terms of policy implementation and longevity. The same could be argued for Jenkins from a Labour perspective, although he did not hold anywhere near the same number of ministerial posts as Butler. Healey was a universally praised Defence Secretary and a chancellor who navigated the dilemmas of the 1970s, while still providing cash for major social reforms. His decision not to join the SDP saved his party, alongside the defiantly resilient leadership of Neil Kinnock. Heseltine was the most imaginative and daring Cabinet minister of the Thatcher era, and remains the model of a Conservative modernizer if the party wishes to move on from Thatcherism. Portillo is a model of a different sort, learning from terrible defeat and changing as a public personality. Like Butler and Jenkins, Clarke was a reforming Cabinet minister who made his mark in every department in which he served. David and Ed Miliband were at the heart of the New Labour project, and therefore close to the centre of power for the entire period of that long-serving government. Given that Labour is usually out of power, the two brothers have had fulfilling political lives compared with those who toil endlessly on the frontbench in opposition. Some of Labour's big figures from the 1980s never got close to government. Although never a minister, let alone prime minister, Corbyn won two landslide leadership contests from the left and wiped out the Conservatives' majority in 2017. Most Labour MPs never come close to realizing their ambitions. Corbyn's case is even more unusual as he had never been burdened by the desire to be a leader.

Yet the ultimate ambition of most of them was never met. There were many reasons why they failed to become prime ministers. Perhaps the most fundamental of them all was that their chances of reaching Number Ten were not as great as they seemed at the time. That is why the stakes are so high in a general election and during a contest in a governing party to replace a prime minister. The winners – those who become prime minister – are likely to be in their post for quite some time. That means mostly in British political life there is no vacancy at the very top.

———

Barbara Castle once observed perceptively of Margaret Thatcher that 'power made her beautiful'. Here Castle did not mean to say she agreed with the right-wing prime minister. She was making a more interesting point, noting that – in ways that were unexpected – power suited Thatcher. When she wore the crown, she did not seem awkward or absurd. This was a surprise to some in Thatcher's party, who had assumed she would not last for very long. Instead, the combination of prime ministerial power and character worked. But it is never clear in advance of a character moving into Number Ten whether power will suit or not.

We will never know for sure what would have happened to the prime ministers we never had. None of them got the chance to be tested. Who might have become beautiful? We can only guess. In contrast, the reasons why they failed to make it to the very top are clear. And they offer as many lessons of leadership as does a study of modern prime ministers.

—

ACKNOWLEDGEMENTS

Thank you to the great team at Atlantic, James Pulford, Mike Harpley and Gemma Wain… and to my brilliant agent, Andrew Gordon at David Higham Associates. I'm also grateful to Peter Knowles and Daniel Brittain-Catlin at the BBC. They bravely commissioned several series of improvised TV talks from me, including on the theme of this book, in an era when most senior BBC managers opt for what they consider to be cautious safety. Most of the talks are now available on BBC iPlayer or YouTube.

NOTES

Introduction

1 Patricia Hewitt, 'Labour's Greatest Hero: Barbara Castle', *Guardian*, 19 September 2008, https://www.theguardian.com/commentisfree/2008/sep/19/labourconference.labour.

2 Interview on episode 203, *The Political Party* [podcast], March 2021.

3 Barbara Castle, *The Castle Diaries, 1974–1976*, Weidenfeld & Nicolson, 1980, p. 168.

4 Andy Beckett, 'Centre Forward', *Guardian*, 2 April 2005.

5 Andrew Rawnsley made this case in the *Observer* on 1 November 2020. The column was retweeted approvingly by many political journalists.

1. Rab Butler

1 Michael Jago, *Rab Butler: The Best Prime Minister We Never Had?*, Biteback Publishing, 2015.

2 Anthony Howard, *RAB: The Life of R. A. Butler*, Jonathan Cape, 1987, p. 60.

3 'Change and Continuity: Reflections on the Butler Act', *Guardian*, 21 April 2004, https://www.theguardian.com/education/2004/apr/21/ofsted.schools.

4 Nigel Lawson, *Daily Telegraph*, 3 October 2004.

5 D. R. Thorpe, *Supermac: The Life of Harold Macmillan*, Chatto & Windus, 2010, p. 103.

6 Howard, *RAB*, p. 41.

7 Howard, *RAB*, p. 322.

2. Roy Jenkins

1 Lewis Baston, 'Wilson. Attlee. Major. The Costs, Gains and Consequences of Devaluation', Conservative Home, 14 October 2016, https://www.conservativehome.com/thecolumnists/2016/10/lewis-baston-wilson-attlee-major-the-costs-gains-and-consequences-of-devaluation.html.

2 Philip Ziegler, *Wilson*, Weidenfeld & Nicolson, 1993, p. 294.

3 Ibid., p. 293.

4 Ibid., p. 294.

5 Speech at a May Day rally, quoted in *The Times*, 5 May 1969.

6 See the chapter on Ken Clarke, who also flourished at the Treasury and never made it to Number Ten.

7 See my chapter on Wilson in *The Prime Ministers: Reflections on Leadership from Wilson to Johnson* to appreciate that the onslaughts on Wilson were largely unfair but made at the time with great intensity.

8 Roy Jenkins, *A Life at the Centre*, Macmillan, 1991, p. 258.

9 John Campbell, *Roy Jenkins: A Well-Rounded Life*, Jonathan Cape, 2014.

10 Conversation with the author.

11 Commons debate on Peter Wright's *Spycatcher*, Hansard, 7 November 1988.

12 'Politics Past and Present: with Dick Taverne', *The Critics* [podcast], 23 June 2020, https://thecritic.co.uk/politics-past-and-present-with-dick-taverne/.

13 Jenkins, *A Life at the Centre*, p. 208.

14 Interview with the author, GMTV, October 2001.

15 From the left, Tony Benn viewed Wilson with the same irritation as Jenkins, but after Wilson's death he noted: 'Harold realized that, like a bird, the Labour Party needed two wings to fly... a left wing and a right wing.'

16 'Politics Past and Present: with Dick Taverne'.

17 *Evening Standard*, 14 July 2001.

18 Jenkins, *A Life at the Centre*, p. 292.

19 Michael Foot's leadership was more expedient and nuanced than the media portrayal suggested at the time or since. There is more on this in the chapter on Denis Healey.

20 Richard Dimbleby Lecture, 22 November 1979.

21 Andrew Adonis, *Roy Jenkins: A Retrospective*, Oxford University Press, 2004, p. 180.

22 Roy Hattersley, *Who Goes Home?*, Abacus, 2003.

23 Jenkins, *A Life at the Centre*, p. 356.

24 Ibid., p. 260.

25 Ibid., p. 333.

26 Ibid., p. 349.

27 Ibid., p. 622.

28 David Marquand, 'The Welsh Wrecker', in Adonis, *Roy Jenkins: A Retrospective*, p. 111.

29 I was on the panel of journalists that featured on BBC One's *Sunday Politics*. After the election in May 2017, we all predicted wrongly she could be gone by that autumn.

30 Roy Jenkins, *European Diary, 1977–1981*, A&C Black, 2011.

31 Interview with the author, *New Statesman*, December 1996.

32 Conversation with the author during the 2017 election. Owen made a donation to Corbyn's Labour Party. He thought at the time that Corbyn was a more expedient and principled leader than Michael Foot.

33 Interview with the author, GMTV, October 2001.

3. Barbara Castle

1 Interview with the author, *New Statesman*, 28 February 2000, https://www.newstatesman.com/node/150817.

2 Ibid.

3 Margaret Thatcher Foundation. Her desire was expressed as part of her New Year message on 2 January 1970.

4 Barbara Castle, *Fighting All the Way*, Macmillan, 1993, p. 346.

5 Hansard, 3 August 1965.

6 Anne Perkins, *Red Queen: The Authorized Biography of Barbara Castle*, Macmillan, 2003, p. 209.

7 Ibid., p. 375.

8 Perkins, *Red Queen*, p. 275.

9 Ibid.

10 Jack Straw, 'Socialism's First Lady', *New Statesman*, July 2003, https://www.newstatesman.com/node/158109.

11 Andrea Boltho, ed., *The European Economy: Growth and Crisis*, Clarendon Press, 1982, p. 174.

12 Perkins, *Red Queen*, p. 297.

13 At least, they were in conversations with the author. They tended to be generous about Labour leaders,

including Tony Blair, but they were scathing about Wilson even though it was Wilson that made Michael Foot a Cabinet minister.

14 Straw, 'Socialism's First Lady'.

15 They were superficial because she had not worked out precisely what the new local tax would be. More than a decade later, she decided on a Community Charge or poll tax, a policy that was a major factor in her fall.

16 Interview with the author, *New Statesman*, 28 February 2000.

4. Denis Healey

1 'Mr Healey, The Man Most Likely To', *The Times*, 2 October 1980.

2 A widespread assumption in the autumn of 1980 was that Labour could well win the next election. The Thatcher government was deeply unpopular at the time. After one opinion poll in 1981 about Thatcher and her government, the front-page headline was 'The Most Unpopular Prime Minister of the Century'.

3 Denis Healey, *The Time of My Life*, Michael Joseph, 1989, p. 324.

4 Ibid., p. 400.

5 Healey refers to this in his memoir but gave me more detail during an interview in 1998, stating, 'The unions were out of control and this made governing almost impossible. By the end I was suffering from one heavy cold after another. I put it down to mental and physical exhaustion.'

6 *Guardian*, 1 October 1976.

7 Healey, *The Time of My Life*, p. 445.

8 Ibid., p. 381.

9 Interview with the author.

10 Giles Radice, *Friends and Rivals: Crosland, Jenkins and Healey*, Little, Brown Book Group, 2003.

11 See the chapter on Roy Jenkins.

12 Gordon Brown was another admirer. In the 2006 edition of *The Future of Socialism*, Brown wrote the introduction. The book was originally published in 1956. Healey wrote no equivalent book of ideological revisionism that has been regularly republished.

13 Michael Foot, *Debts of Honour*, Faber & Faber, 1980.

14 Kenneth O. Morgan, *Callaghan: A Life*, Oxford University Press, 1997, p. 500. Morgan makes the point that Callaghan consulted Foot on all key issues in advance, in order that they maintain a united front.

15 *Weekend World*, 18 March 1983.

16 'At all the Christmas parties around Westminster there was one recurring topic: Benn.' Peter Jenkins, *Guardian*, 16 December 1980. The columnist, Jenkins, was not a fan of Benn.

17 Healey, *The Time of My Life*, p. 501.

5. Neil Kinnock

1 Rob Hayward, 'Why the Polls Were Wrong about the Conservative Campaign', *Daily Telegraph*, 8 May 2015.

2 Neil Kinnock, *Guardian*, 14 April 1992, https://www.theguardian.com/politics/2015/apr/14/neil-kinnock-resigns-labour-leader.

3 Martin Westlake, *Kinnock: The Authorised Biography*, Little, Brown, 2001, p. 720.

4 Francis Beckett, 'Neil Kinnock, the Man Who Saved Labour', *New Statesman*, 25 September 2014, https://www.newstatesman.com/politics/2014/09/neil-kinnock-man-who-saved-labour.

5 Westlake, *Kinnock*, p. 208

6 John P. Mackintosh Lecture, 25 June 1983.

7 Conversation with the author.

8 *The Sun* christened him 'the Welsh windbag' in the autumn of 1983.

9   Speech to Conservative MPs, July 1984.

10 Norman Tebbit, *Upwardly Mobile*, Weidenfeld & Nicolson, 1988. Tebbit argued that the government should have intervened more to help communities dependent on mining.

11 Interview with Adam Price, S4C, October 2014.

12 Labour conference speech, September 1985.

13 Leader's speech, Bournemouth 1985, British Political Speech [website], http://www.britishpoliticalspeech.org/ speech-archive.htm?speech=191.

14 Hattersley, *Who Goes Home?*, p. 153.

15 Welsh Labour conference speech, 15 May 1987.

16 I was covering the event as a BBC political correspondent, and observed Kinnock's almost painful self-discipline,

17 Conversation with the author.

6. Michael Heseltine

1   Decca Aitkenhead, 'Michael Heseltine: "I Would Have Liked to Be Prime Minister"', *Guardian*, 25 November 2012, https://www.theguardian. com/politics/2012/nov/25/michael-heseltine-would-have-liked-prime-minister.

2   Ibid.

3   Ian Gilmour, *Dancing with Dogma: Britain Under Thatcherism*, Simon & Schuster, 1992. This is one of the best accounts of early Thatcherism.

4   Letter to Thatcher, 10 July 1981, Thatcher Foundation.

5   Quoted in Martin Wainwright, 'Michael Heseltine Is Given the Freedom of Liverpool', *Guardian*, 13 March 2012, https://www. theguardian.com/uk/the-northerner/2012/mar/13/michael-heseltine-liverpool-freeman-margaret-thatcher.

6   Gene Robertson, 'Blueprint', *Inside Housing*, 12 June 2009, https://www. insidehousing.co.uk/insight/insight/ blueprint-15798.

7   Conservative party conference, 7 October 1992.

8   See the chapter on Michael Portillo. Labour's Peter Mandelson is another example. Mandelson was an expert at advising others on their images but was hopeless at projecting himself, not that he sought to be prime minister. Mandelson was content to be close to those who were prime ministers in the New Labour era.

9   Alan Watkins, *A Conservative Coup: The Fall of Margaret Thatcher*, Gerald Duckworth & Co., 1992, p. 189.

10 'Interview with Michael Heseltine', *On the Record*, BBC One, 10 October 1993, http://www.bbc.co.uk/otr/ intext93-94/Heseltine10.10.93.html.

7. Michael Portillo

1   Alice Thomson, 'There's Only One Person Who Knows Me – and That's Me', *Daily Telegraph*, 28 June 2001, https://www.telegraph.co.uk/ culture/4724334/Theres-only-one-person-that-knows-me-and-thats-me. html.

2   Patrick Barkham, 'Renaissance Man', *Guardian*, 26 November 1999, https:// www.theguardian.com/politics/1999/ nov/26/thatcher.uk5. The quote is from Portillo's fortieth birthday party in May 1993.

3   The author was in the studio too.

4   Address at the memorial service for Maurice Cowling, at Great St Mary's Church, Cambridge, 29 October 2005, http://www.michaelportillo. co.uk/speeches/speeches_pub/cowling. htm.

5   Speech to the Centre for Policy Studies, 9 October 1997, https://www. ukpol.co.uk/michael-portillo-1997-speech-to-centre-for-policy-studies/.

6 The author was one of the journalists.

7 Interview with *The Times*, 8 September 1999.

8 Nicholas Watt, 'Portillo Did Not Tell All, Says Gay Ex-Lover', *Guardian*, 12 September 1999, https://www. theguardian.com/politics/1999/ sep/13/thatcher.uk2.

9 Opening speech, Portillo's leadership launch, 21 June 2001.

10 He made the observation in an interview with the author in a BBC series on significant political defeats. The prime minister at the time was Tony Blair.

8. Ken Clarke

1 See the chapter on Rab Butler for the parallels in terms of reforming zeal and being part of a one-nation Toryism. There were no similarities in their political personalities.

2 Interview on *The Andrew Marr Show*, 19 July 2020.

3 'Interview with Norman Lamont', *On the Record*, BBC, 15 November 1991, http://www.bbc.co.uk/otr/ intext92-93/Lamont15.11.92.html.

4 *The World This Weekend*, 9 May 1993.

5 Lamont resignation speech, 9 June 1993.

6 See the chapter on Portillo.

7 In 2005, Geoffrey Wheatcroft wrote a much-reported book, *The Strange Death of Tory England*.

9. David and Ed Miliband

1 David Miliband, 'Against All Odds We Can Still Win, on a Platform for Change', *Guardian*, 29 July 2008, https://www.theguardian. com/commentisfree/2008/jul/29/ davidmiliband.labour.

2 Front page, *Daily Telegraph*, 29 July 2008.

3 Front page, *Guardian*, 30 July 2008.

4 Interview with author for *The Brown Years*, BBC Radio 4, September 2007.

5 The interview was with the author. Perhaps out of politeness, David Miliband told the author it was one of the reasons he got the job as head of policy in Blair's office.

6 This was his view in conversations with the author after the war. He was a committed supporter in advance, on the basis of the intelligence that he read. The intelligence, a lot of which was speculative, famously proved to be wrong.

7 The former Treasury minister and Labour MP, Geoffrey Robinson, in conversation with the author.

8 Conversation with the author at the time of the budget.

9 He wondered in occasional conversations with the author.

10 I had these conversations with the brothers and chaired the hustings in Brixton, where I witnessed the behind-the-scenes tensions.

11 Ed tracked down the editor of the *Independent*, Simon Kelner, who was on holiday, and persuaded him not to back David.

12 He did so in a conversation with the author.

13 *Mail on Sunday*, 30 September 2013.

14 He joked in a conversation with the author.

15 George Parker and Jim Pickard, 'The Reinvention of Ed Miliband', *FT Magazine*, 10 June 2020.

16 Conversation between James Purnell and the author.

17 Patrick Wintour and Allegra Stratton, 'David Miliband: The Speech He Would Have Given – if He'd Won', *Guardian*, 10 June 2011.

18 Conversation at the time with Ed's senior adviser, Stewart Wood, and subsequently confirmed to me

in discussions with Ed about his
leadership.
19 Leader's speech, Brighton 2013,
British Political Speech [website],
http://www.britishpoliticalspeech.org/
speech-archive.htm?speech=353.
20 Interview with the author at the Kings
Place Politics Festival, 8 July 2017.
21 BBC News, 8 May 2015.
22 Alastair Campbell, *Diaries: Volume
8, 2010–2015*, Biteback Publishing,
2021, p. 978.

10. Jeremy Corbyn

1 Osborne's view that Corbyn could win
a forthcoming election is revealed in
Diary of an MP's Wife by Sasha Swire,
published in September 2020. Blair
acknowledged that Corbyn could
win in an interview with Ian Katz on
Newsnight in June 2017, soon after the
surprise election result. Both agreed
such an outcome would be disastrous
but they now saw Corbyn as a possible
prime minister.
2 Interview with Kirsty Lang, Kings
Place Politics Festival, July 2017.
3 Strand Group seminar, as reported
in John Rentoul, 'Peter Mandelson:
It's Simply a Myth that Labour Can
Win from the Left', *Independent*, 3
April 2021, https://www.independent.
co.uk/voices/peter-mandelson-labour-
left-blair-b1826082.html.
4 See chapter on Ed and David
Miliband.
5 Patrick Wintour, 'Andy Burnham
Looks Back to 1997 as He Launches
Bid to Be Next Labour Leader',
Guardian, 13 May 2015, https://
www.theguardian.com/politics/2015/
may/13/andy-burnham-labour-
leadership-launch-calls-for-aspirations-
of-1997.

6 Press Association, 'Yvette Cooper
Announces Candidacy for Labour
Leadership', *Guardian*, 13 May
2015, https://www.theguardian.com/
politics/2015/may/13/yvette-cooper-
announces-candidacy-for-labour-
leadership.
7 *The World This Weekend*, 17 May 2015.
8 John McDonnell, interview with the
author, *The Corbyn Story*, BBC Radio
4, July 2016.
9 *The Corbyn Story*.
10 Chris Leslie told the author of
his traumatic twenty-four hours
over coffee at Portcullis House at
Westminster.
11 During the leadership contest, Corbyn
told Melissa Benn, Tony's daughter,
about how he turned to her father for
posthumous guidance and inspiration
as he was going through the most
mind-boggling weeks of his political
career.
12 See chapter on Denis Healey.
13 Ken Livingstone, interview with the
author, *The Corbyn Story*.
14 Interview on *The Andrew Marr Show*,
26 June 2016.
15 Conversation with the author in a
taxi after *Any Questions?* in Brighton,
September 2017.
16 Ephraim Irvis, 'What Will Become
of Jews in Britain If Labour Forms
the Next Government?', *The Times*,
25 November 2019, https://www.
thetimes.co.uk/article/ephraim-mirvis-
what-will-become-of-jews-in-britain-
if-labour-forms-the-next-government-
ghpsdbljk#.

Conclusion

1 *The Andrew Marr Show*, 11 June 2017.

PICTURE CREDITS

Rab Butler and Harold Macmillan (Reg Speller/Stringer)
Rab Butler (Reg Speller/Stringer)
Roy Jenkins (Rolls Press/Popperfoto)
Roy Jenkins and David Owen (Central Press/Stringer)
Barbara Castle as Minister for Transport (Rolls Press/Popperfoto)
Barbara Castle as Secretary of State for Health and Social Services (Keystone/ Stringer)
Barbara Castle and Harold Wilson (David Ashdown/Stringer)
Denis Healey (Manchester Daily Express)
Denis Healey, Neil Kinnock and Willy Brandt (Rolls Press/Popperfoto)
Neil Kinnock (Fox Photos/Stringer)
Michael Heseltine (Derek Hudson/Getty Images)
Michael Heseltine and Margaret Thatcher (Bride Lane Library/Popperfoto)
Michael Portillo at Conservative Party conference (Jeff Overs/BBC News & Current Affairs)
Michael Portillo (Gemma Levine/Premium Archive)
Kenneth Clarke (Gemma Levine/Premium Archive)
Kenneth Clarke and John Major (Michael Putland/Hulton Archive)
Ed and David Miliband outside Number Ten (Carl de Souza/AFP)
Ed and David Miliband at Labour Party conference (Oli Scarff/Getty Images)
David Miliband and Hillary Clinton (Jewel Samad/AFP)
Jeremy Corbyn and Ed Miliband (Christopher Furlong/Getty Images)
Jeremy Corbyn (Samir Hussein/WireImage)

INDEX